"At a time when the enormous attraction to materialistic values has resulted in a damaging neglect of children, *Conscious Parenting* is a landmark contribution to this huge task of stopping the abuse that is routinely enacted upon children. It invites men and women entrusted with the task of caring for and educating children to take up their responsibility with renewed generosity, kindness, compassion and integrity."

— Malidoma Somé, author of *Of Water and the Spirit* and *Ritual: Power, Healing and Community*

CONSCIOUS PARENTING

Lee Lozowick

HOHM PRESS
PRESCOTT, ARIZONA

Cover design: Kim Johansen
Book design and layout: Bhadra Mitchell

Library of Congress Cataloguing-In-Publication Data

Lozowick, Lee, 1943-
    Conscious parenting / Lee Lozowick.
       p.   cm.
    Includes bibliographical references and index.
    ISBN:0-934252-67-X (alk. paper)
    1. Parenting. 2. Parenting--Moral and ethical aspects.
3. Child rearing--Moral and ethical aspects. 4. Parents--
Conduct of life. 5. Moral education. 6. Role models.
I. Title.
HQ755.8.L69 1997
649'.7-dc21   97-23949
                                       CIP

The author gratefully acknowledges the work of
Tony and Robin Berryman in the initial compila-
tion of these transcripts.

Hohm Press
PO Box 2501
Prescott, AZ 86302
1-800-381-2700
http://www.booknotes.com/hohm/

*For my mother and father, Adele and Louis Lozowick,
who raised me with love and faith*

*and for Yogi Ramsuratkumar, my spiritual Master,
who raises me still with Love and Faith.*

CONTENTS

Foreword ix

Chapter 1 *The Context for Conscious Parenting* 1

Chapter 2 *Good Beginnings:* 15
Conscious Conception, Pregnancy,
Birth and Nursing

Chapter 3 *Enough & Never Enough:* 51
Love, Affection and Attention

Chapter 4 *Impressions Upon Innocence* 87

Chapter 5 *Just Like Us:* 133
Role Models

Chapter 6 *Drawing A Line:* 163
The Challenge of Responsible
Boundaries

Chapter 7 *No Excuse! :* 203
On Child Abuse

Chapter 8 *Speaking The Truth:* 227
Language and Honesty

Chapter 9 *Education For Life:* 259
Life In Continuum, The Context of
Education and Home-Schooling

Chapter 10   *Child's Play:*   293
             Emotions, Energy Management
                 and Fighting

Chapter 11   *Body and Soul:*   313
             Food, Health, Sex and God

Chapter 12   *Spiritual Practice for Parents*   345

Notes   355

Recommended Reading   361

Index   364

FOREWORD

Please Read Before Use

I first heard Lee Lozowick speak about children twenty-two years ago at a lecture he was giving on a college campus on the east coast of the United States. At the time I was twenty-four years old and spending a fair amount of time searching for the great truths of life. I remember two things from that first meeting with him. One was a simple, unpretentious sense of openness and lack of judgementalness that I have never forgotten, and the second was the way he said things. Lee spoke with a tone, humor and street wisdom that pierced right to my gut (as you are soon to find out in reading this book), and this was a great shock for me; I had never been around someone so real. I had met other authors of his stature and was hoping to have some light magically turned on—something that would take away my pain forever. Instead, I found myself listening to a man who was clearly grounded in the reality of everyday life, and yet one who had somehow managed to gain a perspective that I had rarely encountered. I decided to read one of his books. Immediately I knew that he would become one of my authors—one of the half dozen or so whom I hold dear in my heart, and read no matter what. I have read his twelve or so published works since then, without disappointment.

This Foreword is titled: *Please Read Before Use*, words which can be found on many products that we purchase regularly. They serve as some kind of warning that lets us know what functions a product has and does not have, as well as how to use the product safely. Somehow I think that this book needs the same kind of consumer information. "But why," one must ask, "a product warning on a book about parenting? This must be just another liberal book on raising children, perhaps with a unique slant, but probably just the same kind of thing that we have read and even thought about before." Allow me to explain.

There are different types of books on these kinds of subjects. There are first of all "face books." They introduce us to the face of things—basic overview material that, if well written, gets us pumped up, but never really catalyzes change. Then there are "how to" books, which give us instruction and perhaps step-by-step processes for us to achieve our goal. The third kind of book we might call a "workbook," which is designed to shift the reader into a whole new outlook, or paradigm, or way of being. Such books are not workbooks in the traditional sense, but in the sense that they work and move us, inside ourselves as well as in the midst of our daily lives in relationship to whatever subject they address. Workbooks knead us in the way a baker kneads bread or in the way a potter turns a pot.

Many of us are already dedicated to the possibility that this book represents. Somewhere along the line we decided that there was no way that we were going to treat our children like one or both of our parents treated us. Or perhaps we were raised by kind, generous, and compassionate parents and we are simply interested in deepening our understanding of how to be all that we can be as parents. In either case, the *Please Read Before Use* relates to my sense that—upon my first reading of *Conscious Parenting* along with my familiarity of the author's style and passion—what you hold in your hands seems to be a workbook.

There is only ever one reason to read or study a workbook, and that is because we have something at stake in our lives; when there is something very important that we want to make happen. After reading this book, I think that the only reason to read it is because we love our children. Actually, it is bigger than that. It is not that we just love our children; there is a part of us that loves all children! Perhaps they reconnect us to our own innocence, or that children represent the possibility of a new and different future for humanity. Whatever the reason, most of us seem to have something at stake with our own children, at least, and this is the kind of impetus that is necessary to make the effort that this book invites of us.

Conscious Parenting is not light entertainment, although Lee's raw sense of humor seeps through the pages. Nor will it be conventionally inspiring to some of us (although to others it will be). We may lose a little sleep over it. It may even cause us to eat a bit of humble pie, or it may make us angry at times. Like all of the author's work, it did some of all this for me. The reason for this, I think, is that Mr. Lee (as his close friends refer to him), walks his talk.

As a professional in the domain of human potential and development, I work personally and intensively with hundreds of people each year. I read dozens of books about my field and related subjects every year. My first hand experience of so much of what is written today is that it is mere philosophy with a bright smile or meaningful glance on the back cover, but not actually practiced by those who preach it. Admittedly, Lee refers to himself as a good parent; not a bad one, but not a great one either. We can leave that consideration to the debating society, but the fact remains, for me, that from my observation he definitely walks what he talks in the following pages. And I think that fact—that this book is based on the blood, sweat, and tears of one of the foremost visionaries of our times—is what calls for a warning. Not to stay away, but just to know that you are holding something very hot, and alive, in your hands.

Surely you will find some "good ideas" in here; but good, even great ideas do not necessarily change us. Somehow, somewhat magically, when words are written by one who has made great sacrifices to live them, they cut through and touch us at our core. Such words reconnect us to ourselves. At least they do for me. It's like the difference between reading a book about Mother Teresa, or one about serving humanity written by an author with a plush home overlooking a beautiful view of the mountains. It's not that the latter may not genuinely serve in his or her life, and poverty is usually not a sign of anything desirable, but I think there is a different place that gets touched in us when we read those who uncompromisingly live their vision. Lee Lozowick is such a man.

Much of what follows in this book you will not find anywhere else. It is a combination of many years of practical experience by the author in raising his own children, as well as his coaching of thousands of other parents in raising theirs. It is a crystal clear expression of centuries of knowledge from the world's great wisdom traditions. All about children, all about parenting, all expressed in contemporary language that we can relate to.

This book is, however, an expression of "no easy way." There is no easy way to raise a child in the western world. There is no easy way to not give in to the superficial pressures of a society that wants our babies to wear pink and that equates love with the price of toys in its advertising. There is no easy way to give children the freedom they biologically demand and at the same time feel like we are keeping them safe—physically, mentally, and emotionally. And, there is no easy way to not leave our children a legacy of our own neuroses.

This book faces "no easy way" head-on, eyes completely wide open, and then it creates the possibility of relationship that we all dream of having with our children. So let's roll up our sleeves and go to work.

—Purna Steinitz
September 1997

❦❦❦

Generally speaking, some basic guidelines around my childraising views have to do with essential continuum concept (see the book The Continuum Concept *by Jean Liedloff) bonding with our children, with full acknowledgement of our children's "basic goodness" (see writings of Chögyam Trungpa Rinpoche), with full attention on the children as long as they seek this attention (understanding that a child raised in a healthy manner will not be grasping and insecure and will reach out of and beyond the parental cocoon as soon as he or she is mobile) and basically to provide an environment of growth that is completely free of abuse, physical and psychic; neglect, benign or sadistic; shaming, verbal, emotional or otherwise; and violence and cruelty. In other words, beyond the natural stresses of illnesses, growth, social adjustments, creative urges and crises and other internal or essential demands that arise spontaneously for the child in the course of their development, the environment of their upbringing is designed to be stress-free in the sense of adult domination and manipulation, conscious or unconscious. The idea is for a child to grow up knowing, tacitly and organically, beyond any doubt and confusion, that they are loved absolutely, for who they are, without the demand for any particular performance, manifestation, achievement, or drama.*

Of course it is probably obvious that for the vast majority, overwhelming majority actually, of contemporary men and women, this is not the case. We, our generation and several before us (perhaps many several

xiv

before us) do not feel so loved. We feel tacitly and organically un-loved, un-appreciated, unfulfilled, dissatisfied, empty and unworthy. We have been raised to view love as a commodity that was available only at a certain price, that price being if we were "good little children," quiet, geniuses, or most likely for most of us so high that it was impossible to "pay." Therefore love, the "thing," was withheld from us because we weren't able to satisfy the insatiable demands of the un-love of our adult social community, this community being parents, extended family, teachers, baby-sitters and even strangers in the grocery store whom our parents were probably more than willing to talk to about our failings (in their eyes) with complete disregard for our presence and the shame this caused us.

So those interested in conscious childraising are attempting to raise children differently, radically, to produce a culture of beauty, joy, delight, love, gentleness, kindness and compassion in which growth produces deep abiding self-confidence, natural happiness and a strong and open willingness to move into life and experience with interest and capability.

—Lee Lozowick
Journal, November 1993

1

THE CONTEXT FOR
CONSCIOUS PARENTING

The responsibility of being with children either in an official capacity as a teacher or parent, or simply as a friend or companion, is literally a responsibility for the future of humankind. What we model for children, how we treat them, how we parent them, is more than *important*—it is absolutely *vital* to their mental, emotional and physical health and well-being and to that of the earth itself (and beyond, as we develop the technology for space travel and extra-terrestrial exploration).

Children grow to be whole adults by living with whole adults, not by having moral principles pounded into their little heads by well-meaning but unconscious hypocrites. Children are like sponges, they can and do pick up everything that they see, hear and sense, not only in the behavior of their primary role models, but even from casual acquaintances. And what they pick up will influence how they grow up, which in turn will have effects on the world-at-large that we can't possibly imagine. One's relationship to children has an impact on many levels of existence. Conscious parenting, then, is not only about the welfare of an individual, but more about the present and future well-being of society as a whole.

WHO THEY ARE

Having children is natural—a part of the ongoing process of life. Besides organically giving children life (which any animal is capable of), we provide them, to some degree, with the education that defines whether they will be healthy and mature adults or psychologically-, emotionally- or even physically-crippled adults. Beyond the obvious sentimentality that occurs when we observe a child's innocence, beauty, freshness and spontaneity (which often, unfortunately, is the primary motivation for some people in having children), there is the consideration of both the responsibility and the integrity called for by our actions and choices with regard to children.

Most children are born pretty much equal, but they show up with vast differences as adults because of the conditioning or education that is provided by the adults in their lives and because of their overall environment. Therefore, we (not just parents but all adults) have an enormous responsibility to provide the kinds of references for children that allow them to grow up to be *who they are*, instead of being crippled by our projections, expectations and our biased demands on them. For instance, there are men and women who can't enjoy a sexual relationship without fantasizing about cruelty and violence, or about the last pornographic movie they saw. People get that way—unable to be naturally loving and intimate—because of their upbringing, not because they were born with those handicaps already in place. One of the characteristics of any mature adult is the ability to be responsible for what is objectively true or necessary, and to bring integrity (in action!) to this knowledge. Most adults have reasonable rhetoric but aren't always capable of acting on the basis of that intellect and clarity. But we must involve action or our words won't be taken seriously. Instead of "the little boy who cried wolf," we have the big parent who cried patience and tolerance yet who demonstrated none.

Parents sometimes superimpose their own unrealistic or twisted expectations onto their children with complete disregard for the child's natural evolution or growth process. They want their child to have the passions they didn't have, or to accomplish what they couldn't accomplish themselves. For example, when her child was only six months old, a mother bought her a grand piano and put it in the living room. That's a *mother's* unfulfilledness being forced on the child, but made to appear as a gift: "You're gifted; you're talented; you're a genius, I'm doing this for you," and so on. This particular daughter grew up to be a great pianist but not because she chose it. And eventually she chose another lifestyle that made her happy rather than the one that made her mother happy.

We have all met others who may be extraordinarily talented or successful in worldly terms, but who are totally artificial, empty or stilted in their ability to feel, to be in relationship, or even just to enjoy themselves or life. This is always the result of a forced formation of qualities that were unnatural at the time. That kind of pressure at any time in a child's life can be damaging, but when children are really young it can set them into a rigid and neurotic pattern that can be almost impossible to break later on. When parents place such a heavy expectation on a child before he or she is even a year old, the child will not just walk around *affected* by that, more likely he or she will walk around *as* that expectation. Up until one year of age there is simply no separation involved in such things. Thus, that kind of programming can be devastating in its manifestations in later life.

I can't emphasize strongly enough that adults need to become conscious parents, that is, educated in how to educate children. We often have no idea of the extreme degree to which a few things said by our parents have defined our relationship to life. With regard to sickness, for example, a few wrong words spoken to us as infants and some of us have become convinced that we have to get sick periodically, or that we are naturally disposed to certain bodily weaknesses. In actuality this may all be the result of expectation and wrong belief at deep, unconscious levels. In these and other ways, adults unconsciously put children in danger. Even if someone has a highly-developed power of attention around children, if their *being* is full of denial, sadism, self-centeredness and bigotry, that constitutes a circumstance of danger for the healthy development of a child.

As I've said, children provide the future for our race. Not that our race *has* to survive, but if it's going to it might as well survive in a useful, life-positive and optimal form. For the race to survive with such possibility, which also means for *us* to survive with our personal possibilities and potential optimized, our children need to be most effectively educated in order to allow this growth its natural expression.

The whole mood of conscious parenting is one of bringing a certain responsibility *for life itself* to our relationships with children. What children should communicate to us are principles far beyond the personal

4

level. If we really look at children clearly we will see the future of the human race, not the future of "a" child. The raising and education of children should be vital to us not only because we are mothers or fathers or teachers, but because as human beings our relationship to our world will either be effective or ineffective. We will either be healing and positive, or destructive, diseased and negative. A man or woman uninterested in the positive education of children, or unconscious to the child's pain of abuse, must in some ways be themselves crippled to the effects of beauty and full feeling in their own lives.

DOING THE RIGHT THING

Have you ever looked in a young child's eyes (young enough so that their innocence has not been seriously stunted) and realized that the child is looking back with absolute and total trust? If one has seen that and hasn't been scared, one can't possibly have been a fully-conscious, competent parent. Period. The responsibility of such trust is a terrifying prospect, as the parent is actually put in the role of a kind of infallible god. If they hurt the infant physically—slap or hit them— the infant doesn't blame the parent for it. Rather, there is complete and total trust. The child would be hurt, confused and afraid, but would still love. What's the old saying? "Power corrupts"? Well, a child's love and trust imbues the parents or adults with real power. A truly competent parent won't be corrupted, but a weak, insecure or cruel parent or adult will most likely (almost always in fact) abuse that power by abusing the child in some way. Think honestly about your adult relationships. Is trust ever abused? If we abuse trust with other adults, how much more likely are we to abuse it, to take advantage of it, with children whose ability to catch us or repay this abuse is far more minimal.

We feel elevated by the innocence and beauty of children, in awe at the essence of childlikeness, or child-ness. "Wonder" is another word that would apply here. One feels wonder at the miracle of innocent and pure humanness. Actually, children are not even describable when they are still predominantly free. We can't just say, "Children are wonderful ..." or "Gosh, children are neat ...." and actually capture this mood accurately. There is nothing that adequately describes such innocence. On the other hand, even the best of children, at times, can frustrate us, annoy us, madden us and bother us because their behavior pushes our tolerance levels. They aren't the problem, we are. Of course if we have brought them up in an environment of abuse or neglect, their behavior might actually be problematic or "anti-social," but still it is we who are at cause, not them. They can provoke pain, distraction, anger and so on for us throughout their journey of growth and discovery. There is no preparation for how "primal" parenthood is; it shakes and stirs up deeply buried elements in parents. If there is anything hidden in us, buried in us, parenting will discover it.

Holding to an aware, conscious course of upbringing and parenting for children can be extremely hard, especially when one tries this alone as a single parent. Finding and getting together with others who have similar values in childraising can be an invaluable resource. Since the tendency to project our needs and desires onto our children is natural (we all do it), we may benefit from regular reminders from outside the insular child-parent bond to help us avoid molding our children to our own neurotic wishes or needs.

Surprising reactions will often come up in us

when we try to raise our children with conscious and objective values. We might be allowing our children to say things and do things that we never could have gotten away with when we were growing up; things that we would have been punished for, even severely. Since those habits and old lessons are still in us, however, the urge will come up to do the same thing to our children that our parents did to us. When our children are disrespectful and sass back to us, we may want to squash them, to shut them up, just because that was done to us when we were young. We may actually be envious of our child's freedom, even when it is us who allow that!

To be able to let our kids talk back to us, and to handle it sensitively without over-reaction—and also without giving them too much license to simply be abusive to us—is a very creative task. We really have to be grown up and know who we are! Then it won't be a problem when the kids say the things they sometimes say, and we'll be able to handle it rightly. Certainly this will be different from the way we were brought up, but that's the whole idea. One parent said it well:

> *From her work as a psychotherapist, Alice Miller reports that our childhood wounding can lie buried and forgotten in the unconscious until we have children of our own. In fact, even though our childhood experience strongly affects our adult choices, dynamics and relationships, these effects may remain invisible to us until we have children. Then we may find ourselves inexplicably acting out toward our children the patterns that were imprinted in us.*

* * *

As far as I'm concerned there is only one way of being with children that resonates and is exactly "on," and it can't be described in terms of being conservative or liberal. We are either "on" or "off" in terms of our resonance with what is objective in the sense of right or optimal for the upbringing and health of the child. Every circumstance has a very specific, objective response inherent within it, and conscious parenting is about developing the resonance to what is objective. Clearly there is some tolerance—none of us, certainly myself included, are perfect parents; so there is some leeway for different personalities, different circumstances, for right timing and so on. Within that tolerance, however, it's not a matter of being conservative or liberal, but of doing the right thing, i.e., making discipline when discipline is needed, being soft and flexible when flexibility is needed. There is no subjectivity to that. Increasing our awareness of this principle in all aspects of childraising is what this book is about.

"AND A LITTLE CHILD WILL LEAD THEM ..."

One of the impersonal values of having children in our lives may be to show us how "unwhole" we are. Because children touch our hearts so deeply, the sorrow of realizing the illnesses of the world based on recognizing what that is to children—how war, greed, cruelty, torture and criminal atrocities affect them—can really spur us on to investigate what it means to be completely whole and conscious ourselves. If one really feels the nature of human suffering, and if one looks at an innocent child who doesn't know anything about the realities of all of that (they just play and they eat and they cry and they laugh), and if one thinks of what it is going to cost for that child to lose their innocence ... if that's not enough of a burr under the saddle to motivate us to want to come out of hiding and to become conscious (to mature in our spiritual and temporal life), nothing ever will be. As long as the child still maintains some innocence, every expression of this innocence should be such a reminder.

It's not so much that children are our teachers because they are wise and they are pure and they remember their past lives and they see auras ... and all that kind of nonsense. (On the other hand, we don't have to bother to become "channels" because our children speak to angels anyway and they'll just give us the straight answers.) Children touch in us the compassion for those who suffer—the unnecessary suffering of so many, due to unconsciousness, denial and closed-mindedness. That pain is easier to see when children are around because of the dichotomy between that type of suffering and the child's vulnerability and pure innocence, desire to be happy, and desire to see others happy and healthy as well.

Any adult who is really sensitive realizes that children will naturally and effortlessly keep us present, i.e., keep us "here and now." They keep our attention, if we let them; they don't let us fly off in the clouds somewhere. In encouraging them to be their own persons, however, the older they get we should not demand of them this relationship of keeping our attention in the same form. Otherwise, we end up just smothering their creativity, and we all become "stage mothers."

Another profound, almost tragic, communication that we can learn from children is how fragile life is. I mean, our feelings are as easily hurt as a child's feelings, but since we don't express ourselves like they do we act like we aren't touched; and that is why, beyond all of the other things that add to our disintegration, such as psychological and emotional confusion, frustration and overwhelm, we can end up after fifty years with a heart attack, a stroke or some other form of debilitating disease that is the result of suppression of feelings and denial of what is actually so for us.

LOVE IS ENOUGH / LOVE IS NOT ENOUGH

Outside of right discipline, or right boundary-setting, which is *the* key to success with children, love has to be the basis on which we relate to them. But we might as well forget about correct or "just" discipline if love is not the context of this discipline. Without the context of love we will end up, in some way or another, harming our children—if not physically or emotionally, then psychologically.

If love is the foundation or the field out of which of our relationship to children arises, somehow we will get through the rough spots—and there are always rough spots. After all, our children may certainly have similarities to us, but at the same time we are all quite distinct individuals, each with our own destiny, personality, born tendencies, resonances and so on. While we may raise our voices at them, be angry with them, lose our temper and be short of patience, somehow the love will always make things essentially resolvable. However, love cannot be a sometimes thing or a response to stimuli. It has to be constant and tacit, and not every adult is willing to recognize that love entails responsibility of such extraordinary proportions.

If love is our primary response to a child, and we are willing to be responsible for that, it will always pull us out of the depth of whatever confusion, frustration or depressiveness we might occasionally feel. No matter how annoying children may get at times in their growth into independence and individuality, if we love them deeply, abidingly and affectionately, it makes it worthwhile—the fights, the annoyances, the misunderstandings.

If we don't love them, but simply bear their presence in our lives, we're stuck with them for a certain period of time; and we often go about destroying one another's peace of mind and blocking the love that could grow or develop. Of course as adults we are infinitely more successful at diminishing a child's beingness and aliveness for the first three or four years of their lives than they are of diminishing ours. But at four or five the tide turns, and they become infinitely more capable of disturbing us than we them. We can dominate and control them, but they can "get us"; boy, they can get us like we couldn't dream of. They aren't naturally disposed to warfare with their parents, certainly, but they are conditioned to such behavior by survival needs. When children are not loved, as infants, they often develop problematical behavior as a way to prove to themselves that they are worthy of attention—any kind of attention. It is all a deep subconscious mechanism. In a successful relationship with children it's really only common sense that we should love them.

Love as a basis for our relationship to our child is either natural or we have to create it. The first part of creating it is disciplined responsibility on ourselves. In practical terms, that means for instance that we don't snap at them when we are having a bad day, whether we attribute the "bad day" to them or not. If a child is whining it is *our* responsibility to hold firm but just boundaries, and to remain calm, loving, affectionate and clear-headed.

Love is not enough, though, if the context isn't appropriate. We might even say that there cannot *be* love if the context is "off." The context we are talking about here is an environment of caring—an environment so deep and accepting, and so intelligent in relationship to who our children are essentially and developmentally, that our children *know* they're loved, without a doubt.

It is natural for us to want the best for our children, and we should cultivate the attitude that we will do the best we can for them—provide the best education, the best care and love and attention. But the sooner the child becomes *his own man* (or woman), *his own boy* (or girl), the better. Every time we see a way in which we can provide something for them, or a way in which something isn't provided but needs to be provided, that should remind us of this vision to support them in being *who they are*. However, many people's lives for years are about having children, raising children, educating children ... and only ten or twenty years after the children are gone do these parents get the point, all of a sudden. (Or don't ever get the point. A lot of people don't and just suffer unnecessary emotional and psychological turmoil.) What's the point? One of the points about children is that they aren't *ours*—they aren't things, possessions, objects to be manipulated, controlled or dominated. A big "point," this.

If a man or woman doesn't have self-esteem, or doesn't develop self-esteem in some way, it becomes almost impossible to be a conscious parent. This vital work of parenting needs to be done from a position of strength, self-confidence and self-knowledge, not from a position of desperation and weakness. And it's very important for children to have self-esteem so that when they grow up and have children of their own they can pass on the principles of conscious childraising without which the world is doomed to even more darkness and suffering than is so pervasive, epidemic actually, today.

GOOD BEGINNINGS
*Conception, Pregnancy,
Birth and Nursing*

CONSCIOUS CONCEPTION

There's a saying that goes, "The road to hell is paved with good intentions." In a moment of passionate love we may look at our partner and say, "Oh, darling, I want to have your child," and they reply, "Oh, yes, yes, I want you to have my child." But then, a year and a half after the pregnancy, the woman's got black eyes and broken arms because the guy can't handle his anger, his irresponsibility and his lack of integrity and discipline. He's ready to leave, and he's drinking himself into a stupor every night because of what, to him, is the burden of a child, a family and a marriage. Yet, in that great moment of sincerity, possibly induced by hormones or neurotic desperation, an action was taken which was completely out of context with the various abilities required to handle it. We don't often think of the long-term implications of our actions, especially when our genitals are screaming for orgasm.

A very popular subject in new-age circles these days is this idea of "conscious conception." Most people think that conscious conception means that when you're having sex you think of what great human being

15

you want to reincarnate as *your* child—like you want to bring Gandhi or Mozart or Bach back to Earth; or Albert Schweitzer or Martin Luther King or Buddha, or someone like that. (Or maybe Mahatma Gandhi this time and not Albert Gandhi. If your family was poor, you might want Albert Gandhi, because then you'd at least be supported in your old age given Albert's amazing gift with creative financing. If you've got Mahatma Gandhi, you'd have to go get beaten up on some picket line, and you might not like that particularly well.) Although, Americans are so vain, so superficial and so self-centered these days that it would be more likely they would ask for Marilyn Monroe, Clark Gable or Groucho Marx to come back and be their child. This is not and in fact has nothing to do with conscious conception, however. It's not only fantasy, it's pure egoism.

Conscious conception is when one surrenders their humanness and their personal process to the movement of the Divine. It has nothing to do with deciding that you want this perfect being, or this Atlantean, or this world leader. It has to do with surrender, with submission to *what the Universe needs or wants.*

In a conscious society couples don't decide to have children because they love one another. The romantically sentimental reasons most people want or have children for are completely selfish: the child becomes an affect of a couple's doting neurosis, and will undoubtedly suffer the personal effects of that neurosis. In a conscious society a couple prays to whatever the Divine is, and says, "What do *You* need? Do You need children now? Do You need a warrior, a wise person, a worker? What do You need, and, you know, at Your pleasure." Not like, "We want a child because *we* love one another, and this child will be the product of *our* great epic love, a demonstration of true love." That's just so selfish, but unfortunately all too common.

The true idea of conscious conception is to surrender the possibility of conception to Divine movement and Divine influence, so that a being who can optimally use the environment that is offered, and who will optimally serve God, is the kind of being who will take incarnation; rather than saying, "Oh, I want a saint for a child. I want someone who will love God. I want someone who will be really honest and well-behaved, who will be a social reformer." I mean, you *can* request a certain kind of being, and anyone who is developed enough in occult practices is likely to get what they want. Such development can be achieved through submission to intense spiritual practices, or it can be accomplished through practice of magical techniques, in which case one is liable to implore: "Keep it in the family—give me another ruler, another power broker, a wealthy person, a genius."

First of all, conscious conception involves an understanding of communications between dimensions or levels of existence. It's not wishful thinking, or like closing our eyes real tight and praying for something and hoping that our prayer will be heard. Rather, one must be able to communicate to the level from which incarnation comes. That communicat█ █eedn't take the form of a verbal supplication. It's █ █rally a kind of "whole-being request" or wish. █ █ *we are* that dimension anyway, so it's a matter of █ █tractly recognizing the significance of the two dimen█ons and focusing "there" for a moment instead of focusing "here" for a moment.

Of course, a loving, affectionate, accepting, respectful and honoring relationship between the perspective parents is crucial. After that, conscious conception is a matter of maintaining this "Being-Presence and surrender" through the period of ejaculation, and some time after, since it takes a little while for the sperm to reach the egg. (Not like maintaining this focus only until the man ejaculates and then, "Ah, conscious conception; ... chill." Then rolling over, having a cigarette, and saying, "Now let's *really* get down to some fun," while getting out the chains and whips, and starting to swing from the chandeliers.)

Of course you will waiver in this "full Being-Presence," which is natural, but it's the ongoing intention which is needed and effective. The context must be maintained for some period of time, but it doesn't have to be held by both the man and the woman. One person can achieve conscious conception. However, it adds to the process if both people understand it and are involved in it. This is rare, but it helps.

Trying to choose the sex of the child beforehand, through diet and other means, is ridiculous. Why even bother? Who are we to take over God's job anyway? The sex of a child is the job of the great process of Divine evolution. Who are we to decide, "I want a boy, I want a girl." My recommendation—before, during and after the pregnancy—is to eat a clean diet, to exercise, to take care of yourself, to think right, and to relate to God right ... that's all. That's that! The fewer expectations you have for your child (children) the less likely you are to diminish or bias your love, affection and acknowledgerement of them when they don't meet and fulfill your expectations. Just let them be who they are and love them "as is" instead of putting conditions on it.

THE CHOICE IS NOT OURS

We don't really create children out of nothing. They come to us from somewhere else and wait for us to serve as their vehicle into this dimension and life. The consciousness of the being who is entering into incarnation picks the time and the place. Often, when people decide to have a child, they "work" at it. Sometimes, once we decide we want a child it *does* become work. But that's really not of much use, or fun either.

In a conscious process of child conception there is no such thing as an accident when it comes to children "coming through," or not coming through. (A lady I know in Germany has had a couple of miscarriages, and there's nothing accidental about that.) The prospective parent could be a saint, the best vehicle in the world, but it is the child who will pick what *they need*; they do what *they want*. Our job is just to kind of hang out, "Need a doorway? Here I am." Once they are born, of course, they need our guidance, love and support, but the essential imperative is still active so we need to let them find that groove, and we need to allow them to grow and blossom in it.

Most people don't think that way, however. Most adults look at these cute, soft, cuddly (and psychologically and behaviorally malleable) little things and think, "This is *mine*, and I love them so much; and am I going to do good things for this baby!" But the child actually already knows what they need the parent to do for them. The child already knows everything we are going to say to them. The blueprint is drawn. They already know when the mother is going to whack them, and when the father is going to lose his temper.

The whole process is all complete magic! And we

need to trust the magic or we will get very frustrated: "I've got to *make* this happen .... My child has got to be like this ... or that." We *are* involved; we're completely absorbed in a circumstance that's entirely magical ... from where *we* are. (From a higher perspective it's not magic at all, it's science; but from our perspective it's all beyond our understanding.) We need to accept and embrace the process, allowing it to unfold with ourselves simply as the "frames" for this "picture."

AN AWESOME RESPONSIBILITY

When a man impregnates a woman he feels very proud of that (as if all men weren't born with the capability, or as if this was some great feat of warriorship or manliness). But really it's no big deal—every man has the equipment. Every male animal, human and otherwise, makes babies. Human men, however, think that they have done something really special, something that makes them particularly and exclusively important, which is their neurotic impulse in full bloom.

Of course, there is the non-neurotic side, which is being profoundly awed by the responsibility of being a guide for someone who, in fifty years, could hold the balance of the world in the palm of their hand. Imagine if your child was the one who sat with their finger on the "Red Button" waiting to begin or avert World War III. You would want to be damn sure that child had a certain sense of perspective and integrity. (Probably they would never have that job if they had integrity, but that's academic. Politics and social philosophy is another issue entirely, so let's stay out of it!)

The responsible side of fathering or mothering a child is to know that, while the child is not really "ours," we will still be responsible for training, education and input so that the child becomes a mature and meaningful human being as an adult (as much as possible), rather than just self-centered and possessive (like the usual adult these days), or even psychopathic.

INFLUENCES DURING PREGNANCY

Throughout pregnancy, and actually at all times, birth should be considered in enthusiastic, exciting and mysterious terms. This is *life* that's happening! It's always a great and wondrous mystery. So, if another child asks, "How does a baby get born?" one might reply, "Only God knows! The sperm and the egg unite, but that itself doesn't create a human being. That simply manufactures the vehicle." Always refer to birth as something to be looked forward to, both in your own mind and attitude, and in talking to others—children and adults.

Women tend to be very excited, aglow with beauty and wonder, with romance and sentiment (not to mention raging hormones), and men tend to be very matter-of-fact and sometimes annoyed by all the excitement. But birth is always about a new life appearing; so it's a wonderful thing, truly thrilling. This mood can and should transcend all gender, cultural or personal tendencies.

People should not sit around with a pregnant woman sharing horror stories about their mother or their sister and what miserable, painful pregnancies and horrendous labors were had by all. Women sometimes talk to an expecting mother like, "Oh, you'll be all right ... but when my mother gave birth, oh, did she have problems ...." That's not only absolutely insensitive but quite stupid. Those discussions are never appropriate anyway, let alone in the midst of a pregnancy. One should always strive to be in the midst of good company—discussing God and divine life, beauty, delight, joy, health and vitality. No difference during pregnancy!

Sometimes, relatives or others may have a clearly stated prejudice against natural childbirth or other choices you might make as a parent, expecting and ongoing. One friend of mine chose not to tell his family, grandparents and so on, that a home birth was planned for his child. Instead, they were told it would be the usual hospital birth, and were very happy, supportive and excited. After the child was born, the relatives said: "What! You had the birth at home? Everything was fine?" When my friend assured them they all relaxed. If they had known beforehand they would have been saying, "Oh, you shouldn't do this, you should have a doctor ...." They would not only have worried but would have totally intruded upon the expecting mother, full of their own fears, doubts, criticisms and so on. This way everybody was both supportive throughout, and fine and happy in the end. It's extremely important to have an extended environment that is as fully-supportive as possible—free of tension, bitterness, disagreement and discord.

Generally, because the life support system in the womb is completely the mother's responsibility and the child doesn't have to do anything about it, that period is most likely a very comfortable one for the child—a period of pure nonlinear sensation, a time of collecting data; of a singular bliss, oneness; life without motive or neurotic demand. The only things that disturb the comfort of that period are severe emotional states or heavy use of some chemical or drug that affects the nervous system. If the mother uses a drug that sedates the being, the being gets born addicted to such sedation. Severe emotions, such as hatred, rage and depression which create brain and body chemistry which threatens the health of the being, should obviously also be avoided. For some women, their body-chemistry can become almost abortive, but usually it is not in large enough dosage or compounded enough to cause a miscarriage or other related problems. However, as much as possible, the mother should try to avoid situations of stress that would encourage this type of chemistry.

One doesn't need to worry too much about eating exactly the proper foods when one is pregnant. If a woman follows those zealous, health-conscious books about what she should or shouldn't eat when she is pregnant, she'll be so busy worrying about eating the wrong piece of bread that she'll be too tense to relax and enjoy her pregnancy. She should simply eat a basic healthy diet—clean fresh food—without too many chemicals and additives. After all, what's the percentage of children born damaged because of average dietary problems in America today? Almost nothing—so small as to be statistically insignificant. What are children born damaged from? Drug-addicted parents, alcoholic or heavy-smoking mothers, physically abusive mothers and fathers; medical drugs that are taken for various conditions, and radiation mutations, and so on—that's what children are born damaged from. Not because of artificial coloring in cheddar cheese. Not from preservatives in whole wheat bread. Parsley, I am told, is a natural abortifacient. Do you know how many women don't know that and eat a parsley leaf (or three) once or twice a week on their fish and in their meals? We have been terrified by the counter-reformation in the health-food industry. Such fundamentalism may be based on data that has some validity, but the right-eousness of it may be counterproductive.

During the whole pregnancy, communication to the child is another extremely useful aspect of conscious parenting. We should say whatever we would ordinarily say to someone we wanted to talk to: "Wasn't breakfast nice this morning?" or whatever. Essentially, we talk to the child the way we would talk to an adult. Not verbally, necessarily, but of course the vibrations of our voice will have an added effect, along with our psychic communications. Say things like, "We're really looking forward to the birth," and "Gosh, it's great you're coming to be with us." Of course it should go without saying that one would only speak positive, healthy and encouraging things. For instance, when a period of worship or some other event has really been wonderful, share that with the child. Tell heroic and mythic stories to the child. Communicate, right from the beginning. [The subject of language usage around children will be covered in greater depth in Chapter 8, *Speaking the Truth: Language and Honesty*.]

The fetus "hears" everything. For instance, if parents are asked, "What do you want? A boy or a girl?" and both of them look at one another and say, "Well, we'll take either if they are healthy, but we *really* want a girl," the fetus *feels* that. It's impossible to insulate the fetus from even subtle prejudices of that kind. So we need to be very clear in our own minds about our expectations, desires and unconscious needs. Clarity or ruthless self-honesty, and consequent intelligence, about such things is the best way to minimize their influences on the infant's consciousness and psychology.

You might ask, does an unborn fetus or an infant respond more to the actual words that come out of our mouths, or to the subtler psychic communication that's behind our words? The answer is to both. The psychic communication is most powerful early on, in terms of behavior. The brain registers language exactly, and when a child begins to learn language, the brain goes back and begins to interpret what it heard before the child even knew what language was.

The overall mood or texture of birth should be no different from the texture of ordinary life, except for details obviously. We should always be living, thinking and being in ways that entirely support the whole situation of pregnancy and birth—demonstrating kindness, loving attention and affection to our mates, to other children and friends, to our own parents, and so on. All of this registers with what will become, in childhood and adulthood, the person's unconscious mind and defining psychology. If we're not living that way initially, when the time comes to become a parent we have a great reminder for paying more attention to their basic needs, because birth is such a significant event. It often shatters our staid and unexamined notions of ordinary function.

This whole mood of kindness, generosity and compassion should be maintained from the moment the child is born, and before birth as well, in how the mother is treated during pregnancy. When I was sixteen (or even twenty-five), my whole idea of childbirth was that women were strong: they could work 'till two weeks before birth. Then, when it was time, they would go lie down, the baby would come out, and a couple of hours later they'd be up and around and back to work. I was a dyed-in-the-wool male chauvinist then (maybe still am). However, from experience in our community—not only with women in their thirties and forties, but with women in their twenties as well—we have learned that sometimes a woman has to stay in bed for a few months to protect both her own health and the child's health. The important issues then become: How is a woman treated by her family and support system when she is in bed? Is she treated like she's taking a vacation when she ought to be up working? Is she begrudged her needed rest? Or is she treated like her body is in a delicate condition, acknowledging that she needs care and attention? One way or another all of this will be communicated to her child. Who knows when a child's appreciation of kindness, generosity and compassion begins? Certainly before birth.

BIRTH CONTROL

We once published a satire issue of our community journal that contained a cartoon series. One illustration depicted me as extremely angry, with my hair wildly out of control. A very pregnant woman, looking overwhelmed, with three children hanging off her skirt, is saying to me: "Oh, you mean, I'm supposed to use the cervical cap *every* time?"

Generally, the more natural the birth control the better. We usually recommend cervical caps, and if one *must* use extra protection, then condoms, rather than any kind of more radical approaches such as surgical sterilization or some kind of sexual yoga. Some men are very good at ejaculation retention and some aren't good at all. (Just because they can't hold back doesn't mean they have to let go *inside*, to be blunt.) I've heard that herbal-contraceptive control and/or temperature and bio-rhythm measurements are absolutely effective. I'm a bit skeptical, however, as I've known cases where pregnancy occurred during and just after menstruation; and one case where three types of birth control were used at the same time—cervical cap, condom and anti-spermicide—and the woman still conceived. If a being wants to be born badly enough, they will still make it through. However, the less cautious we are, or the more carefree, the more unconscious factors will determine the likelihood of pregnancy, rather than conscious ones.

Some say that as long as a woman is actively nursing she won't be fertile. That's usually true for most women for two to three years, although some women are fertile almost immediately after birth even though they're nursing consistently. So it depends.

I think that it would be hard being pregnant again before the first child was walking, but in terms of the spacing of children it's a personal choice. Since the burden of caring for the children is going to fall on the mother, predominantly, it seems reasonable for her to be the one who decides. If somebody wants five kids, and they want them each a year apart, that might be pushing it. I do think it's possible to have two small children and for both of them to really get what they need; but even that is difficult for many people. We aren't all "natural" parents, though we all can educate and train ourselves to be "excellent" parents if we are truly willing to make the sacrifices if necessary, and to make the leaps of maturity required.

BIRTH

Adult members of our community have considered at length—through psychological work, deep self-study and self-revelation—the serious effects that an unnecessarily traumatic birth has had on them, and how to eliminate these effects in their newborn children. In order to establish and maintain a culture of true and natural human values—such as kindness, generosity, natural health and vitality—we believe it is crucial to develop consistent and wise practices concerning the birthing and raising of children. This topic should be one of serious study not only for expectant parents, but for every member of every community—social, alternative, spiritual, tribal or civic. An appropriate birthing culture requires the understanding and support of the community as a whole in order to be an effective reality for the children it serves.

Natural Childbirth

I have frequently spoken about the need to bring children into this world in a manner that will dispose them to best fulfill their capacity as human beings. The best birthing situation is one which, first of all, is natural. Drugs used on the mother can also attack the natural bodily growth of the child. As is typical of our society, however, conventional modern childbirth practice (and much so-called "health-care" practice as well) has become a dehumanized, self-serving institution that overlooks, and in some cases aggressively denies, the realities of positive human life-energy and development.

Steven Gaskin's community in Tennessee was called The Farm (and is still in existence under that name). At one time they had an open policy, which they publicized, that any woman who wanted to have a natural childbirth could come to The Farm for care and treatment, and that any woman who didn't want her child could leave the child at the Farm and the community there would take care of it. Any time a mother wanted her child back, moreover, she could get it. This policy lasted for many years, but eventually, because so many children were left there without their natural mothers, the community had to restrict it.

One can get an interesting education from reading their natural midwifery book (*Spiritual Midwifery* by Ina May Gaskin, Summertown, TN: The Book Publishing Co., 1978). The record of problematic births at The Farm was so small that medical authorities found it hard to believe the data. However, the residents there did have to create a completely modern clinic, including oxygen-incubators for premature births, just to satisfy the authorities, even though they had MD's and nurses on the property. Very few conventional hospital-birth advocates believed what these folks could do with natural childbirth, and how completely effective they became. (After three or four thousand births, you get to be pretty good!) At that point their work became statistically relevant, and an invaluable health resource. In fact, even a Canadian medical journal included The Farm's record in their statistics.

What happened at The Farm is a good reminder that childbirth is not a "problem." It's the human design and was meant to be natural and easy. When a mother consciously conceives and cares for herself, when a woman's life is in resonance with universal laws and principles, her delivery will usually be completely graceful and natural. Of course with some few exceptions. Occasionally, even under the best circumstances—with the best mental attitude, the best health and preparation by the expecting mother—hospital care or a C-section is necessary. In these cases, a woman's mental state of acceptance, her willingness to stay psychically connected to her child (and not tune out or abandon the "project" of birth) make all the difference in the world.

In the births I've seen the process has been very clear-cut and the implications of difficulty (or of no difficulty) quite obvious. In one case, the woman was uneducated about birthing, and was nervous and very superstitious. She ended up having to go to the hospital where she had a long labor and an extraordinarily painful birthing. For years afterwards if anyone mentioned anything about birth she'd wrinkle up her face and say, "Oh God! It's a horror."

My first cousin also had a difficult first delivery—very painful, with long labor. (She's extremely constrained, so that may have been one factor.) Before the birth she was in favor of natural childbirth and nursing. But after the birth she was clear that she would never go through that again: "If I have another child I want them to knock me out. C-section ... I don't care. I just want to get it over with." She wouldn't even consider ways of making childbirth more easeful.

In both of these cases the women were completely unprepared for natural childbirth and, prior to their respective pregnancies, had each lived a life of marked self-indulgence, abusive treatment of their body and notable self-centeredness. The demands of birth were far beyond their references, their willingness to surrender to the needs of the process, or their concepts of serving an "other," in this case even their own child. It never ceases to sadden me how many people are like that—the demands of birth and parenthood are so antagonistic to their world view (their own world view of their personal existence and insularity, not their political world view) that they'll do anything rather than expand to this higher level of conscientious humanhood.

In two other births which I am particularly

aware of the situation was totally different. The women were looking forward to birthing. Each had lived in right relationship to her body and her consciousness; each was thrilled, unafraid, prepared, ready to breathe and ready to give birth at home, with no projected obstacles in the way. Both births were easy and pleasant. Any stress or pain was subsumed by the anticipation of birth and motherhood, and taken sensitively and maturely.

Almost any woman, with rare exception, if she's cultured properly and has the right context, can have natural childbirth at home with a minimum of discomfort. And, some of that requires a joyful and positive support system of friends, family and community. With a first child, the tendency is to be a bit awed as well as a little nervous—not nervous in the negative sense, but some anticipation is likely; some "not-knowing" of what it's going to be like, at least experientially.

Discipline is a crucial element because there will be times during labor in which the woman will think, "I can't take another minute of this." Yet it must go on, and most women have the discipline to be great. (These days, to be "great" is to be what was just ordinary for women of antiquity.) They just keep going!

Of course, there are alternatives—to get a spinal; to have your belly cut open and the baby pulled out. Unfortunately, right at the time when discipline is most needed, the staff at the hospital will offer the alternative. Today, a woman doesn't have to go through with labor to birth. She can just be drugged, rendered unconscious. But the differences in natural birth versus birth under conditions where the mother is unconscious are profound.

TRANSCENDING IDENTIFICATION WITH THE BODY

The conditions of a child's birth affect the child dramatically; they affect the identification that the child will have with its human form. The assumption of embodiment (taking birth as a human) implies that the being will be responsible for an entirely different organism than what it was prior to incarnation. The implications of that include the demand to transcend the illusory identification that it can and usually goes have with the body. Any being will tend to be identified with its grossest level of manifestation, and since the body is the grossest level of human incarnation, we tend to be identified with the body as if that, exclusively, were us in totality, consciousness included. (Many scientists claim that all consciousness is a chemical function of the brain. We disagree.) The responsibility of a human being is to transcend identification with limitations that are, in essence, no more than the result of misunderstandings of our true condition.

To transcend the *body itself* is unrealistic, and in fact simply silly. If you blow your brains out, you transcend the body! But to transcend the *identification with the body* as if it were the entire being, that is necessary in order to become all that is inherently possible in being a human. That's a major responsibility! All of our training and our education ... all of our schooling ... is oriented towards body-identification or psychology-identification. Even learning to read and write, the way it's done, addresses our grossest level of manifestation only. Transcending identification with the body, therefore, as difficult as this may be, has crucial implications—like the end of cruelty, bigotry and violence in the world. The difficulty involved also has its distinctive payoffs. The easier it is to accomplish something in a given incarnation, the smaller the spiritual payoff. It's a little crude to express, but it's like we earn "spiritual points"; and as human beings the potential of building a tremendous, but subtle, energetic bank account is always present (whereas with other forms of life—certain animal, plant and inanimate forms—it's not).

The actual conditions of birth can directly affect how a person manifests in life, in psychological terms. A local midwife told us a story about a hospital birth in which the newborn just slid out of the doctor's hands and smashed onto the floor, head first. The baby lived, fortunately, but someone born under circumstances like that would have a really hard time transcending identification with the body. And treatment like that is more common than we might believe in the usual, conventional birthing situations.

The more directly the body is attacked in birth, the more the being feels that it is immediately going to be extinguished; hence, the stronger hold it takes in identification with the body. Bright lights, a lot of noise, rough handling—all contribute to strengthening the cramp[1]. In the imagination of the being, the body takes on the role of the vehicle of *survival*, instead of the encasement of consciousness, which itself cannot be extinguished.

THE INFLUENCES

The best birthing situation is one which is quiet and peaceful, and not attended by a lot of psychically loud and gawking onlookers. Any people present should understand something about the mystery of birth, and have both an awe and reverence for the process as well as a total resonance to and acceptance of the pregnant woman and her life beliefs. A new being is coming into existence, and that demands respect and honor! Parents, the midwife, and maybe another helper for the midwife, and at most (this is my personal feeling) two more people—close friends, people with whom both the mother and father are comfortable—are enough. One person always needs to be ready to run out for water, attend to errands, answer questions at the door, take care of the phone, and just keep the usual business of the world out; and the other is there as good company, to encourage the child and the parents. The father should be helping the mother to remember to breathe (in order to optimize the process of labor), and helping her remember what she's doing. Unfortunately that is not always the case. In one birthing class, for instance, there was a guy whose wife was eight-and-a-half months pregnant—she was due in two or three weeks—and she was terrified. All her life her mother had told her horror stories of birth, but somehow she still wanted to have natural childbirth. The husband, however, was totally insensitive; to him the whole thing was just a pain in the ass. Every time she'd ask him a question he'd get really annoyed and say, in a disgusted and critical tone of voice, "Damn, aren't you listening to the midwife?" That kind of situation is not very pleasant for the being about to be born who can literally sense, instinctually, such patterns in their parents or other primary adults commonly in the family space.

The context held by the people in the room—parents and others awaiting the child—is very important. Obviously, everyone there should be in a state of alertness and welcoming. If everybody is really nervous; if they don't trust the midwife and are sitting around with minds full of criticism and complaint; or if the mother doesn't want the child, for any number of reasons, such as for moral beliefs (like being against abortion), or if she has been coerced into going to term and is scared and identified with the pain and her internal conflicts, these are clearly not ideal situations.

If the people in the room have a real feeling for, and are genuinely inspired by, the mystery of birth, the great mystery of existence—not simply and crudely by this little lump of blood and flesh coming out of another big lump of blood and flesh, but because a living being who actually has communion with the Divine Source is achieving incarnation—that's extremely important. The being subjectively "gets" that communication, and is deeply, cellularly impressed with it.

* * *

People sometimes ask if there should be certain ceremonies when a child is born. I tend to always lean towards simplicity. Certainly one might light candles, and do other kinds of rituals—like the ritual of earth, fire, breath and water, in terms of purifying the child (all those forms of purification are valid)—but I tend to express radical reliance on the Divine. Radical reliance on the Divine may include some minimal ritual, perhaps a welcoming prayer, but doesn't require a tremendous amount of technical and long, involved ritual activity. A very simple prayer is enough. (I wouldn't necessarily recommend that the midwife, or the midwife's helper, say the prayer. The father could do it, but also it's helpful to have someone else there in case the father needs to be busy.)

If the parents know that now they have responsibility for a being who needs right culture in which to grow up, and if they heed the right kinds of objective influences, that's the important part. If the child grows up seeing their parents express a right relationship to God and Life in general, the child will also have a right relationship to God and Life. If the parents don't, then any number of rituals are just going to be something the child gives up as soon as they are old enough; just like most of us gave up Christianity or Judaism, in some form or another, as soon as we were independent enough to get away with it.

* * *

For the physical surroundings of a birth I prefer a room that's simple and tastefully prepared. If the room is the parents' bedroom, which is also recommended, there shouldn't be dresser drawers open, with clothes hanging out, stuff all over the walls, knick-knacks here and there, and the windowsills full of little pots of flowers. If the parents are part of a spiritual group, ideally there should be some sacred signs of this in the room. The room should be soft and inviting, not one with purple and silver wallpaper all around, mirrors on the ceiling, etc. I prefer quiet colors like pastel green or blue (my favorite is mild yellow). It should be a room in which sexual communion is practiced, not a space of constant interpersonal abuse, turmoil, difficulty and crisis. (Of course, if that were the case, such a couple would be foolish to have a child to begin with.)

I'm not in favor of music playing, either—even quiet, soft music (especially not electronic, "new age" music). If people are just talking, all being in communion with one another and celebrating the event of birth, that is enough.

* * *

Parents have specifically defined roles in birth. The mother's role is just to remember what's happening, and not to get lost in her own subjective projections, expectations, fantasies and imaginings, either because of pleasure or pain. The mother should maintain clear psychic contact with the child, "talking" to them while the birthing is going on, such as: "I can feel you getting ready to come out, and it's really wonderful, and we're looking forward to meeting you," and so on. This "talking" doesn't have to be verbal at all, although it certainly can be. But abstractly the mother needs to maintain communication with the child. She should explain what's going to happen: "You're crowning now, and you might feel a difference in temperature. That's natural, and as soon as you're out completely we're going to let you get adjusted, and then we're going to cut the umbilical cord, and we're going to put you right on my breast ...." Obviously, most mothers will be too busy with labor to maintain such a "cool" focus, but she can hold this intention of communion as a context, and the father can help with the formalities of language, greeting, encouraging and so on.

The father is there essentially to support the mother in, and also to communicate with the child in his own way. Sometimes women get a little delirious. (Sometimes the delirium is ecstasy. A lot of women have tremendous periods of ecstasy during birth.) It's helpful for the father to be there to maintain focus, and also, as one of the parents, to welcome the child.

POST-PARTUM SECLUSION

In traditional China, for the first twenty days after the birth the mother doesn't leave the birthing room, and the child doesn't leave the house. Along these lines, I wouldn't recommend long trips or noisy environments for a time following the birth. There's some disagreement about this, however. Some knowledgeable sources feel a child should be exposed early to as much manifestation as possible (noise, light, color, everything), and that the child should be talked through it (i.e., it should all be explained). I prefer, for the first two weeks, or even a little longer, just to keep the child inside, where it's quiet, protected, warm and secure. By then the child is used to nursing and is adjusted to its parents; and adjusted to breathing and elimination (pooping and peeing) and all of those standard things. After that one can gradually introduce the child to other various environmental manifestations— lights, noises, colors and all the rest— while explaining what it is the child is experiencing, and continuing to assure the child of its safety. You don't want to interpret the child's experience in your adult way, but just to objectively describe things.

Anything that will likely shock or surprise the child should be explained beforehand. For instance, if you intend to take the child outside in the city, where there are cars honking and other sharp noise, you may explain, "We're going to go outside, and there are going to be a lot of loud noises. You're with me, and you can hear the noises and take them in, and observe them, but they do not need to threaten you directly. They have nothing to do with you. ['Hurt' isn't a good word to use.] Just observe them, pay attention, absorb information." So, you should always explain things to the child.

Nothing is really *necessary* by way of follow-up to the birth. The same thing holds throughout conception, pregnancy, birth: know what you're doing; be aware that the child is an individual, and that he or she is conscious and aware. Talk to them; relate to them; turn them always toward the Divine, toward wholesome and natural relationship to life, toward service to others, toward happiness and self-confidence. That's all.

CIRCUMCISION

Circumcision may be performed seven or eight days after birth, as this is what is medically conventional. I would want the circumcisionist to be really relaxed, and to know what he's doing with the scalpel. The ideal circumstance is for the circumcisionist to understand the whole process of birth, and circumcision, and the relationship of man to God and all of that; but that's asking a lot.

Of course I'll be energetically slaughtered here for even bringing up the subject. Most, if not all, of the proponents for the kind of natural and conscious beings, and the healthy birthing practices that we're discussing here, are dramatically and even violently (righteously) opposed to circumcision. So, let's just say it should be a personal, parental option.

NURSING

In his book, *Making Sense of Suffering*, J. Konrad Stettbacher (the therapist who worked with author, psychotherapist and child-advocate Alice Miller[2] in her own healing process) gives a dramatic example of the difference between loving care and abuse of an infant, and the effects on the child's psyche:

... *An infant is hungry and searches for its mother, who reacts adequately to its needs .... It seeks and finds its mother's breast and pleasurably drinks the milk until, satiated and relaxed, it smiles up at her. It allows her to rock it to sleep. After a period of rest, it will awaken and smile, searching once more for its mother in pleasant anticipation.*

... [In the opposite case, the child's needs are not met, resulting in injury to the child's primal integrity.] *Because of the child's vulnerability vis-à-vis the adult world, it can be arbitrarily hurt. The attempted satisfaction of the child's needs—which should be a pleasurable event—comes, as a result of the injury, a painful experience the causes of which the child has no means of discovering. The child is 'all need' and must obey this imperative. Every rejection, every denial, constitutes an abuse. Regardless of the reasons for the abuse, the child feels the injury as the result of its own inadequacy.*

... *An example of such an injury: An infant is hungry. It calls out, screams, but the mother reacts only with impatience. She hastily heats the baby's bottle, barely bothering to check the temperature of the milk, then, frowning, grabs up the child. The infant, its face streaming with tears, reluctantly opens it mouth and tries to reject the hot liquid with little or no success ... instead of meeting with the expected, pleasurable satisfaction of its need, the child is subjected to pain— pain inflicted by its mother or someone else entrusted with its care.... In the future, as soon as the child senses a need, it will be gripped by fear and vainly attempt to escape the situation. The injuries inflicted upon its body and soul—give rise to latent overreactions in the system that constitute a burden and simultaneously generate constant fear.*[3]

Negative experience abounds in everyone's life, and the psyche is prone to being affected by it. Only a whole Self, grounded by experiences of satiety and fullness, can serve as an anchor in those times. By far the best time to get experiences of satiety and fullness is in childhood, and the earlier the better. That way, they are elemental enough in our basic makeup to be stronger than the negative experiences that we encounter later.

This satiety and fullness comes, in childhood, from having our needs met. Plain and simple. As a baby, if you are carried when you want to be carried, put down when you want to be put down, given quality attention as a matter of course, fed when you start looking for the breast as opposed to when you have to scream for it, then you are most likely to be basically, elementally satisfied. You have this beginning experience that the world is okay, and that you will be provided for. You belong and everything's all right, and that serves as a tremendous anchor for the rest of your life.

In light of this I continually wonder why more of the people who are supposed to be conscious and aware aren't nursing their children? That is even more curious given the degree of attention to pure food with no chemicals ... and no this and no that ... which many people have today. Why would they give a child a bottle, and not the real thing? Children *can* tell the difference! Glass ain't your skin, no matter how warm the milk is; I can tell you that. This kind of contradiction, however, would pose no problem for a hypocrite. Of course, there are random physiological problems that make it difficult for a woman to nurse her child, but those are few and far between. The predominant problems are psychological, and there is no excuse for denying a child this intimacy with mother simply because the mother is so self-centered.

The wonder and power of nursing, and the bonding this creates, is beautifully described by an experienced mother:

> *The newborn infant sleeps in the family bed and is carried on the mother or father's body when the parents are awake. During the day, the infant sleeps and wakes feeling the rhythm of the movement of his mother's body, just as he did within the womb. He observes her face and other faces; the changes of light; the smells and sounds of human activity. His daily life is full of touch, affection, closeness, and the stimulation of the life that is around him. When one lives in a communal setting, ashram or community household, this provides the infant and growing child with even more of the warmth of human commonality, and an opportunity to integrate into the greater web of life.*
>
> *The mother nurses the infant whenever the child is hungry. There is no need for a schedule of feeding imposed by an adult; the child knows when she is hungry and asks to nurse. Because the child is carried on the mother's body, the child does not even need to cry, but simply nuzzles toward the mother's breast and the mother responds. This is the beginning of a relationship in which the caregiver respects and responds to*

the child's expression of her own needs, rather than the adult defining the child's reality for her, dictating what the child should need and how the child should respond.

We recommend that during the infant's first six months, the mother devote full attention to the infant during nursing. This means that the mother does not read or even, in general, carry on extended adult conversations during this time. Nursing is an intimate part of the establishment of bonding between mother and child, and it is a time for the mother to be present without distraction. It is an opportunity to look lovingly into her child's eyes because eye contact is one of the most important aspects of human bonding. Any mother having paid even minimal attention to her child during nursing will have noticed how total and steady a child's visual attention is on her gaze when the child is nursing. This attention should be met and held.

As a general rule, we recommend that nursing should be "on demand," and allowed to go on as long as the child is actively nursing and as long as the mother *can* nurse physically. Ideally, nursing would continue for three to five years—but that depends on the circumstance, on the child, and on the mother and the mother's health. Many women find nursing for that length of time very difficult. I suppose that if one were fully psychologically healthy there wouldn't be any difficulty. Once the child starts biting the breast and scratching, even mothers who are completely in love with their child, and have not even the slightest wish to curtail this activity, feel that nursing can get to be tremendously intrusive. Since a child intuitively feels that mother's breasts are a part and parcel of his or her given rights to do with as they wish, it is often necessary to set appropriate boundaries around this. A child can easily get used to nursing gently and sensitively. (Although *not nursing at all* is not a boundary; it's a punishment to the child, even if the adult doesn't mean it that way.) If the child is biting the breast, the more common and traditional treatment is to flick him in the nose really hard, so that after a couple of times he'll never bite again. We've not advocated that method. Rather, a mother can talk to her child and say, "You know, that hurts. You can bite your toys, or your rubber duck, or a carrot stick ...." And the child learns pretty quickly. Nevertheless, every time the child gets a new tooth, they may want to try it out. When this process is repeated frequently, it is understandable that the mother can feel personally threatened or victimized.

So, a lot of women will want to stop nursing earlier for many reasons. Some women are embarrassed in public, but that's usually the last of the reasons. More often, the decision is because nursing uses a tremendous amount of energy—the woman may need to eat large amounts of food and will be hungry quite often, thus provoking the whole psychological neurosis around food. Sleep deprivation can be another reason. For lucky mothers, the child will naturally, and often very quickly, learn to sleep through the night, like the parents. But sometimes children don't; and a mother may feel that it is just too demanding when her child is waking frequently during the night to nurse.

Because of her physical health, one of the mothers in our community had to stop nursing when her child was only about two. The doctor told her, "If you keep nursing your body will weaken to a degree that is dangerous to your health." This mother had internal health problems since she was a child, and she contracted hepatitis in India and never fully healed. The nursing was physically more than her body could naturally take.

If the mother is healthy and *can* breastfeed but *doesn't* —because she's got a job and she needs to stop the milk flow, or because it's inconvenient, or whatever—the child will feel that, and will compress their range of feeling experience to accommodate the mother's range of feeling experience, instead of staying open and vulnerable, which a child normally is. Therefore, the child would compromise his or her emotional life, and end up stunted and incomplete in their ability to express feelings. However, if a mother has physical problems and *cannot* breastfeed, the child will also instinctually know this, and the adjustment will be more natural and freer of trauma.

As children get older it is easy for them to understand that there are certain circumstances where nursing on demand doesn't work—on a public bus or in restaurants, for example, where the negativity of people watching is counterproductive to the positivity of the child's experience of being able to nurse on demand.

Nursing is very comforting. A child will almost always want to nurse either when their feelings are hurt, when they're embarrassed or ashamed, or if they are physically hurt. Sometimes nursing at those times may proves difficult, depending upon the circumstances. Nonetheless, even if we have drawn clear and appropriate boundaries, it is important to put the overall health of our children before our own small discomforts.

In my understanding: anything that disturbs the infant's security in relationship to food and comfort is taken by the raw instinct of the infant as being a threat to it's literal survival. For instance, if you are a nursing mother and you take a shower while your child is asleep, if your child wakes up and starts crying, you know (as an adult) that if you don't nurse the child for a half-hour they're not going to starve. You know they're going to be fine; but the child does not know that. A child begins to feel threatened when it's hungry and it isn't immediately fed. As an adult you may say, "Give me a break. I can't be nursing the child every fifteen minutes, every time they give a little whine." But to a child, when they are hungry and not fed they assume instinctively (not intellectually) that they are going to die. Of course there is a major difference between actual physical hunger and the desire to nurse as a form of emotional comforting. If a child is breast-fed whenever they are physically hungry they will be less likely to be traumatized, even mildly, when the boundary is eventually drawn to not be allowed to nurse solely for the emotional security of it. As they get older and become more cognizant of the relational aspects of their world, they will clearly understand just and right social boundaries. But if as infants they were denied the kinds of love and affection that allowed them to tacitly feel loved and secure they will have a habitual reaction, unconscious, to boundaries, and this habitual reaction will overrule whatever rational intelligence might apply under healthier circumstances.

What happens next? The child cries for a half-hour, assuming they are going to die, but then, all of a sudden, they get food. So, even though the child knew instinctively they were going to die because they weren't fed when they wanted to be, somehow, obviously, they are still alive. They survived. That is the beginning of the survival strategy—the start of the program:

"I have to do this to get my needs met." [This scenario reinforces what was noted from Stettbacher earlier. Although it is based on the author's opinion, it is also shared by much of modern psychology. For our purposes here, it is vital to appreciate the essential connection between early feeding experiences and the psychological and emotional development of the human being. The implications of this infantile survival strategy will be covered in the next chapter, when we focus on the need for love and attention.—*Editor*]

How To Stop, Consciously

When a woman has some idea of when she is going to stop nursing, or when the child will not sleep in the parents' bed or room anymore, the parents can begin a little ahead of time to prepare the child for the transition. There are different viewpoints, of course, on how to wean your child.

With one child, who nursed until she was five, her parents started preparing her when she was around four-and-a-half. "At five we are going to stop nursing," they said, and every time they'd say that she would say, "No we aren't." But, when she turned five she actually made no argument. The same thing occurred about moving from the family bed and getting her own room. The parents said, "In a few months you are going to have your own room ...." Now you would imagine this would seem great to the child, but she would say, "I don't want my own room." Once again, however, when it was time to get her own room there was no problem, because the parents had previewed it: "You're growing up. You're getting to be a big girl now. Things change as you grow; circumstances change," and so on. In both instances the transitions were explained in terms of how exciting it is to be getting older and learning new things, as if stopping nursing was a great adventure, as if getting one's own room was a gift of responsibility. This allowed the transition to be graceful and free of argumentation and difficulty.

In conclusion we must again emphasize that nursing is a part of the biological program, at least as much for the mother as for the child. The difference is, of course, that the child is innocent, uncomplicated and instinctual. To a child, to be deprived of this need—without the exception of the mother being physically unable to breast-feed—is to be rejected and abandoned. An infant does not have the intellectual sophistication to reason out mother's neurotic psychology. A child has no recourse but to armor itself against this pain of rejection by repressing its feelings and adapting to the situation, which to varying degrees, depending on the rest of the family health or lack of it, always produces aberration in adult behavior, or in the natural course of developmental growth. For the mother, by the time a woman is an adult, her own complex psychology is already firmly in place, and the immense volume of unconscious neurotic directives make the task of ease-fully following her biological imperatives a very very difficult and tricky process. The mother's resistance to breast-feeding (when there is resistance) is highly unlikely to be simply overcome, even in the face of the certain knowledge that to deny this intimacy to her infant risks debilitating the child in various ways for a lifetime. It's almost like if we can't see it we refuse to acknowledge its viability. But again, we must empha-size the importance of nursing in the mother-child bond, and in the overall health of the child's self-image and self-confidence at all stages of the child's, the ado-lescent's and the adults life. To deny both child and parent any element of the natural, organic developmental program is to handicap both in profound, sometimes subtle and sometimes very blatant ways. Consider this deeply, for the health of your child or children may well depend on it.

——— 3 ———

ENOUGH & NEVER ENOUGH:
On Love & Affection
and Attention

LOVE & AFFECTION

Alice Miller once described an individual's child-hood in a city where there were earthquakes—where buildings were falling down, and people getting hurt. Literally, the child's whole world got shaken up, but because he had a secure family environment he came out intact and unscarred, either psychologically or emotionally. The point is, there is no substitute for an infancy and childhood grounded in a truly loving, bonded and affectionate family, although many people try to make up for the lack of this in their lives through accumulating power, territory, fame or possessions as if true security could be found in such fleeting and ephemeral domains. Many people, in fact, collect "love" as if it itself were a thing, and as if getting a big enough quantity of it (through children, lovers, affairs and so on) would create ultimate security.

I want to share with you a story that makes an important analogy to the need for showing love and affection to our children. Quite a few years ago we were looking at a piece of property out West, and we asked the owner whether there were any mines on the land.

The guy understood immediately that we were concerned about the possible danger for children.

"There are two open mines on the property, about thirty feet deep. Funny thing," he said, "once, one of my kids couldn't find his dog. Dog was missing for a long time." He went on to tell us that for two months everybody assumed that the dog had been out in the woods and had gotten killed by a big cat—a puma or something. The man was walking around the property one day and found that the dog had fallen into this thirty-foot well and couldn't get out. Amazingly, the dog was still alive after two months! Skinny, very skinny, but still alive.

They rescued the dog—pulled him out, brought him back to the house, fed him and nurtured him, and he came back to health. Problem was, there was a big difference between the dog before he fell in the well and after. After he fell in the well, once he got a little health back and was feeling more energetic, he started killing all the chickens on the place—anything he could find he'd grab and kill. So they had to get rid of the dog. There was nothing else they could do. The dog would attack anything edible.

When the dog was in the well he basically survived on rainwater, and maybe any little rodent that fell in; there was nothing else down there. So the dog developed a disposition of scarcity—purely instinctual of course; not in the way human beings do, in all of their amazing intricacy. After this well experience where there wasn't enough food, anything that had to do with food, even when the dog wasn't hungry, was desired in a completely vital way. One could say that the dog went mad. He was still a pet (still nice to the folks he lived with), he just had this disposition of scarcity—he could never get enough. The dog could eat and be full, but could never, in a kind of instinctual way, collect enough food. So he'd kill the chickens even if he didn't eat them, a purely instinctual response to a hunger that was in his memory, in his cells, but not still active in the present time. Made no difference to the dog.

It's amazing that as thinking, self-reflective, intelligent human beings, we do the same thing. How often, at some time in our childhood, something happens to give us this feeling of scarcity. And as adults, even when such conditions of scarcity are totally unrealistic, we still act as if they were actually real, here and now.

There are two basic dispositions that human beings have: they either feel loved or unloved. Children either know they're loved or they feel unloved with the concomitant feelings of worthlessness, uselessness, insecurity, or of being bad, a victim, etc. (If in the first two years of a child's life they know they're loved, we can breathe a sigh of relief even while we may be fighting "tooth and nail" with them later on.) Of course, this knowledge of being loved or unloved becomes an unconscious motivating factor very quickly, and it is so total, so pervasive, that to uncover it as an adult, through therapy or some other means, is extremely difficult. It is like invalidating our entire life's program; and the resistance to that, as you can understand, is overwhelming.

It happens for all of us: If as children we know we're loved, essentially we will have a hold on life, a stability that requires no proof or reinforcement. It just is. We'll still have the usual stresses of growing up, and even unavoidable neuroses, but such things will be met and taken in stride. They won't "derail" us. Environment can be a big factor and the whole aspect of Madison Avenue conditioning and many other influences can affect us, but nonetheless we've got something that's really crucial! Children will have self-respect, creativity, confidence and capability if they *know*, if they feel, they are basically and essentially loved as they are, and for who they are, free of parental demands and expectations to be something other than what they are.

If a child doesn't know they're loved, or feels unloved (which is epidemic in today's world), then, all their life they attempt to find love from the position of scarcity; like that dog. As adults, they usually don't act this out in as obviously unrealistic or as vital forms as the dog did, but this is their conditioning. Being intelligent human beings, they are able to consider what this type of behavior would mean to those they live with; or its potential effect on their boss, so that they can keep our jobs, and all of that. But still, unconsciously, they seek love from a position of scarcity and lack, and this plays itself out in an infinite number of idiosyncrasies and personality quirks and twists.

Commonly, a girl child who feels unloved will flash on her father, and will always tend to relate to men in a way that indicates that she can never get enough love. No matter what a guy does, it won't be good enough. "You don't pay enough attention to me." Or, "You don't spend enough money on me." Or, "You don't love me enough ... you aren't interested in my life ... you don't care about my dreams." There's always something. If it's a little boy who feels he hasn't gotten enough love, he often flashes on his mother, and as an adult he becomes someone who goes from woman to woman always feeling the empty hole of unlove, always feeling misunderstood and never loved enough, acting towards women as if they needed to mother him instead of be with him as an equal. Obviously, both situations can develop into mild or severe sexual aberrations. When a child grows up feeling that they are unloved, it's extremely hard for them to deal with the emptiness that they constantly feel, unconsciously and often consciously as well, because that's what human beings need most—we need love; not in the sense of a mating relationship, or enough sex, or lots of praise, even, but a deep, comfortable and familiar kind of reliable, tangible and abiding love.

This love is evident in cultures in which people must rely on the security of a family—like native or Indian cultures. Among the less privileged in these cultures, several families often live in the same house in only a few rooms, and in fact, these large extended families may be the only security a child has in his or her life. There's a real difference in the kind of closeness that people have under such situations. A feeling of scarcity may apply to food if they're starving, or to something else, but not to love.

Some of you must have felt that kind of abiding love, but it's very uncommon in the U.S. Maybe some of you who have strongly ethnic families have felt that love, because of the deep bondedness and commitment to the extended family clan. Perhaps you can't feel it with your Mom and Dad, or between brother and sister, but when the whole family gets together—the aunts, the uncles, the grandparents—and there's a mass of warmth, affection, humor and acceptance, then you can feel it. It's palpable, and there is a delight in such company. Ideally, that love would not be solely and exclusively relegated to blood relations, although we tend to have a certain feeling for blood relations that we don't have for other people. If we achieve this bondedness with any group, however, that's what real community is.

THE DEADLY EQUATION

Very early in life, probably at several months of age, we began to realize that the objects of our unconditional love and attention could either return that love or deny it. The condition of scarcity, this feeling that either there wasn't enough love, or that we would never get enough, arose when we were denied that love. This is always a great shock because to the infant it is unimaginable. The child doesn't have a choice: to love or not. The child can only love, and so expects this of others. But when an adult does not love the child, the effect is so devastating that some form of withdrawal or "closed-down-ness" must result. Such denial usually wasn't done on purpose, with intention, of course. Our parents *tried* to love us. They *thought* they loved us. But they were too self-centered and unconscious to be aware of what they most likely thought were insignificant actions, but which were actually forms of aggressive manipulation, abuse and unlove towards their child (such as laughing at us when we did something that they thought was funny, but which to us, as an infant, was terribly serious).

The feeling that we got from that unconscious treatment was something like, "This is too painful to be *love*, so therefore it isn't. And if it isn't, then I am not loved." But also, we noticed that there was something that worked, in the sense of getting our parents' attention. Perhaps when we wiped our dirty hands on Mommy's clean white blouse, Daddy laughed, and we sensed this to be a positive response to us, to our literal being. We then equated this "acknowledgment" with love and went about trying to recreate it. When we next got a negative response from Mommy (often something a child does innocently and spontaneously is cute, adorable and endearing, but becomes contrived and false when it is redone with intention or purpose), we became confused and deeply hurt, reinforcing our defensiveness and caution and this feeling of unlove.

As adults now, we need to be child-responsive in our parenting. We can try to see their lives from *their* developmental perspective, and thereby avoid giving this whole problem of scarcity to our children. Sometimes we will miss some things that we really don't want to miss, but if we give them attention early on in life, the rewards will easily be worth whatever sacrifices we have to make, whatever changes we have to effect in our unconscious behavior and unexamined attitudes. The best thing we can give a child—more important than formal education—is the knowledge that they are loved, wanted, enjoyed. If for the first two years of a child's life we have to starve ourselves of adult "food" (metaphorically speaking) to give that child the right kind of attention, then we should starve!

To give a practical example: Many mothers who care for their children with this kind of attention become so hungry for "a break" without the constant presence of the child (especially if they have a "family bed" which allows the child to sleep with the parents, and which can mean an almost twenty-four-hour-a-day companionship), that they'd be tempted to ignore the child or deny them loving, affectionate presence for an hour or two (or five minutes) just to have a quiet, uninterrupted "adult" conversation with their mate or with a friend. But putting our own imagined "needs" over the real and necessary needs of our child is not worth the price. When a child has to yell "Mommy" over and over to get our attention, it should be clear that we've shut the child out, that we've been in a trance, unresponsive to the child's needs because we've felt the need to serve ourselves and our hungers ahead of our child's.

Children need and want firm and just boundaries. Within that context, they also need overwhelming amounts of loving, exclusive attention. This is what allows them to develop self-worth, confidence and self-trust.

PREPARATION FOR THE DISCOMFORTS OF LIFE

A child who is properly loved during the first year of life is a big enough human being to be able to assimilate, respond to and adjust to many negative circumstances in their lives. On the other hand, a child who feels unloved is usually so disposed to take all negative situations as direct reflections on, or as proof of, the fact that they are unloved and unlovable, that they will respond in such circumstances as if they are being personally attacked, rather than responding directly to the situation itself with clarity and creativity. Feelings of unlove generate unconscious, "blind," habitual reactions, instead of sound, intelligent and objective responses. For example, why is it that there are always a few people who, as horrible and shocking as what they see and experience may be (even in a war situation) are able to integrate that shock and became more humane as a result? Whereas with others, such an experience drives them mad; makes them more violent, more angry and darker human beings than they were before. Could it have something to do with childhood-instilled feelings of self-worth? For instance, in the Mexico City earthquake, in the Indian earthquakes, in the earthquake in Italy some years ago, there were ten to thirty-thousand deaths. In such situations, one who was left alive would have some extraordinary suffering to observe and deal with. Ideally, one would want to serve by helping people out, by giving people who lost their homes a place to stay, or food or blankets. Our capability for serving in that way, rather than just breaking down or walking around entranced and despondent, might very well depend upon how we were loved as children.

In the first years of a child's life there are plenty of discomforts: fevers, wet diapers, loud noises in the environment; parents may fight, playmates may do disagreeable things or act in quite aggressive ways. Even with the best parents, there are going to be upsets for a child. No matter how attentive the mother is, there are going to be times when she is out of the room just when the child wants her and starts to cry. But, if the overall context of the child's life is one of security, safety and love, then the discomforts will be a side issue, easily subsumed in the child's attitude of self-confidence and self-worth. By nature, of course, some children are more vital, more fiery than others, so we can't expect that *all* discomforts will always be met with external manifestations of unending patience and serenity. Overall, however, a child's inner response *can be* big enough, not deeply divided, not upset by the usual life-stresses and strains.

If we had the security of feeling tacitly, non-problematically, unconditionally loved, not only would we have the ability to put up with things that have nothing to do with us, or things that can't be helped (like traffic jams, or even unexpectedly getting fired from a job), but we could also put up with exchanging comfort for discomfort (i.e., replacing discomfort with a more viable or comfortable situation, and visa versa if it were useful), when it was socially relevant. For instance, when visiting in-laws (with or without our new child), we might have to bear a circumstance that we feel is extremely uncomfortable—like tolerating our in-laws' negative or life-denying language, their physical or psychic aggressiveness, or their abusive shaming. (Of course, our in-laws might be the loveliest of people; so might our own parents; so might our co-workers. Unfortunately, these same people don't necessarily understand the way that we feel it's important to be with a child, or to talk with a child.) In any case, this circumstance presents a very reasonable need where we may wish to exchange comfort for discomfort. If we had that security as a child, we would be able to do that easily and with the greatest diplomacy. We would make the best of it. If we didn't have that security, it would be nearly impossible.

THE HORRORS OF CONDITIONAL "LOVE"

Many people who feel basic unlove have unconsciously developed a mechanism whereby they can imagine themselves loved if they meet certain conditions. These conditions would obviously be the ones that were used as bribery (or blackmail) by their parents in order to earn affection or attention (both of which, in desperation, an unloved child will equate with love). An example might be a parent who has a stated expectation (or unstated, but highly charged) for their child to be a musical or artistic prodigy, or to get all top grades in school. Such a child is very likely to equate what the parent expects/desires/demands with the condition necessary for being loved (or to get love). This conditioned neurosis will continue throughout a lifetime, if left unexamined, unacknowledged and undealt with, and will motivate all that person's choices, actions and responses to various situations.

That is exactly what is going on in Bosnia, where the children have been forced into the mold of a cultural definition and not allowed any individuality in expression. The racial hatred between the Muslims, the Serbs and the Christians is not possible to reason out with sane discussion. Those people have no living individuality, but can only react blindly and violently to the effect of mass psychosis. When the Communist government was ruling the country, the religious mass psychosis was subsumed by the political mass psychosis. But once the government was gone, then we have what we have today. The same thing is true of the Cambodians slaughtering the Vietnamese. There is no racial, social, cultural or religious exception to the physics of human psychology and consciousness.

A rigid ego is simply not able to enter into the creative process. How many of us have found ourselves entering into a process of creativity, entering into previously unknown territory (certainly this applies to spiritual life, in principle, on a different scale), and found ourselves panicking; literally afraid that we wouldn't be able to "come back." Yet, that's the whole point: if we do give ourselves to our art, or to our lover, or whatever, "we" won't come back. We will be altered, changed, transformed; we will have grown as a human being, sometimes even immeasurably. But most people are so terrified of "not coming back" that they won't let themselves fall into such brilliant opportunities. A secure ego realizes that it won't get lost (in the sense of being diminished or even going mad), for there is no danger. A mature human being can allow themselves to fall into a love affair, into deep intimacy or vulnerability. Obviously, when the entire self is entering into a relationship with the Divine, a relationship in which the self will be consumed, there is also the fact that the more secure the ego, the more willing we are to allow Divine Influence to have its way with us, so to speak. The more rigid our ego, the more distrust there is, understandably of course. Rigidity is caused by projections, expectations, bigotry, righteousness and so on.

TRANSCENDING UN-LOVE

Have you ever heard a child crying, "I want my Mom"? If only a child ever *really* knew what they were asking for. Never in the history of mankind has a child ever said to their mother, "I want you," and consciously known what they were saying. How could a child have such a truly sophisticated or refined concept? Usually, a child under such circumstances wants comfort, security, a firm and just boundary, or help in "power-tripping" another child or another adult (besides Mom). Of course we can't ever convince a child of what they *really* want, until maybe they're about thirty-five or forty years old. (They'll still be a child at that age, but they'll have something that's much more susceptible to a different type of conviction. Which is fortunate for all forms of self-development or transformation, the sanity of the world and the continuation of the human race.) The bottom line is, they want to know *who they are*; but in psychological terms they want the ability to feel love. Unfortunately, nothing in the usual psyche's bag of tricks can produce that after unlove takes hold; not even a lot of good and genuine loving. Although a lot of steady, trustworthy loving and genuine respect and acknowledgement *can begin* to repair the rift, that's important, even though it can't entirely make the difference. Only "rewiring" from childhood life-choices of unlove can fully make the difference.

All of our therapy and our unbelievable amounts

of work on ourselves are simply about getting back to the point at which we decided that we were unloved and then remaking the decision otherwise. Most people will never do that—they just don't have the patience, fortitude or the guts. The few people who do manage it are touted by the therapies that they have been taking and held up as examples to others: "Look, you can do this as well." But most people just *can't* do it because it takes such tenacity, such commitment and such a willingness to voyage with ruthless self-honesty through one's pain and loneliness that the average person simply will not persist. Most won't even begin.

To feel unloved can really slow down one's spiritual work, if one is involved in such things. Maybe it's subtle, but if someone is really serious about their transformational work they don't even want subtle interferences. For some, feeling unloved is an obstacle that has to be dealt with and gotten out of the way as a foundational step, nothing more. (There is no need to embellish and exaggerate it.) It is useful to have the attitude that, "This belief system is attempting to divert everything to its own uses, it's own vision. I have to get this out of the way, because then I can necessarily have more integrity in relationship to the Divine."

The feeling of scarcity *can* be transcended in the realization that there isn't any scarcity, since we all have a reference point for communion with another human being. And while it's true that people are invulnerable, resistant, territorial, protective, defensive, and on and on and on (we could give a whole list of tendencies that people express to avoid even basic, clear communication, not to mention communion), because they're afraid of being hurt and taken advantage of, victimized, abandoned ... the usual standard things ... nonetheless, this reference point for communion still exists. Absolutely! Even if we feel unloved and unlovable, at the same time *we have loved*. Children *love* their Moms and Dads and brothers and sisters and aunts and uncles, and even everybody and everything—cats and bananas and thunder .... So, we do have a reference point for deep communion. But, we may not have a reference point for the appropriate *response* to love or communion when it comes towards us. We may well be too blocked by our obsessive, and usually compulsive drive to get the very thing that we won't believe when we actually get it! We do have a reference point for a kind of one-sided communion, and we usually don't realize that it can be a two-way street. What we *can* do is the "giving out" of love, not knowing if it will be returned (and usually not believing it *can* be returned in fact).

That's why some people struggle so hard with this work of becoming truly human. They don't believe they are lovable; that in fact they are loved. I don't mean intellectually. One doesn't sit down and say, "I'm unlovable." I mean primally. We don't *know* we are loved, and it's very hard to do this work when that attitude pervades everything; because even when people love us, we may be grateful and vulnerable, feeling something ... some glimmer of reality ... but we are still doubtful and suspicious. "Is it real?" "Can I *trust* it?"

Expressing Affection

It is natural for me to watch parents with children very closely—a lot of my inspiration for writing comes from observing dynamics between adults and children. A common phenomenon is evident when parents, or aunts and uncles, say to little children, "Come and give Mommy a hug," or "Come and give Uncle John a hug," or something of the sort. Sometimes children *love* to give the people they love hugs and kisses, and shower attention and affection on people they are close to. Sometimes they simply don't.

Such responses from children are exceptionally pleasant because children are so innocent. When a child strokes us, with no solicitation, we know that it's real. (Sometimes this real expression even lasts up to their teenage years.) When a child hugs Mom or Dad with all their might, it's totally genuine; not some "peck on the cheek" protocol-thing that they do when they are expected to and have been trained to do, to meet the expectations of polite society.

I used to be so "laid back" that when my first child, the way children do, would just come up and hug me with all her enthusiasm, delight, joy and fervor, it would disorient me. That kind of spontaneous affection is completely wild, and I was a pretty up-tight kind of guy. That's the way children are. They don't naturally fawn over you, they don't stroke you the way adults desperately stroke their loved ones, out of need and pain. They will just run up in a burst of affection and give you a great big squeeze and run off. No problem and no underlying motive.

It often strikes me as both sad and unfortunate that we rarely trust ourselves enough to drop our expectations and just let children be spontaneous with their affection towards us. If we stop to think of our own displays of affection, even if we're unceasingly in love with someone, we don't pet them all the time. There are times in which we touch, and times in which we're involved deeply in some work task, or consumed with some fascinating distraction. It's not that we don't love our "significant other" at those times, but rather, we are being spontaneous to our loved one in a way that is not *directly* offering attention (which, nonetheless is always tacit, always just shimmering and simmering under the surface). Shouldn't we be willing to let children have that same freedom?

Sometimes, even sensitive and intelligent adults aren't willing to give children the space to express their love at their own pace, in their own way:

"Where's my kiss this morning?" they say, as the child goes out to play.

"Oh yeah, I forgot," the child answers, as they run back to do their duty.

The way to encourage those we love to express spontaneous affection is to express it ourselves.

For children, the whole dynamic of "give Mommy a hug" is indicative of our attempt to structure our environment to suit *our own* insecurities and *our* survival strategies. We structure our environment by compartmentalizing every event, and we then have an automatic response for every conceivable circumstance. It would be a lot more enlivening for us to be more spontaneous and genuine, to allow the universe, or life, to unfold according to *its* momentum, instead of trying to play God, so to speak.

Children can get used to realizing that warmth, love, affection and attention can all be fully present in a look, in a touch, in a glance or a big hug. It doesn't have to be a constant and overwhelming immersion in physical or gross level attention. That's something that's very important to communicate to them. Otherwise, when they get to our age and fall in love, every insignificant momentary lapse of attention from their partner seems to be a sign that he or she is either paying attention to someone or something else, or doesn't love them. Such a person will have an intense and obsessive attention on their lover, because they've constantly got to know that they are loved. They are always, in unspoken ways (or spoken ways) whining at their lover, begging them to give constant feedback in dramatic physical gestures that indicate that they love them or care for them. Such insecurity and tension is not the most pleasant mood in which to live.

The biggest destroyer of love is that kind of desperate and often aggressive need to be recognized all the time – that clinging, needy grasping. Children need to learn that communication is more than a lengthy diatribe or monologue, or a twenty-minute hug, or four hours of non-stop block building. They must learn that a complete communication, full of warmth and love and gentleness, can be given in just a simple brush of the fingertips across an arm, or just an "uh huh." How are they going to learn that if we don't feel that and express that to them with genuineness and happiness whenever we feel it? The time is always right to express our love for our children. We don't have to wait for just the perfect moment. In fact there is no "perfect moment" when it comes to the natural expression of feelings of love, caring and affection

* * *

If we love our children, and if the way we relate in loving them is by hugging them, then no matter how difficult any given developmental stage may be, we should not stop hugging them. (Up to a point, of course. If they're twenty-seven and they've got their fourth conviction for dealing heroin, we don't have to treat them like they are three years old and cute as the dickens.) To withdraw spontaneous and genuine affection as a punishment to them, whether conscious or unconscious on our part, is simply wrong. For instance, when you walk in the dining room and find your best set of china—the set you treasured more than *anything* in your whole life—in splinters all over the floor, don't stop hugging your child for three weeks because you're so furious with them for an accident. If you normally hug them every day, then hug them every day, *and* let them know that you are very sad that the china is broken. Don't stop hugging them, and don't keep blaming them for something they probably suffered (and maybe still suffer if you keep that suffering evoked) great remorse over.

What counts is action. Action communicates. Even if you aren't *feeling* it, keep acting loving, and before you know it, you will be, no matter what you feel like.

"EQUAL" AFFECTION

One of the most damaging things to a young boy or girl is when affection is shown by the father to the mother, but not by the father to them; or by the mother to the father, but not by the mother to them. Some adults find it easier to give affection to their mate than to a child. That is very unfortunate, and is always the result of some childhood conditioning of the adult's that has become a part of their neurotic relationship to life and is usually quite unconscious. (I have further observed that when such a manifestation is pointed out to the adult, they usually defend themselves—quite vigorously—and proffer all kinds of explanations, excuses and reasons why their neurotic behavior is justified or proper.)

If there is more affection shown to the other parent than there is to the child, the child will almost inevitably assume that the difference is because they are in some way worse than or less than the adult who is getting more affection than they are. This is not only devastating to the child's self-esteem, but can significantly alter their entire matrix of feeling expression. To the child, it usually seems like the other parent gets "more" anyway, but if we try in some sense to be scrupulously equal, they will feel and appreciate it. Obviously there will be some dramatic differences in the form of affection between parent-child and parent-parent, but children learn fairly quickly that different situations each have their own unique qualities and properties. This is important to understand.

If one is a single parent, then affection to friends is what must be balanced. Keep affection to friends and affection to one's child both clear and well defined.

* * *

Parents with more than one child will definitely notice that they don't relate to their children exactly the same. After all, children *are* different from one other—unique and individual. Therefore, parents will normally have specific relationship idiosyncrasies with each child. But, the underlying context of potential joy, appreciation and love should be the same for all. Certainly one wouldn't treat a one-year-old the same as a seven-year-old, or the same as a fourteen-year-old—we would give them each a different kind of response and attention because they're different people with different needs and different developmental processes. The form of our relationship to our children will vary, but never the love. That is a constant.

Often a child will ask a parent, "Who do you love most, me or my brother?" or "Why do you love my sister more than me?" or whatever. That's a very profound moment, when a child comes with a question like that. At that point it is tremendously important for the child's entire development, for their world view, for the healthy personality and psyche we would wish for them, that we honestly let them know that, even though different people may receive different forms or gestures of attention and acknowledgment, that the love is equal.

For example, in my own case, a very deep friendship exists between one of my stepdaughters and my daughter, who are very close in age. This friendship has lasted into their adult years. One of the reasons for this friendship is because (I don't know how I pulled this off, I was a pretty terrible parent at the early stage of my education) I tried hard to treat them both equally in the sense of not favoring my daughter over my stepdaughter. This became apparent to them as they grew. What in the first year or two of their lives together was a competition for my affection (experimenting to discover if I loved one more than the other) was completely obviated once they realized I wouldn't "play favorites."

Even when one child is the aggressor and the other is the victim, we should still treat them equally in the domains of love and fairness, even though we might respond to them differently. After all, the roles can shift practically moment to moment! To one child we may say, "That's enough, that's too rough," or whatever, and not to the other. But we don't have to say to the other child in an affected, patronizing tone: "That's okay honey. Your mean brother won't throw your dolly out the window again."

When one treats children equally in these domains, it speaks to a child's instinct, to their deep selves. When they see that they aren't loved more for being sweet and submissive, and they aren't loved less for being aggressive, then when they get to a certain age they'll naturally feel self-respect and confidence. And beyond that, their relationship to others will tend to be more fair and equal, based on clarity rather than hidden competitiveness, greed and insatiable needs to control and dominate others. I think people who, as adults, are sadistic, mean, intensely greedy, or who demonstrate some other negative and aberrant behavior patterns were in some twisted way rewarded for that behavior when they were children—and not being treated equally was probably the least of their parents' abuses. These children were either denied love, or somehow trained to expect love in the form of intense attention, even negative, only when their behavior was "naughty."

All children need acceptance, support, encouragement and acknowledgment. That *speaks* to children! They think to themselves: "If I'm not going to get dramatic reinforcement for being mean, then what should I be mean for?" It is not natural for children to try out cruelty, violence, teasing or shame just to see what kind of a reaction it gets. They see these traits in others and copy them, or they experiment with their own vast landscape of arising emotions and feelings to determine what the world context for such behavior is.

They may get reinforcement (intense attention) from the other child they're being mean to, but who they *really* want reinforcement from is the parent. If the parent doesn't support it, that says something meaningful to them. They will conclude, "Well, I don't need to do this. It's not getting me the love I want"— which is the original, organic association that a child makes. Whatever they do—even negative behavior— they do for love. If they don't get love (or what they have come to associate as love—this primary attention, recognition, acknowledgment) by behaving negatively, they will just stop the negative behavior at a certain point. At least they will stop if they are still young enough, or innocent enough, to have not become totally crystallized in chronic habit patterns—patterns which their unconscious mind has deemed to be "who they are," entirely. At that point, the individual has absolutely no conscious volition in relationship to these mechanical behaviors.

Boys are very different from girls in many ways, beyond obvious physiology; but we should treat them equally where attention and acknowledgment are concerned. Don't hug the girls more than the boys. As a parent of a boy and a girl, be affectionate with both, even if one child seems to be more responsive. If one child gets straight A's in school and the other gets just average grades, you can acknowledge one for scholasticism and the other for their sense of rhythm, or mechanical skills, or whatever.

BALANCE OF AFFECTION: MALE AND FEMALE

Many children spend their time with women, essentially —with their mothers, female childcare people, or an aunt or older sister. When they have the chance to be with men they really engage it, because they want the kinds of influences that men carry, influences that are significantly different from the feminine. This is a tremendous reminding factor for men, in terms of their importance in the whole childraising domain.

It's amazing to see a man who really pays attention to a child. For most men, their whole image of being a man in relation to children is, "Pat 'em on the head, plop them on your lap once in a while, and then let the women take care of them and give them affection and understanding." Yet, as society becomes more enlightened, i.e., more mature, we are realizing that children need healthy role models—male and female—in their lives. Twenty or thirty years ago, what man would ever stay home with the children while his wife went out, or even went to work? That is changing now, as we realize the importance of this kind of balance. Children need the company of psychologically healthy men to round out and fill in their own healthy psyches. [This subject will be covered again, in depth, in Chapter 5, Just Like Us: Role Models.]

In many families, especially single parent families, either the father takes care of the kids all the time or the mother takes care of the kids all the time. However, the children need the opposite role model in their lives to balance their own masculine or feminine energy. Children respond in different ways to masculine and feminine energy because these energies are different, very different. They have different qualities, moods, textures.

Masculine energy doesn't mean aloofness. To actually make the movement to touch a child would create for some men (and for some women, too, but women are more natural at it), manifestations of fear, even terror. Literally they'd start to sweat; they'd start to shake; their body would heat up—all the things people do when they're afraid of something or embarrassed about something. It's shocking that what would seem to be such a natural function isn't for a lot of men. This is due, of course, to their own lack of balanced affection as children.

For a lot of boys, when they're little, Mommy

hugs them and kisses them and that's okay, but they don't get that kind of feeling attention from the men in their lives. As a result, it's genuinely rare for young boys to be affectionate, although it is very natural, as natural for boys as girls. All children are by nature extremely affectionate. In many cases when there was very little touch, however, the child has grown up cold, literally hesitant to touch others. And they have suffered for it, mightily, both as children and as adults.

Children respond to touch, and this is especially important for men to understand. We don't have to graspingly fondle them, and hug them and smother them. All we have do is rest a hand on their back or arm, with genuine feeling, love, care and affection. There's no mystery to it.

ABOUT SPOILING OR SMOTHERING

The whole idea of spoiling a child (*To spoil or not to spoil, that is the question ...*) is a big one for most parents. Certainly there is a smothering and domineering kind of intrusive parenting that is devastating and diminishing for a child, but most of what the repressed, life-negative world calls "spoiling" is just what I would call normal affection and normal parenting. (People say that I was spoiled. But, I can't have been because my mother still refuses to move out West and live with me. If I had been spoiled she would have been out ten years ago. She'd be living with me and I'd be whining at her; and she'd still be buying my pants and sweaters and making me cinnamon toast exactly the way I like it ... and only she can make it.) So the next time you're out somewhere and somebody says to you, "Oh you're spoiling that child rotten," grab your child and kiss him or her and say, "That's right!"

A friend who has a newborn, recently told me that she feels so much love for her child that she just wants to lie around the house all day and kiss him and hug him. She was worried about smothering him with affection, and if there was any danger in that. The consideration we had, which might be useful both in terms of relationship to our family and children, and to anything really, even our plants, was that *no amount of affection is too much*. What makes a mother a "smother mother" is not allowing the child to be themselves. If one uses affection as a form of punishment/reward, a form of control, as a bribe as a manifestation of our own insecurity and neediness, or to make a deal with a child, this causes problems. For most adults, when we give a child love and affection, somehow in our minds we think that because we gave them so much affection they owe us something, and what they owe us is for them to be *good*—to do their schoolwork, to practice the piano, to stop teasing their little brother or sister, whatever. This is *our* version of good, of course, and it could be anything, like, show no fear at the doctor's or dentist's office; practice speaking quietly; sit still two hours every day .... Whatever it is, it is always subjective.

However, if we are offering simple, loving affection that asks or demands nothing in return and that isn't motivated by desperate insecurities, no amount is too much. We will still have to figure out when to draw boundaries, when to make delineations for our children. Every mother and father has to do that, because children need boundaries to figure out how human society works. But, no amount of affection will smother the child if the affection is clean, adoring attention that has simply arisen out of love, simply because they *are*. They don't have to *be* anything, they just *are* what and who they are. That is the miracle.

What smothers a child is to not let them learn their own lessons, be themselves and talk back to us sometimes when they have to. I'm sure some of us, the first time we ever talked back to our parents, got slammed and were made to "stuff it" with no recourse. It must have been a singular experience; it is for all children. It leaves them confused and angry. Children need to be able to express themselves in a way in which they feel safe, secure, heard, and still loved and accepted. Most children, when they disagree with their parents are made to feel bad, wrong, rejected, uncared for and unloved. At the same time, I suppose there's a way of educating children so they learn to discuss their disagreements with us without becoming insolent and overdemanding, and so on. That's for every parent to figure out—in process, so to speak. So, let them be children. They'll grow up soon enough.

ABOUT ATTENTION

It is wise to be developing a culture in which our children are given an ideal, elegant, sensitive, compassionate, attentive upbringing. "Attentive" is more important than a lot of the other descriptors—one can be a raging son-of-a-bitch (relatively speaking), a somewhat bumbling, impractical, foolish sort, and one's children will still develop self-confidence and self-esteem out of which their ability to act creatively and with integrity, and to make clear distinctions, will be strong and active. If we just give them a certain quality of immediate attention, what they're going to get is that they're cared for, and that they mean something.

RESPOND IMMEDIATELY: TELL THEM YOU HEAR THEM

If a child says, "Will you fix my toy this after-noon?" and you say, "Uh huh," and then don't fix it, they not only very quickly start to demand more and more, but they feel let down, abandoned and unimportant to us. They also begin to realize that you are unreliable and untrustworthy — obviously not a healthy relationship between children and their parents. Don't just absent-mindedly say, "Sure, sure kid," and then space out their request. Don't brush them off with a quick "Okay" knowing you are likely to forget it. Turn to them, give them your full attention and tell them you'll handle it, and when. Then, do it at the time you promised (or before), but not later. We should have clear, intentional presence of mind when we communicate that way to our children.

Nine out of ten times we should hear a child the first time they call. This immediate attention to their needs is a form of acknowledgment that they are important and useful, but beyond that it is an affirmation that they *are*. If children don't feel they are being heard (which, given most adults' distraction quotas is an accurate perception), they start screaming for attention over and over, getting louder each time. "Mommy, MOMMY!" Pretty soon we get frazzled and say, "All right, all right." But we shouldn't have to get annoyed at them for screaming at us. If we had been listening to them to begin with, and said "Yes?" the first time, in most cases they wouldn't have to go any further. Yet, an amazing psychological phenomena exists, for example, in a mother who can hear a child murmur in a whisper during sleep (when both sleep together in the family bed), and yet during the day, not hear the child call her name until the sixth time, even though she's awake and the child is standing right next to her. The subconscious is always paying attention, and even though neurosis is guided from there, it manifests on the outer conscious levels.

Children can grow up maddeningly demanding for attention because they really don't know we have heard them, and we adults need to examine why our children believe we don't hear them. There is always a reason, and children are usually very accurate in their unconscious (or conscious) reactions to our behavior. Because we have filters which interfere with clear self-observation, we are often quite unconscious of our actual behavior. When we have free attention we hear our children when they call for us.

One way to let children know that we are paying attention to them is, when they say something more than once, to reply, "I heard you the first time, and ... " (of course, we should only say this if we *were* paying attention and we *did* hear them; we shouldn't just say this for effect) "... as soon as I'm done I'll give you my attention." Then, if the child still clamors for us it's okay, because their attention span is short and they live now, in this moment, not "later." But, make sure they know they have been heard. We need to be ready to interrupt our "important" conversations with another adult as soon as a naturally convenient break comes, to give our child what they need, and only then go on. Obviously if they need something that will be involved and time-consuming we can tell them clearly that we'll help them as soon as we finish our conversation, and then finish it without undue indulgence.

However, suppose that meanwhile they've peed in their pants, and they say, "I told you...," I would say, "You're right, you did tell me, and in this case I didn't pay attention to you soon enough. Thank you for telling me, and next time maybe I'll pay attention to you sooner." As an adult, one shouldn't be so shamelessly ignorant and so blatantly selfish as to say something to justify one's own lack of attention, or to make the child feel like their being obedient was wrong, like: "Why didn't you go by yourself? You didn't have to wait for me. Now look, now I've got to throw your clothes in the wash ... as if I need more clothes to wash."

A lot of people disagree with me, because if I'm with a child and I'm involved in a task, like working in the kitchen, and he has to go to the bathroom, I drop everything and take him to the bathroom. I've had more than one person say, with obvious distaste, "They can wait a minute or two." I don't know. I don't think a child should be forced to hold going to the bathroom if it isn't necessary. It's more likely our casserole can wait than their pee or poop.

Give the little duffers a break, you know, they're only kids. Give them attention in the first three years, and it is amazing what they learn from this, and how competently independent they are wanting and able to be. When they're only two years old we might think, "What do they know?" Everything! They need to be heard the first time they call, so that what they know is not denied and suppressed. Before they get to be five, six or seven is when to acknowledge them, because by then it's too late.

Unfortunately, some children have gotten used to constantly yelling for attention because that is the only way they know to get it. Even when someone gives them attention right away they keep yelling anyway—they don't know they've got it. In such cases it's a matter of giving them regular assurance that they *do* have our attention. When a child has that habit it's very hard for it to subside, and very hard to turn things around.

RELAXED AND NATURAL ATTENTION

Within our community, adults give each other lots of recommendations about ways to be with children: "Do this ... Don't say this ... Be positive ...," on and on. But, when we are actually with children it is important not to be quoting rules to them. No child wants to hear about some "expert" who told their Mom and Dad how to be with them. They want honesty. They want to be told what is real for their parents, not someone else's reality. Education about childraising is meant to be embodied—lived as one's own—not simply parroted, like a record player with a broken needle. (Remember those? I'm dating myself here).

If we're hanging out with the kids and a child says something inappropriate, or does something inappropriate, what do we do? Do we remember all the stuff we memorized about how to deal with children, and pull one of those tricks out of the bag? Of course not. To have a relaxed and natural attention with children means that: we are there, the child does something, and we respond naturally, from the body [in contrast to responding from the ideas or "shoulds" presented by the mind]. We respond lovingly, and like a creative problem-solver. (The two are not mutually exclusive.) We needn't worry about whether we are making a mistake. That doesn't make the kind of difference that leads to neurosis in the child if we are honest with them.

Debbie, a woman I know, is an example of someone who is natural and spontaneous with attention. If a child needs something and comes to her while she is busy, she just stops, gives it to them with full attention and then goes back to her work. She attends to children in a very natural, warm way, and that's it. She doesn't

80

need to follow them around. Once they've gotten what they need, they don't feel driven to keep her involved.

We may think we need to give children *constant* attention, but we don't. If a child has given us that impression, we can be sure it's because we're not giving them what they need when they need it, or haven't in the past. No child needs our constant overseeing. They are content in their own world most of the time. We've all seen that when children are playing make-believe and dress-up, building a fort, or whatever they do, they hardly need us. They *do* need to know that our love and attention is reliable, and that it's there waiting in case they need to tap it at any given time. So, for instance, they play, and every once in awhile they run up and hug your leg (when they're little and can't reach up to you) and kiss you. You look down, kiss them and smile at them, and they go back to playing. A minute ... ninety seconds ... and they know that they're still meaningful to you and that's the end of it. They feel such tacit unconditional love for us, their parents, that they assume we feel this way about them. They feel this way about us until we prove that their assumptions are untrue. That's the beginning of the end of their innocence, and of their deep and unmotivated happiness. A sad day.

The attitude and the mood we bring to our work has a great impact on our children. We can be really busy with something—our whole attention rapt in our task, obsessed with getting this thing done—when a child comes in. If our priorities are straight, then no matter how wild we are, even if we are flying around the office doing a million things, if they need us, we'll immediately shift to what's necessary for them. We won't bark at the child and tell them to come back later (they won't *need* later what they need right then). If we bark at them it means that we're *identified* with our work, instead of resting in our essential being. Is it worth possibly shattering a child's faith and trust in us because we're too busy to give them a rubber band or a glass of water?

If our attention is on *our* opinion of the moment (the opinion that the child is "a pain in the ass," for instance) because we need to get back to cooking, they're going to stand around the kitchen and break things and knock the flour all over the floor until they get our attention; or they will slink off into some other space and sulk, deepening the unconscious need to rebel and act-out. We can count on it! When a child is a year-and-a-half old, they're sucking up *everything*, and crystallizing it all into a world view that may well last a lifetime; and will definitely underlie all behavior, and influence and inform all opinions, beliefs and manifestations for their entire lives.

Of course, all of these considerations apply to our relationships with other adults as well. Actually, if we don't apply them to one another, the likelihood of us applying them to children is very small. When we are with children we need to realize that they are other human beings living with us. They have the same needs, the same hopes and the same capacities to give and receive love, even if their developmental stage is not the same as ours.

For my children, I would wish that they be caring, compassionate and socially aware, and have some sense of the difference between pouring sulfuric acid smoke into the sky from some factory, and another kind of relationship to the environment—the difference between killing the Earth and feeding the Earth. I would hope that they would have that kind of a sanity, but I can't make them have it. Yet, if we raise children with caring love and attention, they will naturally come to meaningful ideologies, philosophies and lifestyles. They may not come to this meaningful lifestyle or ideology where we live (i.e., in their home-town or in our chosen field of work), but they will come to it on their own. We don't need to train them to be good, socially-aware adults. If we give them love and attention for who they are, they can't come to any other conclusion. (Not that they can't, academically, but they won't.) Who we want them to be may or may not be a part of the program. It depends on whether our expec-tations are a result of love or neurosis.

Give children all the attention they need and want in the first few years, and they will naturally have wise and mature independence when they get older.

CHILDREN FIRST—THE HIGHEST LIFE PRACTICE

If the predictable routines of our lives are inter-rupted by the moment-to-moment needs of our chil-dren, even if our special times are interrupted, I rec-ommend that we spend the time helping and being with our children, and that we not put *anything* in front of the child's needs, unless we have to. That is the higher practice; that is really what is needed.

If we have a doctor's appointment or a dentist's appointment and can't be with the child, occasionally we will have to make exceptions, but then only for a valid reason. If, on the other hand, one were at an inspirational meeting and the child were to say, "Why do I have to stay here? I'm bored," and the adult were to reply, "I have to hear this lecture. You know my well-being depends upon it ...," boy, is that going to teach them something about hypocrisy. (Of course, an adult

83

in that circumstance wouldn't know they were being hypocritical; they'd really believe their own excuses.) The child is instinctually connected to the Universe. He or she knows that no lecture means the difference between success or failure in someone's life, spiritual or mundane. It's very important to not burden a child with adult desires that don't or can't apply to, or include, the child.

In two-parent families the child is often fortunate, because one parent is usually available to play with them and care for them. But, suppose you are a single parent and you want to hear that lecture ... go to that movie ... sleep with your new crush ... and you can't get a baby-sitter, or you don't believe in baby-sitters, or whatever. (Basically, I discourage *any* baby-sitters before a child is two; even family members, like grandparents or the parent's siblings, although most parents can't handle that—they've got to get out! It depends on how committed one is to the purity of one's parenting, which in other words means how committed one is to the overall health of the child's psyche—which obviously extends to their bodies as well, i.e., "mind over matter" psychosomatic technology. I suppose if someone was exactly like the parent, and had exactly the same life principles and relationship to children and so on, they would pass as a baby-sitter; but no one really is a satisfactory parental substitute.) So, if you desperately want to hear that lecture and the child doesn't, my recommendation always is: leave the lecture and do something with the child that they will enjoy.

When a child is our responsibility, we should not force them to conform to circumstances that *we want to be in* because we don't want to "miss" something. Either take the child out to play, or if they seem to want to stay, but are being overly exuberant, talk to them and express the fact that the circumstances demand a certain kind of behavior, and that the kind of behavior they are animating is not the kind of behavior they should express in that space. Don't ever tell them, "Children should be seen and not heard," even if you are joking. They won't get the joke. It's bullshit besides. Absolute garbage! A lie! Sometimes children *should not* be heard, and sometimes they should be. Some spaces require quiet, some do not. Children should have a time in which they can scream and yell and make noise and bounce off the walls. What else are they going to do with all their energy? The essential life principle is— whatever the circumstances require, we should pro- vide. We should be responsible for what our child needs regardless of our personal preferences. We never *miss* anything ... like a lecture or a night with our lover. There will always be endless numbers of lectures and endless nights of possibility!

If we are responsible for a child, we sacrifice our petty desires to their needs, even to their desires in many cases. (If we don't want to be responsible, per- haps we shouldn't be a parent in the first place.) We need to be responsible *no matter what*, and understand that everything depends on circumstances. Especially if one is alone with a child, and the other parent isn't there to take them to the park while we listen to the lecture, a lot of parents will just whine at the child, act- ing more childish than the child, instead of acting in a just and fair way.

It doesn't matter how we feel, the point is to do what is wanted and needed. If our child is unhappy in one environment we go to another environment. If they're unhappy in that second environment, we go to a third environment. We keep entertaining them until they're happy; and if they're happy, we certainly should be as well. How we feel cannot be the motivating factor for action. Who cares whether we've got a "real emotion" associated with the child at that moment or not.[1] It doesn't matter. The child doesn't know the subtle differences coursing through our complex psyches. All the child knows is whether or not there is nurturing, and whether there is a response that served. That's all. The imperative is to serve.

Let's say one wants to go to the bathroom, alone, without the child. It's important that we are able to give that up, if necessary, without resenting the child, because resentment or blame would undermine the whole point of sacrifice. Besides, it won't hurt us, or them, if they watch us pee. It is really pretty uninteresting, and they'll probably get bored after a few times and leave us to our own devices in the bathroom. If we deny them the freedom to observe us however, they may assume that we're keeping them from something really wonderful; and they will feel angry, left out or threatened. (And, if what we do when we pee *is* that fascinating, perhaps we'd better take a deeper look at ourselves, hmm?)

Our children need boundaries and education, of course, but what they need most is us, our acceptance. And remember, those early years will be gone, long gone, before we know it. So, treasure them while they are in progress—don't ignore children's needs. Put the child first—that's real practice. In fact, there are times in which the regular tasks of life *are* higher practices, but we often tend to not view those things in terms of their actual importance. Seeing what's needed and wanted in the moment, and fulfilling it, is a very high practice, always.

4

IMPRESSIONS UPON INNOCENCE

*O*ne of the most painful things in the world is to watch the destruction of a child's innocence, not by Wisdom, which doesn't destroy innocence but sobers it with the experience of reality, with the deepening of compassion and the broadening of experience in general (and so with the growth of skills for life), but by disillusionment with the child's natural expectations of adults.

A child has no reason to expect an adult, or adults in his or her world to be less than completely reliable, loving and attentive, natural and Whole, Psychologically healthy, clear and strong, and Psychically alert and responsive. Innocence does not expect abuse, cruelty or handicap but only expects, instinctively, that which it knows to be the only spontaneous manifestation that is perfect, free, and obvious in every given moment. Yet what innocence is often confronted with is the strategy of survival, the psychological cramp, selfishness, neurotically affected motivation in the unconscious, insecure, or just plain confused adult. Such a response promotes disillusionment and a natural suppression, a burying of innocence in order to avoid pain, blame, and life-doubt.

Wisdom on the other hand is the progressive maturation of innocence as it is (also confronted) exposed to the realities of the human condition: the laws of mind, the realities of the underworld, the conditions of the middleworld, even the mysteries of the upperworld. This should not be avoided (a child shouldn't be protected from "harsh realities") but allowed to discover these things in their own time and place, at their own speed as a natural outcome of growth and education. But on the other hand we shouldn't excuse our neurotic idiosyncrasies, and their effects on children by assuming our selfishness and presumptuousness (cruelty) is just a lesson our children need to learn, just part of growing up.

There is a very fine line, a subtle boundary, between that which produces wisdom without shattering or imprisoning innocence and that which certainly makes its point, even is a learning for the child, but is a learning of defense or self-protection and a disillusionment to Natural innocence and to their natural trust of their parents and other loved ones.

In fact it is so painful to see the erosion of innocence, not only in progress but in hindsight (to see how it has occurred, or that it has occurred, to feel it) that I wish for most people that they never realize their role in it. I think the remorse, if one had the depth to feel it, would be literally unbearable. I don't think most people are strong enough ....

Journal, May 10, 1990

* * *

The knowledge of the painful aspects of human existence does not necessarily destroy innocence—but it does destroy naiveté. There is a certain kind of innocence, like the innocence of Buddha when he was prince Siddhartha (before he left the castle and saw the sick man, the old man and the dead man), that doesn't know the harsh realities of life as it is. But, there's also another kind of innocence, one that has to do with a type of equal vision, that actually *needs* the knowledge of life in all its glory and its misery—the light and dark—in order to blossom and flower. It's the kind of innocence that sees Blacks and Reds and Yellows, and Gays, Catholics, Jews and Buddhists as all the same. That kind of innocence needs information, an "awakening" about the world as it is, to be able to fully develop. Basically, for innocence to remain, a child needs wisdom in his or her life, not just space or education. (Some of the most highly-educated people in Europe, in the nineteenth century, for instance, were cruel, harsh and lifeless individuals, but they were very highly "cultured.") How such knowledge will impact consciousness and psyche depends on both the sensitivity of the child, and on how the knowledge is imparted.

We should keep children innocent as long as possible. One of the results will be that when they finally start to be shocked by the lack of innocence in others, their own innocence will generally be big enough to absorb it. Whereas, if the child is too young or too delicate, they may not have enough depth, enough "density," to absorb the shock of the lack of innocence in others. Their mother's own innocence may be shut down or suppressed in the face of the pain of others, which is another reason to allow a child's innocence to be strong, and so abiding in their being, on many levels, that when they are confronted by the "horror of the situation" (as G.I. Gurdjieff called it), they can roll with it or subsume it, rather than be turned-off and driven inward by it, or capitulate to it. If they are too weak, then the tendency is to "go with the winners." And, in numbers, power, strength and resources, those lacking innocence are certainly the "winners." Jim Morrison said, in one of his songs about the "flower child"generation of the sixties, "They got the guns but we got the numbers." But it's not like that anymore. Now "they" have both.

The longer we can keep a child's essence[1] freed up, the better off they're going to be later on. We should try to keep a child "childlike" as long as possible, and not banish the "kingdom of Heaven" too soon. If we can keep a child innocent until they are six or seven, we are doing miraculously well! When they get to be twenty-five, that will have been of immense value. Their life, in terms of its purity, integrity, compassion and kindness, will show profound effects of this innocence having been kept alive and nurtured during their childhood. As teenagers, they might have a little trouble (or they might not)—this individuation process is definitely an intense time, even for the most conscious individuals. If we have kept a child basically innocent, i.e., kept them from crystallizing[2] until they're ten years old, the peer group pressure on them is going to be crushing. A whole gaggle of ten-year-olds aren't going to want a strange and unusual ten-year-old around; they are going to want to ostracize them—get them out of the group; torture them, the way ten-year-olds torture, which can be pretty painful. At the same time there is a deep attraction, or undeniable magnetism to such innocence. The innocent child will always find those others who are innocent like themselves. There are friends for all of us. So, there may be a few rough years for a normal child like that, but later on the payoff will be astronomical.

IMPRESSIONS

Children, in their innocence, have all their "doors" (i.e., sensory and emotional doors) open, and so they accept whatever they see without discrimination. Meaning, if they grow up in an environment of illness and dissonance they accept that as if it were supposed to be true, as if that were the way *all* life is (rather than *some* life, as in "... some are sick, some healthy"). Their entire worldview, the full spectrum of their perspective, is then filled with the dissonance of their early life experience. So, we should introduce as broad or deep a spectrum of life to our children (within reason—not to expose them to murder, torture or war) as possible in their formative years. This means different types of music, art, types of people, cultures and so on.

What a child gets to see, and who the child is influenced by, are obviously vitally important issues. First impressions—those made earliest in the child's life—tend to be the strongest, since these impressions are let in without any discrimination. If the child were reasoning it all out in "child understanding," he or she might think: "This is the first time I've ever seen this kind of behavior; and since these people around me obviously know what they are doing and how it is, this must be the way it is and always will be. Therefore, I will judge all similar things according to this." Babies don't actually use such reasoning, of course, but the impact is the same, because this is the unconscious's perception at that developmental stage. These first impressions serve as a template for every subsequent influence that comes along.

We, as adults, take for granted everything that we know—we have identified completely with it all. But this little person, whom we are talking to and living with, doesn't know *anything* that we know—we have a twenty-five or thirty year jump on them. They have neither our wisdom, life-experience, skills and academic training, nor our bigotry, our pessimism, and our subjective, biased social and political beliefs. Everything that we tell them is all fresh, all new; so whatever we introduce them to and the way that we introduce it to them is what they will pick up as if it were the one and only exclusive reality. They'll pick up *everything* about it—not just the content, but context as well—including our subtle and unspoken attitudes and feelings in the way that we introduce them to a space, for instance. Therefore, we ought to be truly mature and clean, unprejudiced and free of conditioned falsehoods so we don't transfer these to our children.

THE KINDS OF "IMPRESSION FOOD" TO FEED THEM

In spiritual as well as social communities, in all cultural milieus, there are vast differences of opinion among parents about what kinds of "impression food"[3] are healthy for a child. Some people say to give them everything: the more impression food—the more varieties, the more colors, the more sounds—the better. I'm not that liberal. Let me give a few important examples.

Books ... Stories ... Movies ... Music

In giving children life-positive initial impressions there are so many good children's books to choose from: books with a good story line, with lots of color, good characters and good points to make—like kindness, service and generosity. Some of the books in most children's libraries, however, are not very good, even if they are vastly popular. The imagery may be wonderful, the pictures and artwork may be beautiful, but the language is awful. Many popular children's books are full of stupid, insulting, negative language. Even many children's book authors have no idea what kind of education is healthy for growing, impressionable children. Wonderful visuals never make up for life-depressing language.

For myself, when children ask for stories, and if I can remember them, I tell them Zen stories, and Sufi stories, and stories about saints, instead of the traditional fairy tales. Most children love stories about Jesus. A child of five thinks it's great that Jesus got out of the boat and walked on the water, and that the apostle Peter said, "Hey, I'd like to do that." And the child says, "Yeah, I'd like to do that!" Children's imaginations are so fantastic, so bright; it's good to give them positive, healthful imagery to take off on, rather than scary or gruesome imagery. I would tend to read books to children that are more realistic and life-positive rather than either cruelly violent or "light and lovey" idealistic.

Fairy tales contain numerous underworld archetypes. In a book I read recently the author suggested that fairy tales could be used either to great advantage or great disadvantage with children—the difference was in how the fairy tale was read. If the fairy tale was read very matter-of-factly, if all the stuff about nasty dragons and witches and children and ovens, and whatever, were read without undue dramatization, then (in the research this author did), children never had nightmares. If the fairy tales were read from the viewpoint that demons were bad, and "out to get" the hero or heroine, and if the reading emphasized this overly heavy play of light and dark, the children developed an unhealthy relationship to their own underworlds.

Some people say children *should* have fairy tales about monsters read to them; that they need to learn that there are monsters in life; that life is not totally one-sided ... and all of that. I think it depends on the fairy tale, however. I don't particularly recommend the raw, original versions of the Grimm Brothers tales. Too grim.

As I've said, for me it's vital to preserve a child's innocence as long as possible. That's why I recommend discrimination in terms of "impression" food. I would keep the blood n' guts and the dark "evil" comics, and all that bizarre sexual perversion stuff away from children for as long as possible. So, with a small child I might go to a movie in which there was death, but I wouldn't go to a "slasher" movie. I might go to a movie in which children would see violence, but I wouldn't intentionally take them to a movie in which the idea was just to scare one as much as possible, or to be as bloody and violent as anyone could handle.

Would it be hurtful to a child's innocence to take them to a movie which is about AIDS, or should the parents wait till they start asking about those issues? Clearly, for an eight-, nine- or ten-year-old it depends

94

on the child; I wouldn't say there's a straight rule. It depends on the rest of their experience—who else is inputting data to them; what they already know; their sensitivity, and things like that. Chances are that for a child of that age those issues are already present, and many children probably talk about them with one another. (I don't know if children talk about AIDS specifically, although I would guess they do since it is so prevalent in our society; but certainly they talk about war, death and discrimination.)

With the *Star Wars* movies, for example, if we tell a child the story of the movie and make certain points about the Emperor, and the good side of The Force, and all the mythic archetypes—if we tell it in a way that communicates certain "higher" ideas, certain principles, then there's some value in it. If we just describe battle scenes, it's as useless as anything else.

Children tend to flash on the more dramatic visuals ... on the battle scenes. Usually at age three, four and five, the visuals are all they get. The *telling* of the story, however, communicates something else. They'll always remember the battle scenes (there's no way for a child to see that movie and not have the battles, the soldiers and the storm-troopers get in), but what they *hear* will get in on a different level. Children can begin to understand about metaphysical principles at seven or eight years of age. To them, the ideas are not that unusual; just physics. To most children, what is supernatural is just natural; that is, before we condition them to be suspicious and closed to the "unknown."

We should give them life-positive impressions "to eat," possibly even to the point of playing special music for them, like the Masses of Bach. What children see, hear and sense, and what they learn from what they see, hear and sense, can dramatically affect their connection to all aspects of life. There's no hurry to educate children about negative impressions—the violence and cruelty of life. Those impressions are going to come along anyway no matter what we do. In our culture, any child who rides in a car and looks at billboards, or any child who leafs through a magazine with lots of pictures, can't miss the negative impressions.

TV Impressions

One of the saddest aspects of technology today is that children, even infants, are exposed to so much television, so many video games, and so many movies at such a young age. Among other experts and child advocates, Joseph Chilton Pearce, author of *Magical Child* (NY: Bantam, 1977) and *Evolution's End* (San Francisco: Harper San Francisco, 1992), says that even an ostensibly loving parental situation could be highly compromised for a child by television that is present from infancy. The imaginal faculties aren't present when a baby is born. They develop later —at three, four, five, maybe six years. Pearce says that if one sits children in front of a television, it's like feeding predigested food to their minds. They're getting images that they don't have to learn to create on their own, and so the imaginal faculties don't develop ... and this is crippling to them. As they grow, these children can't imagine, they can't visualize, they can't project. Consequently, they are denied some of the brilliant facets of healthy development; their development of creativity is left flat and lopsided.

Anyone who has ever walked past a television set with an infant who has never seen one before, knows how totally fascinated they are by it, no matter what the subject matter. That bright screen and that imagery ... it's tremendously hypnotizing. Even black and white TVs ... (Are there such things anymore? Dating myself again.)

The longer a child can be given to find their own way and to learn through natural-paced means of development without sophisticated mechanical "help," the longer their innocence will last; and the more understanding, breadth and depth that child will have. This contemporary rage about getting children on computers at three and four years of age is terrible—a travesty. The longer children can be allowed to develop within the limits of their organic nature, in their own way, the longer they'll be innocent. At a certain point, they'll keep that innocence even through periods of sorrow, grief and tragedy.

With television, computers and video games we are stunting the growth of an entire generation. While on the surface it may look like progress, in actuality it is a dangerous crime against nature and evolution. So, keep things like television, horror movies, video games and similar kinds of impression food away from small children as long as possible. Certainly expose them to "lights" and "noise" and "color," but even discriminate as to the types and sources of that input as well.

Toys

Toys are a big influence on children, so the types and varieties, even the material toys are made of are relevant to the child's growth and education.

A newborn baby doesn't really need an entire jungle of stuffed animals around it. It's hard to develop a value for things that way. We might want to avoid giving children lots of toys all at once, like at

Christmas. But instead, give them a few things at one time, and then a few more things six months later.

Of course children, once they begin to crawl, walk and run will find things to play with everywhere—a big empty refrigerator box or stove box can be the most wonderful play house; every screw, piece of gear, old rag or stick or rock becomes a new fascination. Certain basic toys, like a wagon or a tricycle or bicycle, like roller skates or a pogo stick are fairly essential. Building blocks of various sorts are great. The point is that children are so essentially and naturally creative that it is healthy to allow that creativity a great leeway of expression rather than to stifle it beneath a mountain of mass-produced plastic toys. A few will do as a supplement to all the things they normally find around the house and neighborhood.

Also, we might want to censor gifts from family, or others. If someone sends them a gun or a TV set, or something else that just doesn't work in the culture we are trying to raise our children in, we might show the gift to the child and say, "Grandma sent this to you, however this doesn't fit in our life. This doesn't work in our culture so we're going to send it back or return it to the store, and you can choose something that you like that works for us all." That way we are honest with them. By the age of four or five they're ready to hear that kind of explanation and to accept those things that serve the education they are getting. They even come up with such suggestion themselves.

Let them pick things out of the garbage (not the compost) once in a while, like that fantastic mold that your new stereo came in. Let them play with lots of different things. Don't give in to your tendency to mold them into totally pragmatic little adults of four years old.

98

Influences of Playmates

Children receive strong impressions from their playmates, and as far as what influences to expose them to, every parent has to decide his or her tolerance level. I have zero tolerance: the *innocence* of the children's playmates, not the playmates' habits, is my criterion. I am a vegetarian, but I don't care if my children play with meat-eaters (or television-watchers), as long as the meat-eaters and television-watchers are basically kind, generous and life positive. I would try to assess those qualities in children's playmates as much as possible ahead of time, i.e., before the children got together. Children tend to like everybody, so the younger they are the more I discriminate for them. The older they become the less I do. I figure that if I do it properly when they're young, then they'll learn discrimination for themselves.

Obviously, there are times when such choices are extremely difficult, even impossible to make. If we go to a wedding and every one of our long-lost cousins is there, we can't easily separate our children from playing with the multitude of nieces and nephews. But it's only for one afternoon. In another circumstance, we may be forced by necessity to leave our child in a day-care situation where we certainly can't choose the other children who will be there. In such a case we should choose the adult care-person with very exacting discrimination.

As far as I'm concerned, it is almost as important that a child's playmates not be shaming, abusive and overly manipulative as it is that parents and other close adults in the child's life not be. At the same time children form very deep friendships, deep bonds, for reasons we often cannot know. So, I would discrimi-

99

nate, yes, but I wouldn't be so zealous or so righteous that I ended up protecting or buffering my child so dramatically that he or she ended up totally incapable of relaxing and enjoying a wide variety of types of people.

Clothing and Shoes

We distance our children from the experience of being bonded to the Earth by forcing them to wear shoes when they are outside playing. As long as they are playing in our own space, or an understanding neighbor's space, children should not be coerced, in any way, to wear shoes, but should be encouraged to play outside with no shoes, summer and winter. (Not in the snow, of course, but a little cold won't hurt healthy feet.) Obviously (again, at least it should be obvious), this does not apply to city-dwellers, but only to families with a yard or a little green space. Cement or blacktop isn't earth.

When adults wear shoes even to walk into their own yard for one or two minutes to hook up the hose, it communicates to children that feet are tender and delicate and need to be protected; and more deeply, that the Earth itself needs to be buffered from us. A child who spends a predominant amount of their childhood barefooted, whether they know it or not (and whether the parent knows it or not) is going to have a feel for things that no shod child can possibly have—that's the way of nature and natural living, in tune with subtle energies. When they are forced to wear shoes all the time, they are denied something that neither we nor they fully know the value of, but the evidence of that value is undeniable as they mature.

Another aspect of this same principle applies to clothing. In a country environment we may want to encourage younger children to wear less clothing. In cities or densely populated areas, however, to allow a child to run about naked might attract unnecessary and unwished for attention. But, when allowable, nakedness is a wonderful thing to encourage.

Children's pure love of and delight in nudity is unquestionable. If we let them, they'd go naked all the time. So, whenever they can, going naked will help them develop a healthy attitude towards their bodies. (This assumes, however, that their adult role models aren't totally ashamed of their own bodies, or aren't shaming the child in those sadistic ways that so many adults are unconsciously active in, like saying, "You are *so* fat. Doesn't your Mommy feed you anything but butter?" And, "Cover up, you nasty little flirt." And so on.)

It certainly wouldn't hurt for parents to bathe with their children, either. Especially as the child gets beyond infancy, same sex parents may really enjoy a bath with their child until the child begins to enjoy bathing alone.

Travel

We went to India with some of the children when they were just four and five years old. Many people thought, "How can a four-year-old appreciate the depth and the breadth of Indian culture? It's just a waste of money, energy and attention to bring children on a trip like that. And, it's terribly dangerous to their health besides." But, these same people didn't realize that the cultural influence on a four-year-old will be ten times what that influence is to a thirty-year-old. Most of us have no idea the kind of perceptive capacities children have. It is absolutely unbelievable, awesome even. We certainly observed this with the children who traveled with us. They are now teenagers, and the subtle impressions they absorbed are still feeding them in so many ways.

My recommendation has always been that whenever children can be brought into vastly unusual cultural environments (as long as these environments are sane, life-positive and not dangerous to the child's life), we should just bring them in! If there are dissonant elements, we would simply explain the elements. In India, for instance, almost everybody got sick for a day or two. Very sick. When the children were sick they would just throw up and the next morning they would be fine. It was nothing. It didn't bother them in the same way it bothered the adults. The children were fascinated with the beauty and the interesting things all around them, and the illness was just something that they got through without undue attention to it. On occasion, on that trip, a few of the children didn't shit for two weeks, and it hardly bothered them (psychologically and mentally). But, if an adult didn't shit for two weeks, my god, they would be so obsessed with their elimination problems that they would barely be able to remember that they were in a different culture.

A child's ability to literally just "eat" impressions is magical. It's wondrous. Even when the body is struggling with some small stress, the being—the essence of the child—is soaking up useful and valuable impressions like a sponge.

Other Adults

Alice Miller spoke about being an "enlightened witness" for a child. If there is no one in a child's life who will acknowledge who they are, who will be a reliable ground of kindness, generosity and non-abuse, then they have no chance to grow up healthy. But, if even one person is being a "witness" of the child's inherent innocence and self-worth, it could change a child's whole life forever. Often, a friend of the family fulfills such a role when the parents or close blood relatives do not (or cannot). For instance, my parents were always introducing adult friends to serve as mentors and such enlightened witnesses for me in areas that they (my parents) were less facile with.

In terms of other adults in general, I've always welcomed many "different" people to our community for a time—days, weeks, months or even years. Many of my students, however, feel uncomfortable with the energy that certain guests bring. These students must then come to some resolve about their view of how to handle a great variety of influences, some of which are not very pretty. Considering both what is "transformation-useful" and what is good for our children, we often allow guests whom we wouldn't want living with us, but guests who do add a color, for a short time, that is not usually present. I wouldn't want to keep an environment *totally* free of some of the elements that are, in a sense, "dark" or not ideal role models for children. Those elements can offer tremendous opportunities for everybody involved, both psychologically and "chemically," in the mix. We don't want children to grow up totally one-sided, totally imbalanced; even if the weight is all on the side of the "light" impressions. Of course, I would never allow anyone to commonly keep company with children if that person was *in any way* dangerous or abusive, cruel or violent towards the children. But, people who have unusual habits or twists of psychology (such as a brilliant or masterful artist who, by personality, was withdrawn into their own genius to the point of very little outer expression) that type of "different" can be useful.

A lot of the people whom I find especially useful for what they have to offer are the last people that you would want your children with as sole role-models. Every individual, then, has to come to some resolve about allowing children to be exposed to some potentially negative elements to help them view their world in all its variety, while at the same time assuring that the positive role models are the most impressing (which they will be naturally to a child whose innocence is intact), and that the children are safe—secure in their protection from being overly exposed or impacted.

UNDERWORLD INFLUENCES
ON CHILDREN

As adults, we wrestle with underworld elements, with the dark side of human nature—perversity, cruelty, bigotry and so on. When our work has that dark, difficult or painful feel to it, it is often because we have failed to acknowledge and deal with our own underworld in a matter-of-fact way. When fear, disgust, sorrow and anger come up, we need to deal with such energies simply, as natural and genuine parts of ourselves, and not define these underworld elements as being "bad," dangerous or unhealthy, necessarily. Obviously, there are external elements: war, torture, violent crime and man's unconscionable inhumanity to man (and woman). But, even the ability to deal with these unavoidable ingredients in the stew of life in a healthy way has to do with our own relationship to those same internal qualities in us.

For instance, if a man, for whatever reason, feels violent towards a woman (or towards all women, which is typical, though it usually just manifests towards the woman he is in relationship to), how he deals with those feelings is either going to be a very healthy example for a child who happens to observe this, or a terrifying and possibly traumatic event for the child. A child's mother cannot be brutalized—physically, emotionally or psychically—without this having a devastating effect on her child. And if it's the father who is doing the brutalizing, the effect is even more devastating.

Many of us are still struggling with tremendous demons that are the result of impressions that we received as children—impressions that we didn't have the worldview to interpret as an intelligent adult would have; impressions which didn't enable us to deal matter-of-factly with our own childhood demons or those of the adults in our close environment. And we didn't have understanding adults ("enlightened witnesses," to use Alice Miller's term) to help us integrate, understand and digest these impressions.

If we are able to relate to the sometimes pervasive darkness and underworld-ness in our own unconscious, our children will be healthier than any of us, and healthier than most anyone else in fact. The epidemic of ill health and other sordid physical and psychological conditions in our society is, in some part, due to an inability or unwillingness to deal with the underworld, in addition to a lack of education about actually what the underworld is. We are never taught about the underworld, nor how to live with it, be friends with it, and still relate to the world as compassionate, hardworking and impeccable individuals.

The underworld is one third of reality. In

shamanistic terms, there is the underworld, the middle world and the upper world, and to be afraid of the underworld is to strategize one's life around this fear. Children will learn that, and emulate that fear in their life. When it comes to parents, or anyone, teaching children about the more unpleasant things in life—such as cruelty, bigotry and criminality in some people or in the world—it is important that the teacher have a good connection to their own underworld, to their own darkness. To be friendly with the underworld is to have the straightforward attitude that "bad things happen," or however we might phrase it. We needn't be fascinated with the grotesque or the horrific, but it makes sense to be aware of the existence, the reality of it, and have a healthy regard for such things. We can never avoid entirely such influences in the world at large. Even hermits have such elements within themselves.

As adults who are serious about wishing overall health, sanity and balance for their children, we need to hold for them the whole "no problem" context towards life. [*Editor's note:* In speaking of this "no problem" context, Lee is not referring to any naive optimism which fails to see the pain, cruelty and the insanity of the world at large. Rather, he means an attitude of "this is simply the way life is," which rests on an abiding trust, a sense that our lives are ultimately in the hands of God. If we are living from this context, this will serve as an invaluable type of role modeling for our children. In applying this attitude to the situations that arise in our children's lives on a daily basis, as long as we are attending to their needs with reasonable common sense and discernment, we can drop obsessive or neurotic overprotectiveness, or over control.] Numerous factors will show up in our lives that look like they could be detrimental. But if we hold a "no problem" context in general, what would be negative elements under most circumstances will not have that effect. Rather, children will learn about the underworld open-eyed, strongly, and with wisdom, not with fear and suspicion. They will learn to make distinctions and to have discrimination (which they already have to a really extraordinary degree). And they'll be able to speak these distinctions for themselves, which is absolutely denied to them in the ordinary world.

When I was very young, one of our close family friends was a severe alchoholic who use to get falling-down drunk every party. I was always asleep by the time he got "sloshed," but conversation amongst my parents scrupulously avoided this subject. I was unaware of this until I was in my twenties! I was not harmed by this lack of knowledge but neither was I educated for some harsh realities that I encountered in college and beyond. Fortunately I was quick to learn and not particularly prone to self-debasement or weaknesses of self-abuse, substance or otherwise. Still, what I was observing was shocking, and in many cases unimaginable, and still is.

It is interesting how intellectual concepts don't get translated into a lack of innocence unless there's traumatic experience attached—and then innocence goes pretty quickly. If the experience is held in a context of "no problem" or "this is the way life is," however, the child's experience is broadened or deepened without recoil (i.e., negative reactivity), and the underworld elements in our lives will not affect our children, behaviorally, in a dark or negative way.

EXPLAINING INFLUENCES
TO CHILDREN

In terms of raising children, given their state of innocence and receptivity, one should attempt to do two things: first, as far as possible, provide an environment of health, gentleness, respect and clarity, even though sometimes that's not possible. Second, if the environment contains dissonance (which most environments do to some degree or other), the adults in the environment need to contextually recognize the dissonance *as dissonance*, rather than as accepted normality, and communicate that to the children as being one element of many in the landscape of their lives. Thus, if an environment contains an element of clarity and discrimination in relationship to what is healthy and creative, children will respond to that subjectively, even if objectively they're responding to the noise, the violence, or whatever else is in the environment. If one is in a situation with one's child, let's say, where one witnesses a car accident where the drivers get into a loud, violent fight that the child is staring at, wide-eyed, one would use that opportunity to explain how such reactions are unneccessary, and a function of unmanaged anger and feelings of stress, and so on —and explained in a way a child could grasp, not with a doctoral dissertation.

When taking a child into an unknown environment (unknown to them), I've mentioned before that we should tell the child what will be going on, ahead of time. For instance, if one were going to a place where there would be a lot of screaming and noise (the floor of the Stock Exchange, for instance, or a panty sale at K-Mart), one would prepare the child: "This is where we're going ... and this is the way it is there. This is not life-threatening and there is no danger to you." Without that warning, children will often take in these impressions in a way that causes fear and apprehension. Often, the energy of competition ... push and shove ... great vital impatience ... affects children as if they were the object of that energy. So, we want to assure them ahead of time that they are not the object, and that we will keep them safe and secure. We don't need to be concerned with whether the child is old enough to understand literal language (a one-month-old or a three-month-old child might not), but they will get our communication at a feeling or sensing level. They definitely understand the intention and the mood.

Now obviously if an adult is the hysterical type who thinks that a child needs to be protected from everything, from every little feather of a negative impression, that will be communicated at least as strongly as the dissonance in the environment. So, the whole recommendation is that adults be relaxed and life-positive with their children; and that requires quite a bit of the adults. On the other hand, if the adult is the other kind of hysterical type who forgets they have a child with them in the heat of their negative or overblown reaction to something, the child will get that as if it is directly threatening to them. So, equanimity in general with our children is a good idea.

Essentially, it's almost impossible to eliminate all dissonant elements from any environment, not that one would particularly want to anyway. On the other hand, a lot of the dissonance for children is created unnecessarily because adults are somewhat ignorant of children's needs. Of course there are the obvious examples of violence and abuse—adults who don't really want their children push them around and wish they weren't there, and so on. But much of children's negative conditioning comes because adults don't know that television is worse than, or at least as damaging a drug as alcohol or nicotine. Or, because adults will fight with one another, creating deep conflicts and fear in the child.

The first time a child sees cruelty, the most important thing is that we are honest with them. Witnessing cruelty from one human being to another, a child will look at us, with a look that says, "Why did they do that?" It is helpful to be able to explain these things, and never to justify such violence through silence, denial, or attempts to distract or shield the child from such realities.

It is inevitable that a child is going to notice adults screaming at and slapping or hitting children — in the supermarket, at the toy store, pet shop, at the movies and in the park. Simply explain the truth of human mechanicality and habit-pattern conditioning to them. Don't try to hide them from it or explain it away with some absurd reason. And, explain it to them so they can understand it. Don't give a child a clinical dissertation on abnormal psychopathology. A small child can't comprehend war and criminality at the level of neurotic motive, because they don't have those motives out of which to understand. Wait until they have the depth of understanding to know what it is, before you go into such detail. And don't *ever* make a joke of it, as in: "Hey, watch out now, don't ever do that [throw a box of cereal out of the cart, or whatever] to Daddy, or he might have to act like *that* Daddy towards *you*." Even if we're laughing or using a tone of voice that another adult would understand as joking, a child won't.

In speaking to the child, then, one may use the

approach: "There is never a good reason, or rarely a good reason, for cruelty. Some people are frustrated and angry, and the way they express that is by hurting other people, and that is definitely not the best way to handle such things .... " Use that kind of generalization, which is true, but not overly intellectual, complex or sophisticated. Of course, we have also got to be able to tell the child how to handle such things positively!

All of this doesn't mean that we should take a Pollyanna-ish attitude toward the world for children. Some adults are so afraid of their own underworld that they have made all of life into billowy white clouds, unicorns, rainbows and pastel shades, and strains of pathetic, wispy electronic new age music. Certainly children should not be "beaten over the proverbial head" with gruesome tales of man's inhumanity to man, but neither do they need to be unrealistically shielded from such things. I would not keep picture books with photos of war atrocities around for a two-year-old to look at, but I wouldn't hide *Newsweek* or *Time* from eight-years-olds either. Often, in looking at the pictures in these magazines, the children will see dead bodies. The first time they come across such pictures they will say, "What is that?" and even cry sometimes. "Why would anyone do something like that to somebody else?" We don't snatch the magazines out of their hands as if the horrors didn't exist, we just try to explain it to them when they run across it.

If in the child's first introduction to the Civil Rights movement or the apartheid of South Africa they ask, "Why do white people hate black people?" we need to know why ourselves, and be able to clearly explain the nature of hatred and prejudice. If we are in denial about our own biases, it will be most difficult to honestly relate to children around these issues. We need to know, in our own being, that people do these things to one another. We need to feel the horror of it so that we have some compassion—in both our relationship to the broadening of a child's education, as well as to the shock these things are to a child's innocence—so that we don't push a child's curiosity into a paranoid terror of such realities, leaving the child quivering, shaking and afraid, in a shell of misinformation, confusion and paranoia.

To use an extreme example: in a state of war, children are going to see horrific things —their friend's mother blown to pieces, for instance. There is no way that we can make such things okay, but we might say: "Yes, this is a terrible thing, and when you grow up you don't have to perpetuate it." I would even say: "It's not right, but we don't control everybody and we can't make everybody do what's right. We can't make people be kind to other people. Some people are just very violent and very cruel; that's how they get their frustrations out ..." or something like that. "These people are not conscious," would be another way of saying it. "They're not conscious, they don't understand. If they were more conscious they'd be different." I don't use that kind of language every day, because the concept is often too obscure for a young child. But we might use that language every once in a while, so children get the idea that they are individuals who have a choice in terms of their ability to be conscious, and can choose integrity and right action even in the face of peer group pressure.

Sometimes, in such extreme circumstances, they will be shocked but fascinated at the same time. They may want to see what's going on. Suppose the whole family was huddled in the basement or in some cellar while the city was being bombed. The child might insist: "But I don't want to be here, I want to be upstairs." That's when the parent must say: "Well, we can't go upstairs until the bombing stops. Then we'll go upstairs as soon as we can and maybe when we get upstairs the walls will be broken down. Maybe not, maybe we'll be lucky." There is no way to make that kind of tragedy acceptable. A lot of cultures say, "Be strong"—which usually translates into suppression, as in: "Don't feel." I would always allow children to grieve as fully as they needed to: let them cry, yell or scream out their anguish at man's inhumanity to man in such situations.

THE INFLUENCES OF
SUFFERING AND DEATH

In the ultimate scheme of things children know what they're getting themselves into, in the sense of consciousness existing in pre-birth and pre-conception domains; consciousness that can see ahead into incarnation. There are two kinds of suffering for children. There's the suffering of the fact that there are inherent limitations in organic incarnation, and that this needs to be lived out; which is "pure" suffering—not a reaction to anything, just a given element to the physics of existence. Then there's the suffering that is a reaction to a world of crime, illusion, war, pain, brutality, violence, confusion, and on and on.

It's very easy for a child to come into incarnation and be buffered against this latter type of suffering in such a way that would build in them a denial mechanism—a mechanism that would not allow them to be moved by what's wanted and needed in the moment, spiritually and socially speaking. It's relatively easy for a child to be protected from this type of suffering in a way that does not give them the innate motivation to work against it. In many traditional cultures, however, particularly cultures with a strong relationship to the Absolute, a child's upbringing is designed to not allow that buffer to take effect.

Poverty, suffering and pain—in India, one gets the whole scene. Before we went to India, most of the adults in our group (naive, middle-class, bourgeois) had never been to a Third World country, and had never seen *real* poverty and sickness. Everywhere they'd look they would be horrified. "Oh my God, the ugliness, the filth, the suffering, the pain." They walked through India full of this sentimental view of things—it wasn't real compassion, for they were being sympathetic to their own feelings of fear and revulsion, not to the Indians. Certainly there is plenty of suffering in India, but there is also a whole different viewpoint.

On the other hand, our children were fascinated, not turned off by what they saw! In certain parts of India there is so little food that animals are treated extremely cruelly, because food that animals would normally eat, people could eat. The dogs are kicked and beaten whenever they are seen. In one area we visited, all the dogs were the worst-looking animals one could imagine; they all had diseases ... all their ribs were sticking out. The adults would lament, "Oooh, that poor dog." Seeing a starving puppy staggering around in the streets, the adults were horrified. But the children had this fascination: "Is he going to die?" "When is he going to die, and can we watch?" Tremendous innocence. Many times we had to caution the adults to allow the children to have their own opinions and to let them see life just as it is, without superimposing the adults' neurotically-conditioned biases on them.

Children don't have the same fear of death that adults have. Four- or five-year-olds sometimes ask, "When am I going to die?" For them it is just very simple. But if you look at a forty-year-old, everything about them is saying: "I'm getting older. I'm afraid of pain, breakdown, the unknown and death. No, no, aaargh!" Adults have this tremendous denial and fear of death, that children don't.

In Benares, a holy city in India where people come to die, all along the river there are big cremation grounds. Wood is piled up, the dead body is thrown on, and some more wood is piled on over the body. Butter is thrown on to make it burn really hot, and then the fire is lit. Sometimes the body isn't bound really well, and once the fire starts, even if the body is bound, the ropes burn, and an arm pops out or a leg pops out. The children thought it was great: "Wow, look at that!" While the adults might turn their heads away and say, "Eewwww!" feeling that it was very strange, even horrific. But the children wanted to stand and watch.

The Indians have this custom where they smash the skull of the burning body at a certain point, so the skull doesn't explode. (The brains cook! Like a can of food put in the oven and baked would explode at a certain point of heat, the skull is the same.) If one doesn't break the skull, BOOM! The kids would wait and watch: "When are they going to smash the skull?" A number of the adults really had to be careful not to condition the children that it was ugly, or awful, or weird or wrong, but just to let them make up their own minds.

One way that the children in our community learn about death is through the compost pile. A few years back a number of them got involved with the compost pile after they had carved up some pumpkins into Jack-o-lanterns. The pumpkins were "alive" when the children carved them, but then they saw the pumpkins go onto the compost heap and watched them decay over a period of some weeks. That was just awesome and incredible to them. One of the most amazing things that they had ever seen—birth, disintegration and death in two weeks!

It's also useful for children to have the idea of continuum, so when something dies, their goldfish or a budgie or something, the parents shouldn't be devastated for the child. Often children are curious rather than devastated. If we get them another one they are perfectly happy. We teach children the idea of continuum through *our* responses: Life goes on and on, and one form becomes another form of life. The dead goldfish buried in the garden becomes part of the rose ... or the zucchini.

EXPOSE THEM TO
DIFFERENT MANIFESTATIONS

When raising children, give them as much exposure to different manifestations as one can, so that when they grow up they aren't limited to one or two very narrow experiences. That's the thing that's really fictional or fantasy about the Tarzan stories. I suppose it's academically possible, but practically speaking, someone raised in that environment probably wouldn't have the fluidity that Tarzan had. They wouldn't be likely to adjust, and so quickly, with so few difficulties.

When we were traveling through India we

stayed at a small ashram that had a girl's orphanage and school associated with it. One of the girls, then thirteen years old, had been found living with a pack of wild dogs. She crawled on all fours, ate and barked, and went to the bathroom like one of the dogs. She had been discovered at age eight or so and had been in the orphanage/school for five years, but still had not fully learned language or human ways of living. And while she was an extremely happy, bright, curious girl, she was noticeably different from anyone else there, and not overly enthusiastic about trying to adjust to human society. Rather, she survived with the minimum of effort. The wild dogs most likely had a wiser culture to her.

That happens to some children. They grow up in an environment that's so isolated they only learn one or two manifestations—they only learn one tone of voice, for instance. If they are with an angry parent, all they ever hear is this angry tone of voice; all they ever see or feel is that angry manifestation. If they are in that environment long enough, it's all they might ever learn throughout their life. Learning skills can atrophy if they aren't used, stretched, demanded of. When such children grow up, just to learn to speak in a different way is excruciatingly difficult.

In motivational training sessions, like the Dale Carnegie course, every once in a while someone shows up who has only one form of communication. To be able to change that pattern is highly improbable. Sometimes people see how limited their one mode is, and they just break down and cry because they can't get out of it. Some people learn only one emotional response and have a similar conflict.

Harry Chapin did a song called "Bummer," about a little black guy who grew up in the ghetto. The opening lines are: "Whenever he cried he got a fist in the face so he learned not to show his feelings." That guy had one manifestation. He was a bully in grade school, dealt dope in junior high, and got sent to prison at sixteen, where they "turned him from a junkie to a hater".[4] When he went to Viet Nam he did great. They put him in a tank and he just went around killing people. That was his manifestation. No emotion except rage, and he used that one to the advantage of the troops. Finally, he was on a tank crew with a bunch of guys and they came into an ambush. He shot it out. The men who came in after him found everybody dead except him. He was lying in his own blood with a smile on his face (the first smile that he ever had his whole life) because he went in to save his friends. He had this realization that the only thing he was good at was killing ... violence, and in this instance it served. It could have saved people's lives. As the story goes on, the second smile he ever had was when he got killed robbing a store. He died with his medal of honor in his fist. A touching song. Harry Chapin was a very brilliant balladeer—one of the best of our era.

So, some children only learn one emotional manifestation and it's very hard for them to be happy with their lives in such narrow confines. It's like they are in a prison without bars, but also just as incapable of being "out." The more manifestations one has at their grasp, the better. For instance, one could introduce a child to classical music of various composers, rock and roll, jazz, blues, opera, folk and live concerts, acoustic, electrified, recorded music ... or, one could introduce a child to Mexican, Italian, French, American and Indian foods, and so on, and to artists, mechanics, nurses, salesmen, etc.

Children should grow up not being shocked by

psychic phenomena (supernormal, metaphysical or parapsychological), or by the consideration of life after death. They should feel the ordinariness and naturalness of every kind of curious and magical event. As I've noted before, such things should be natural to children because such things are real, and even commonplace, if we ourselves are open to both seeing them and experiencing them. So for instance, it is often interesting to talk to children about people like Satya Sai Baba, Uri Geller, Swami Rama or Swami Premananda.[5] The children will ask, "How did they make those things out of the air? How do they do that? Can I do that?" Personally, I don't try to explain to a three-year-old that "everything is energy" and $E = mc^2$. I just say, "I'm not sure how they do it, but I've seen it; it's real; and it's amazing isn't it?" I want to introduce children to the wealth of phenomena in our world.

Some children will look like they have only one manifestation, very quiet and reserved, for instance, but let them take part in a theater skit, and all of a sudden, "My God, I never knew they could do anything like that!" They become totally gregarious and outgoing! Sometimes children learn something when they are a year old and they never show it until exactly the moment when they feel like showing it. (That's proof that things we learn when we are little are "in.") In a circumstance in which certain things are needed, we will see how incredibly skilled and brilliant children are. But, we must *let them be* this way, not suppress (or compress) them to the degree that they are so insecure or scared that they do nothing. Neither should we train them so arduously as to demand they be highly skilled, beyond their natural tendencies, in many areas and able to perform on command.

Part of the dance for us as adults, then, is

unlocking all of the things that we have relegated to the "closet," or to the "attic" of the psyche; things that are tremendously expressive and valuable aspects of our being. The other part of the dance is training all the potential aspects of our being that we have shut down as children.

THE DANGER OF DEFINING CHILDREN TOO NARROWLY

Children are voyagers, explorers, adventurers. They live in many different realities and domains at the same time. To the average dull, conditioned adult, there is only one dimension, and every predictable mechanical human lives there. This is limited by belief systems that are usually arbitrary, and most definitely defined by the illusions, misconceptions and projections that were assumed to be exclusive truth, based on childhood psychological presumtions. To the child, in touch with their imaginal realms, any moment of perception is only one intersection that they have shown up for a certain period of time, and that shifts in the next moment to somewhere else.

Children function in many realities, and they *don't* know they function in many realities in the intellectual way we are discussing it here. They are trying to be just like us; they are trying to "get" this thing called life, trying to figure everything out, and they are all over the place. It is really useful to understand that about children and to allow them full freedom for discovery. Let them, even encourage them to explore not only the vast and complex dimensions of psychology, but the deep and abstract subtleties of parapsychological dimensions as well, which they all do and will continue to do if they aren't conditioned that such alternative realities are weird, scary or evil.

Let's look at a practical example of how adults limit children. When an infant looks up and smiles, the adult's first response is, "Yeah, that's funny, isn't it?" because, first of all, the adult thinks he or she knows what the child is experiencing, and secondly they think, "Why would the child smile if something wasn't funny?" For an infant, however, a smile is not necessarily a response to something funny. Neither is a laugh. When infants laugh, it is not because anything is funny, it is because they are delighted, full of pleasure. Free delight produces laughter.

Infant children don't even have a concept of "funny." They don't live in a subject-object consciousness in which there is anything separate from themselves to laugh at. They contain all things, and their laughter is pure enjoyment of this state. I mean *really*! Nothing is ever funny in one sense of the idea. How could anything be funny when there is no duality? How can we as adults be laughing *at* something, even innocently? We can't be. We can only be laughing in or as innocence, joy, delight itself. But, in our illusion, we imagine that we are laughing at something or someone separate from us.

From infancy, we tell children or train children that there are certain very narrow laws and that is the way to read reality, like: When somebody laughs, they are laughing at something external to themselves; something has made them laugh; something is funny to them. When a child starts to cry or whine, in all the ways that we say, "Oh, you don't like something? You don't like that?" or, "Oh, you're uncomfortable," we are telling them what *our* rules are—what we assume about them. Maybe they are not uncomfortable at all. Maybe they tapped into the fact that five hundred people just got killed in India in some Hindu-Muslim riots. We have *no idea* what goes on for an infant! They could be crying over something going on in the far reaches of the galaxy, but we are always defining, defining, defining, defining and limiting by those definitions.

Better not to define anything. They don't need our definitions. Children are smarter than we are. If our sensing mechanism could sponge data the way a child's sensing mechanism sponges data, everybody would have an IQ of 2075 (and some people imagine that in 2075 A.D. we will all have IQ's of 2075, but I for one seriously doubt it, and that's a diplomatic way of putting it).

To whatever degree, infants do come in with "something" already intact—some potential, some essential qualities, beyond just the genetics they are given. This is so delicate an issue. Unless we, as adults, are really perfectly mature ourselves (and who is?), it is very difficult not to bias our relationship to the child in one way or another because of our beliefs. Even in positive ways a child can be diminished or "cramped" in the full expression of their karmic and subtle destiny.

There is too much of an expectation or projection about *"our* child." For instance, one of the points here is not to dwell on who the child looks like: i.e., "Wow. They look exactly like their Mom (or Dad)." To make such statements in front of the child is to program them to be like that person as well, rather than to be themselves. The subconscious scanning system of an infant or small child will pick up spoken and unspoken implications. The more energy (or bias) an adult has towards these views, the stronger the child impresses it and takes it to heart, body, and mind as they grow up.

It's obvious when a child looks like their mother or father. Even newborns have certain characteristics that are clearly like one or the other parent. Why state the obvious? Why indulge, dramatize, talk about, consider, or joke about the obvious? "Oh, he looks so much like his father, I wonder if he'll be an artist too ... or as good at languages?" Life would be a lot cleaner if we simply left it to "What's obvious is obvious ..." (so as not to weight the child's self-views), without editorializing and making projections that fence the child within them. Without these projections, we are liable to have a more spontaneous and innocent relationship to the child. He or she will also be freer to grow into their own essential self, instead of into who they believe they are supposed to be.

Long before a child is a year old it will be obvious if they have an inclination towards some skill—towards music, or towards mathematics or art—beyond every child's delight with sounds, colors and discovery. We can certainly make instruments or resources available to them and give them opportunities to learn. If they want to take these opportunities, we can then give them every chance to absorb these influences, but we don't need to add a lot of personal, opinionated projections onto that. Just keep it as simple as possible.

Parents love to tell stories about their "little darlings," and I understand that. "Oh, my daughter did the cutest thing, listen to this ...," or, "Do you know what my kid said?" and so on. We relate these endless, lovely little things because we love our children, and because their learning experiences, their candidness, innocence and delight are so endearing. But, when we tell a bunch of people at a party what our child did, all of those people and their energies weave into that child's life in a more intimate way. Every time somebody that we have told about our child comes into their aura, their memories of what the child did influence that child's life in terms of the adult's expectation, projection and so on. (Yes, these influences are almost always psychic, not physical, and are usually extremely subtle, but they do have an impact, usually invisible to the rational observer, but present nonetheless.) Some of these principles may sound far-fetched or overly subjective to the average adult. But children function in many subtle realms as well as the gross realm of the five senses. It pays to acknowledge the reality of this. The less our children are defined by other people's opinions, suppositions and imaginations, the better off they'll be.

We don't need to make definitions for children; all we need to do is serve them, respond to their actual needs, not our projection of their needs, and keep them from getting hurt. Really, that's all we need to do— make sure they don't fall into a fire, or pull down a pot of boiling water on their heads, or fall out of a fourth-story window. The best thing we can do for children is keep them safe.

Children need right limits. When we tell a child the rules, like, "Fire burns," or, "Running in front of cars is dangerous ...," that's not defining them. When we teach a child elegant protocol, that's not defining them. The "definition" is, "Aren't you cute," or "Listen to how smart she is," or "Look at that nose," or "She always dances when music is put on ...," holding them to one point of view, or action, or set of parameters. "Defining" is giving them our subjective and particular content for their lives. We should want to set and hold the context of their lives, but let the content arise naturally in the course of events.[5]

124

We've all been limited. In some cases the limitation is obvious. In one woman's case, when she was born her mother saw "PIANIST" all over her. This woman grew up with a piano in front of her, literally from birth, and I'm sure her mother told everybody, "She's going to be the best. She's going to be the *best*." Well, she is the best. She was touring at seven years old, and she polished her training in Vienna with the most renowned teacher in Europe. But, even in a positive sense, that kind of definition crystallizes the psychic structure of the being, and feeds other areas in which that crystallization is not valuable. This woman herself says she's more essentially a violinist, and that she's more inclined to dance than music. But, it's a pianist that she is! So the question arises, could someone who is truly extraordinary at something be more optimally fulfilling their destiny in some other way? That *is* the question and the issue. I assume that we have natural inclinations, and to fully explore those (rather than having skills superimposed on us) is optimal.

I'm sure many of your parents, when you were little, called you specific names and told stories about you to your grandparents: "Oh, she always poops in her drawers." And you grew up defined by that. All your adult life, that was your definition, as subtly as that may manifest as an adult (or not so subtly!). "Oh, he always gets colds in the winter." "Always!" This is not just superficial conditioning—it's total psychosomatic conditioning, yet very effective. You were forced into a behavior pattern that is narrow, limited and usually extremely difficult to alter.

These habitual, mechanical, thoughtless and unconscious limitations have to be cracked forever. Not just altered into a new limitation, but changed completely such that we can move fluently between any manifestation as needed—from genius orator to being "at a loss for words," from brilliant artist to the most ordinary person.

We don't *have* to pass on our learned, habitual definitions and limitations to our children. If we work hard, and if we have integrity, and if we are responsible, they will be too, and as themselves, not as duplicates of us. If we aren't, we can *make* them act like responsible people by forcing them to wash the dishes and do whatever we make them do, but they won't necessarily *be* responsible. They'll grow up and marry someone who will do all that stuff for them. Some of us well know, from our childhood, that if we had a hardworking and liberal parent, we rebelled, got lazy, did what we did in high school and college—lived in a pigsty, slept with everything that moved (or whatever we did), and then, when we got our own apartment, and into our own serious relationship, we were as responsible as our family was.

We don't teach kids responsibility by explaining to them the laws of the state. We show them integrity, and they'll participate. If we don't show them reliability and responsibility in our actions, they will participate to whatever degree they may feel like at the moment, but they won't likely get it.

As a general rule, for an adult to be able to offer some help to a child who is already crystallized (i.e., stuck in an obviously narrow and limiting definition which was conditioned by other adults), one might provide a child with the broadest, deepest spectrum of manifestations possible, without force or pressure to change or "perform." That is why a fantastic trait to encourage in children is their ability to investigate and follow the urges and voices of their imaginations, their curiosities, their explorations. Give them the freedom to discover their own interests, and to pursue these things in the relentless, amazing and profound way that children do.

CONTINUITY IN THE HERE AND NOW

In the organic world—the animal world, the world of psychology, mind, body and biology—it is very important for children to feel a sense of continuity, and most children intuitively know the reality of this. For example, children often want us to tell them stories about when we were little. They also love to ask, "Tell me about when I was a baby." They want to know that they were loved, and they want to know that they're alive, really. They want pictures of themselves and their activities. This "physical" thing is important to a lot of children, and they are fascinated by it. It's a way of tangibly recognizing the reality of this gross incarnation. They want to know that they have a history. They want to know their mythology, the symbols and archetypes of their incarnation. They want proof that they exist in *this* dimension.

For many children, actually getting *into* themselves as a new incarnation can be a difficult task. One woman, for instance, says that when she was born, and for a couple of years after, she was totally disoriented. She didn't want to be here on Earth, in a human body— it was all so limited. She remembered where she had come from, and she hadn't wanted to leave. (Once we are here though, then we've got to be here ... we've got to do this trip ... and there's no transformational growth vehicle like this one. As long as we are disoriented from the other world, we can't be *here* and be working. That's a very simplistic explanation, but absolutely true in essence.)

We are doing a very radical experiment with our children in our community-culture, however, because we have a practice of not having shoeboxes and souvenir books full of photographs of our child doing everything: riding a horse, trying on their new shoes, wearing a little pink bow, playing with the kittens. Rather, we are encouraging them to rely on *being here now*. We are asking them, in one sense, not to have history to rely on, except memory (which, as adults, they'll learn is quite unreliable). So, we are working to have our children be with the present *fully*, as it is, with as little pre-conditioned data as possible—that data which normally programs everything, throughout one's life, based on its biases. Our tastes, our cultural preferences, our relational skills, all may be tainted (positively or negatively) by childhood environmental or circumstantial events; but the point is to be real, to be with things as they *are*, not as some subjective historical impressions designed them to be. Of course, everything is influenced in a sense anyway, no matter what we do, but the idea is to relate to our lives, as they unfold, for what is relevant now, rather than from what was relevant "then." By the world's standards, that's unhealthy ... not to have all this history.

What we're doing is much closer to the way tribal peoples are raised—connected, bonded to the Earth. What tells a tribal child that she or he is here is that they feel their connection to the Earth in a way that isn't dependent on something that is self-referenced. Rather, existence is referenced by the tribe, and the ongoing rituals of the tribe and their relationship to the Earth. Certainly tribal peoples have deep myths, but they are cosmic, universal or tribal myths, not individ-

128

ual or personal (although there is significant familial, lineal or ancestral acknowledgment). This is history arising out of an objective context, rather than subjective biases.

In limiting the number of photographs we take of our children (we do make some exceptions, so there are a few pictures here and there), what we are doing is experimental— although before cameras, photos weren't even possible anyway. When we follow these principles, however, our parents, brothers and sisters are often convinced that we are doing serious damage to our children by denying them the satisfaction of having tangible proof of their history. To the psyche of the contemporary world what we are doing is probably bizarre. Conventional people believe we're denying our children a right!

With photographs, every adoring adult who defines a child by a special photograph is actually affecting that child! When a possessive, neurotic grandma (and thank God for the healthy, sane, wonderfully-wise grandmas and grandpas and great-grandmas and great-grandpas, of which there are plenty) takes a photograph of a granddaughter, do we have any idea of the kind of psychic energy matrix that the grandparent lays on the child? Everyone who the grandparent shows the picture to is psychically projecting onto the child. Of course, as we've noted before, everyone does that just from hearing stories about the child anyway, but a picture gives people an accurate "target" so to speak. It's like a honing device for psychic projection. Again, all of this is quite subtle in relation to all the forms of physical and emotional abuse that parents and other adults often perpetrate on children, but even such subtle influences—the psychic ones—have their effect.

When grandma looks at the picture and says, "That's my granddaughter," there's no distance between grandma and granddaughter—that connection eliminates the distance even if grandma's in New York and the granddaughter's in California. That's what prayer healing is based on. If we really want to help someone, even the weakest prayer will be effective because it's the intensity of intention or desire that is the strongest element of success. If we couldn't care less, but are just doing it out of obligation, one would have to pray their brains out before the prayer would touch the other person at all. That's the principle.

As far as I'm concerned, it's nice to send a picture of the child to the grandparents once every several years or so, so they aren't totally out of the child's life. I would do this unless the grandparents lived near the family and saw their grandchild frequently. Then I wouldn't feel the need for a picture even that often. Remember, this is my personal opinion. I am considered mad in many circles, or at least a fundamentalist-zealot child-advocate.

Taking home movies of the kids may even be worse than the photographs. The object fascination and curiosity that some people can pour onto a child are like a form of contamination. Every child has an atmosphere around them, and a relationship to us as their parents. The average individual has no energy to disturb these, but some certainly do. When they place their energy on a particular child, it affects the atmosphere of that child's developing process. It may be subtle, to most people, but it's undeniable to someone who is sensitized to such things.

In the ordinary world, nothing much happens to the individual as the result of the subtlety of someone looking at their photograph, because most people are so dense and rooted in such habitual mechanicalness that someone's "looking" doesn't have any effect on them. But in a life lived in a more conscious, refined way it does have an effect, because such a person is less buffered.

* * *

Every time my mother visits she sees my grown children and says to me, "You've done such a good job," but she won't listen to a word I say about raising children the way in which I believe, as outlined in this book. So, just raise your children consciously and don't feel the need to get agreement from family or friends. There is no "popularity contest" to this. It is all for the health and happiness, for the overall well-being, of the child.

JUST LIKE US:
Role Models

Every child looks for role models, for heroes. For me (and most of my contemporaries) in sixth grade it was Davy Crockett. What did any child ever do in those days but sing the "Davy, Davy Crockett, King of the wild frontier..." song? It was a national epidemic, and our whole dimension of consciousness (besides a Coke, a hot dog, a piece of candy and our budding sexual awareness) was wrapped up in old Fess Parker (I still remember his name forty years later).

Who are the heroes nowadays? Davy Crockett wasn't cruel or vindictive. He had some honor, some integrity, even some innocence. But, where are our heroes today, where are our role models? Mom and Dad? Mom's busy working at being a complete woman, holding down a job, indulging her artistic skills and competing with Dad. Dad is busy working long hours to "make ends meet" (*which ends, I'd like to know?*), struggling with his sense of manliness, and being outraged by the contemporary social and political climate.

As children we went to church, or synagogue or temple, and our parents pointed out the priest, the minister or the rabbi. Well, a child doesn't have to be very smart to see through those external appearances in most cases. "That's our religious role model? Our spiritual role model? Forget it," we say. "I'd rather be wandering lost in the wilderness."

A lot of you know what I'm talking about. You went to church when you were six years old, and you saw hypocrisy and immaturity. Or, you went to the synagogue for this really sacred Jewish event, and you noticed the rabbi, covered with jewelry, in a slick suit, checking out every mirror in the room and flirting with all the married women. Children don't miss these things. Even if children aren't sure what to make of it all intellectually, their feeling response is accurate.

One woman I knew described being an eight-year-old at church and seeing the priest offering the Communion wafer while women would grab his hand, caress it, and suck and fondle his fingers. And he was "digging it" ... totally indulging it! He might not have touched any of them further, but that was how he got off. And this woman said, "I was only eight, and I looked at that and said, 'Religion stinks. I'm supposed to believe in this shit?' " And it got harder from there for her. Innocence shattered! Children are very bright and sensitive and not easily (if ever) fooled, at least not bodily.

Of course, not all religious authorities are so neurotic, but then again the training they receive is not about psychological health and sanity. Or, more realistically, the criteria for being a priest, minister or so on doesn't demand true human maturity. Lots of big problems with power, greed and sexual perversity slip through, not only unnoticed but totally ignored. Where *are* our spiritual role models?

Children will have to choose role models, that is

for sure. And often parents make these choices for their young children by, to some degree, defining the environments their children are exposed to—such as violent movies, totally inane television shows and even more violent video games. (Somehow, a sadistic psychotic who falls in love and loses the game, a tear dropping from his broken-hearted eyes, is not my idea of a great, healthy role model for an impressionable child.)

Who are our social and political role models? Men who lie, steal, are sexually perverse and totally unreliable? Our media is so slanted, so biased in its marketing scenarios that we end up with role models of greed, self-centeredness, vanity, seductiveness and promiscuity. We become so busy "getting our needs met" that we don't even know that anyone else exists (except as resources to meet our needs) let alone having the inspiration to really serve others in their needs.

* * *

A child's basic patterns are usually set by the time they are three. When they get older, we can see it so clearly—it is just like they were trained in a school to act a certain way, when all they did was live with someone for two-and-a-half years. We may wonder, how much can a child learn in several months? Yet, we see how dramatically they absorb the attitudes of the adults around them, right from birth. It is amazing how often, in cases of divorce, the child is still so much like the adult who left. It is undeniable. And it's not only genes; it's physical influence after birth.

Children are not going to grow up intentionally doing something different from all the adults around them. They *want* to be like us. So they will speak like us, move like us, act like us. We don't have to bitch at them, "Do it this way, do it this way." Just be an appropriate role model and they will follow suit. A child instinctually knows right human behavior from twisted or aberrated human behavior. If the child's role models are living rightly, the child will follow their behavior and grow up sane—psychologically and personally strong and balanced. If a child's role models are living lives of neurosis, psychosis or depravity, the child will copy the behavior in the same way, but grow up deeply in pain, suffering the internal (and usually unconscious) crisis of the conflict between what they know instinctually is right, and how they are actually living or behaving.

When they become adults, then, our children will look for people to be in relationship with who are like their role models were. If we have been role models of adults who are gentle, understanding and considerate, then our children will grow up and look for that. Gentle, considerate upbringing basically perpetuates itself. Our children will spread in their lives what they learned from us. If we are gentle, considerate and understanding, they will seek that kind of person to be in relationship with.

We might say to our children, "I just want you to be happy," but if we are violent to them, how can they possibly be happy? They are going to grow up and get into relationship with someone who is going to be violent with them as well. If they grow up being beaten, they will unconsciously seek to replicate their childhood, as adults; and more than likely they will enter into relationship with someone who will badly mistreat them.

Of course, occasionally the chain is broken by a conscious adult. But our contemporary society is exemplified by those who cannot break the pattern, people who even go so far as to justify their abuses by putting the blame on the victim, like a robber who falls down a set of stairs in a house he is robbing, or gets hurt by the house owner who surprises and overpowers him, and then sues the victim of the crime.

If we want our children to be happy, we must treat them with love, attention and consideration. They will be happy, and will find people to live and work with who are like that too—considerate, loving and gentle. It's common sense, quite linear really, and that's the bottom line.

If we are cruel, they will try to be cruel. Sometimes they won't even be able to, but they will try. If we are constantly angry, they will be angry; if we are violent, they will be violent, no matter what words we tell them. So our primary responsibilities as parents are: don't be cruel, don't be violent, don't shame our children, don't neglect our children. Be respectful, responsible, reliable. Everything else will take care of itself.

THE DEFENSE MECHANISM

As parents, it will be either our automatic responses and conditioned reflexes, or our conscious behaviors that will model most strongly to our children. When children are "knocked out of their Essence," so to speak ... when they lose their innocence ... they will start to develop defense mechanisms against objectivity— against the truths they know inside. It happened to all of us to varying degrees. A defense mechanism kicked in because somebody we trusted implicitly told us, by their behavior, to "defend ourselves" against clarity and truth. Trusted individuals in our lives— parents, teachers, siblings, uncles, aunts and so forth—

told us by implication to develop these defense mechanisms against seeing life as it actually is, and instructed us, through their behavior, conscious and unconscious, in how to view things through subjective biases. We were not necessarily told by direct instruction, but we were told by action, or by how we were treated; and we didn't know that we had a choice, i.e., that we did not *have* to listen. In fact, these trusted others gave us the conditioning commands which first imposed the illusion under which we then functioned; these same commands now continue to keep this illusion in place.

For example, when our child comes home and says, "Morgan bit me," or "Mickie kicked me," if we turn around outraged and shriek, "What! That little bastard!" That's it—they see and hear that, and up comes the defense mechanism against understanding, generosity and compassion.

"Randy told me that it's really great to eat poison ivy."

"What! What a dumb thing to say. Well, Randy is *wrong*." There you go again!

Try this instead. When the child says: "Morgan bit me!" say: "She did? Well that's how people are sometimes. How does it feel now?" The child may stand there surprised, as if to say: "Aren't you going to have sympathy for me?"

Our attitude could be: "I do have sympathy for you and you look fine. You're not bleeding. There's nothing wrong with you. You could walk home on your own two feet to tell me you got bitten. Don't make more of it than it actually is."

Commonly, mothers tell their little girls to do this or that in relationship to appearances ... like, every time her little girl puts on a cute little dress, mother's reaction is so dramatic, so indulgent and so reactive to the child's "cuteness." That's teaching the child to develop a defense mechanism against simple enjoyment, without vanity or fanfare. The mother doesn't have to *say* anything, like: "A little girl should always wear pink frilly dresses and never wear pants, because she always looks like a boy when she's in pants." But, if whenever the little girl puts on a dress, mother "ooh's" and "aah's" and "coos" and sighs, and when her little girl just wears pants and a T-shirt, mother is just her ordinary inattentive self. Then the child cannot help but draw conclusions that emphasize appearances over beingness. When we make such things significant, we train the child's defense mechanisms.

Children are incredibly perceptive when it comes to even the slightest gestures or shifts in tone of voice or facial expressions, and the conclusions they draw from what they see and hear are based on a two- or four- or six-year-old logic, not on a trained, intelligent, wise, experienced adult logic. A woman once told me that her mother never let her pierce her ears, telling her that no man would ever marry her if she had "holes in her ears." This student is now a middle-aged adult, and her ears are still not pierced (even though she finds the clip-on earrings, that she wears all the time, to be a tremendous discomfort). What does a child do with such totally subjective input? Turns it into a lifelong religion.

Children catch everything we do ... and I mean everything! They can be in another room, but if they can still hear our tone of voice, or if they see our posture, they get every nuance. They're being trained quite methodically, whether we want to give them this training or not.

This defense mechanism is not in itself "bad," however. It can work to our advantage or our disadvantage depending on its context. So, for instance, it is possible that, despite an adult's inhibitions and repressions in some areas, he or she may still have the context of a positive primary relationship with their child. If the mother is a loving parent, and her relationship to her child is therefore loving, she still may have a terrible fear of blood ... or spiders ... or she may hate scrambled eggs that are too wet. It could be anything ... an inhibition about dealing with the dog who was hit by the car, and whose insides are spilling out all over the front lawn. She could be in the house freaking out, screaming, "John, John, get that dog out of here. I can't stand it." That could be an inhibition that might not inhibit the child essentially in the development of a positive image and a positive ego/self axis, because of the positive, loving relationship that *already* exists as context or ground.

Overall, a strong relationship can usually stand a few bumps. However, given the mechanics of the developmental process, and the fact that we can't out-guess how such behaviors will affect a child, as the old adage says: "Better safe than sorry."

DON'T ARGUE IN FRONT OF THE CHILD

When parents get angry, it's not necessarily going to devastate the child. We don't have to be "perfect" role models in front of our child and repress everything that might be a little negative. It's just that we have to be completely self-honest and never blame the child for our own problems. If we are fully loving, affectionate and acknowledging of the child, although they may dislike parental squabbles, they won't be traumatized by them. (Obviously parental squabbles are not full out fist fights. Such parents couldn't love a child properly.)

When parents share their bed with the child, and the child is asleep and they start fighting, the child will start fussing and immediately wake up. If they say to the child, and mean it, "It's not you. Mommy and Daddy are having an argument. You have nothing to do with it. It's not about you; we just have some difficulties right now, and we'll work them out fine," the child will go right back to sleep and sleep peacefully, even if the parents are really going on at one another. They want to feel safe and secure in their parents' love of them, and they never want to be the cause of or source of a disagreement between their parents.

As children grow older, I recommend that you don't argue with your mate in front of the child unless you can keep the argument to a lack of criticism of the other person. If we can keep the argument to a discussion of facts, perhaps, or preferences, that's one thing, even if voices are raised and it gets hot. If arguments between parents tend to deteriorate to where one is screaming really deprecating things at the other person, then, no matter what we have to do, we should not do that in front of the child. Children can't make sense of such abuse of a loved one coming from someone who is equally loved. It *must* create conflicts, crises and divisions within the child ... and always unhealthy and very emotionally painful ones. Frequently a child's actual physical health difficulties are the psychosomatic result of their conflict and confusion about parental loyalty.

If we are in a relationship with a partner and we have a child, and if we see one way in which our partner, through their behavior, is "shutting down" our child, we should take all the ways that they *aren't* shutting the child down, and work to keep those other areas *awake* in the child. (Of course, through our own behavior we would also be working to balance in the child those areas that our partner was unhealthy in, thereby strengthening the child in overcoming those weaknesses which were picked up from the other parent.) Then, when the child gets older, he or she will be able to take care of their own un-awake, or "sleeping" areas. We should do that instead of arguing or fighting with our mate all the time. Then we can have a wonderful relationship with both our mate and our child. The result is that everyone benefits.

As I've said, we don't have to play some role of the perfect adult. Just be self-honest and be honest with the child. If we break down and cry we can just say, "Everyone has their limit, and I just met mine, and it's not you. It's not your fault." They'll go, "Okay." That's honest, and they can accept that because children observe adults, and they see the stresses and strains that their parents hold.

We need to be willing to be embarrassed in front of our child, to cry in front of our child, to not be able to hammer a nail in straight in front of our child, especially if one is a man whose son thinks he can do anything. If we guard our vulnerability and our humanness from our child, we also sacrifice a tremendous amount of "food," i.e., nurturing, that we would be getting from that child, and keeping such food from them as well.

DON'T COMPLAIN TO YOUR CHILDREN

Another useful thing to remember is, don't whine to your children, like, "Ohhh, life is so awful, nothing ever works for me, I'm *soooo* unlucky." That's whining. Don't complain in front of children. Remember, you are the parent or the caretaking adult. It is very unhealthy for a child if you become the child, psychologically, and make *them* into the parent—your confessor, the one whom you need confirmation, acknowledgment and support from. And, you should never fall into the terrible habit of making your child play the role a mate should be playing. Often, in a divorce or some other single-parent situation, or even if a couple is together but only one parent is doing the parenting, the parent is so desperate for the kind of partnership that mature adults should share, that they unconsciously (sometimes just from sloppy weakness, sometimes from deep neurosis) begin to put their child in that role or position. You must have seen a forty-year-old woman flirting with her twelve-year-old son as if he were her husband, yes? Such behavior cannot help but influence the child in unhealthy ways, and often inflicts lifelong damage on the child's abilities to have healthy, fulfilling adult relationships. Such a woman might say, "Oh, it's so hard around here without your Daddy and there's so much work to do. Oh, it's so difficult, I don't know what I'd do without my little man to help me," etc. The child comes to think that they need to parent the parent; that they need to take care of the whole family.

If we complain in front of our children they will think that they need to take care of us. Whatever our mate is not doing, our child will think they need to do it. For example, if they see Mom crying and they say, "What's the matter?" and she says, "Daddy and I had a fight," they will always ask, "What about?" If Mom says, "He works so much I never see him; he never helps me out around the house; and he never just brings me flowers. He never just thinks about me, he's always so busy working ..." or whatever; if she complains to her children like that, they will start either resenting the other parent for hurting her, or they will try to do those very things she is asking for, imagining that she will then feel satisfied, happy and fulfilled. Such behavior is truly touching, but not worth the division it must create in a child who is both torn between loyalties and acting as parent when they should only be a child.

Instead, if the child comes over when we are crying and they hug us, we can just hug them back and say thank you, rather than complain to them. If they say, "What's the matter?" we can say, "I'm feeling sad today, it's just nice to be hugged," that's all, and leave it at that.

THEY WILL CHOOSE COMPASSION

Children have a real sense of integrity, human integrity. Human beings—complete human beings—left to their own devices, have an abhorrence for inhumane acts. No normal child is without this. But in the U.S. these days, with the proliferation of cocaine use (crack especially), women drug-users, alcoholics, even nicotine and caffeine addicts are giving birth to babies who are already addicted or disposed to addiction. We are learning that children born addicted to drugs, or children who in the first couple of years of life are taking drugs because of their parents, grow up with abnormal human feelings. No emotion, no conscience, none! That's very scary to think about. Such a child could kill a brother or sister and feel nothing. Literally, nothing. No remorse, just, "Oh well," and go on about his life.

Normal human beings will have a genuine sense of compassion, an abhorrence for violence and inhumanity, for torture, for war, for brutality, for rape. It's *in us*, it's ingrained; that is who we are as a race, with the inherent possibility of living conscious, compassionate, self-reflective lives. So, it is very useful to allow children to develop their own opinions, because if we give them opinions forcefully enough, they will react against those opinions only because they want to be their own persons when they grow up. They may well do things that are less than what we would wish for them only because they are reacting to having been conditioned. If we let them come to their own opinions, they will come to the kinds of opinions that we will honor and respect. They will feel and do charitable things for other people; they will feel deeply for the state of the world. Role-modeling such compassionate humanity is one of the best forms of environmental stimuli to allow children to feel that innate compassion in themselves and to learn how to practice it.

Many four- or five-year-old children have tortured some bug; killed some insects or tortured some mouse that they caught. (I would guess even Mahatma Gandhi or Albert Schweitzer did this when they were young.) When I was growing up I had all kinds of animals, and even though everybody felt I was a very gentle child, I did my share of pulling wings off of flies. I don't know why; children just do that. I suppose it's all experimental. For an adult who witnesses this behavior, it is easy to try to lay an attitude on the child. Certainly we should answer children's questions honestly, and be there as a guide, but we should try not to superimpose our opinions on them too forcibly, even when we think our opinions are the most refined, compassionate, best opinions a human being could have. Let children observe us and come to their own conclusions.

I learned from observing my father who had tremendous social integrity. He was gentle, non-judgmental and non-critical, typically. But, he also had a passionate political ideology. During the McCarthy era in the U.S. he got blacklisted. He wrote for the *Republic*, a socialist newspaper during the Depression in the '30s. As he got older, however, he left the most active of these political involvements behind, although he always maintained an acute social/political awareness based on his love for dignity, peace, kindness, and humanity in general. He had his art and his family to care for.[1] I learned from living with him, not from him telling me what to do and how to be. I didn't even know I was learning, but I was.

One of his pictures was of a protest march, with police on horses clubbing the protesters. It was a self-portrait, but without looking at it carefully you could not identify his face. I was looking at it one day, and my mother said, "Do you know what that is?"

I said, "It's protesters."

She said, "That's us. Your father was in a protest where the police came on horses and clubbed everybody down."

I was dumbfounded, "He was?" Previous to that I had no idea.

My parents had high social ideals and spiritual ideals—but I wasn't force-fed any of it. I was allowed to discover my parents' lives and loves in my own way and in my own time. And somehow, instinctually, I cleaved to the basic goodness and compassion that they demonstrated, instead of to other influences in my youthful environment (like a viciously cruel friend, or mean and drunken adults—parents of a sometimes friend or two, of mine).

If we show children the wisdom of right living, the older they get the more they will recognize who is happy and who isn't; and who is strong and who isn't; and who is confident and who isn't. When they see the contemporary idols—the rock stars, movie stars and sports stars—being less strong, and less confident and happy than we are, they will intuitively review their education and will begin to flash on what our training of them has been.

Children will make certain considerations, draw certain conclusions, and just tuck them away for future use often long before they manifest changes in their behavior based on those ideas. Our job as parents is to be consistently straight and strong, loving and supportive, and not expect to see immediate responses on the surface when a child learns an important life lesson about generosity, kindness, non-prejudice or whatever. If we look for subtle clues, they will be there!

So, have faith in the good example that you have set, and your faith in your child (in their inherent goodness, inherent brilliance and inherent integrity) will prove to be well founded. Not only that, but they will *feel* your faith in them; there is no substitute for that.

THE MOTHER'S ROLE

THE DIVINE MOTHER

Commonly we say "Father" in referring to God, because we've culturally masculinized the Divine, but basically it's as Mother that we look to and for God. When we don't get the essential love and mothering that we need, we can doubt God, or that there even *is* a God! The following edited excerpt [adapted from *The Alchemy of Love and Sex* by Lee Lozowick, (Prescott, AZ: Hohm Press, 1996), pp. 6-9] expresses this idea and further implications in greater detail.

Psychologists tell us that children perceive the world nondualistically for the first several months of life, at least. But practically, they are totally dependent on "Mama." If they are hungry and they cry, Mama is there (or should be). If they are cold or hurt or lonely, some "other"—Mama— is there (again "or should be," if Mama is at all a responsive and loving parent). But a child does- not see Mama as being separate from himself or herself, as coming from "out there" to give food or comfort. To a child, Mama is like an extension of the child's own body. The child's world is indis- tinct—there is no Mama and me, there is only this inclusive experience of sensation, need and fulfillment.

At a certain age, perhaps six or seven months, or earlier, the child's perceptions begin to change. He or she begins to see Mama "over there"—and she represents to the child the great and mysterious "other," or God.

The child doesn't see or make intellectual or scientific distinctions between "woman" or "man." Rather, he or she gets a whole, organic imprint (mental, physical, psychic ...) of essential "womanness" or essential "manness." And the imprint the child gets of woman is quite distinct from that of man. The child sees Mama as god. It is understandable. What does Mama offer? Touch, warmth, attention, care. In some uncon- scious way the child knows that he or she grew in and came out of Mama's body. How much more "creator" can she be? It's not the same for Daddy. He didn't carry the child, Daddy didn't feel life inside him, and the child didn't bond organical- ly to man in the way he did to woman, even if the genetic code is half his.

No matter what we want to think or say about it, a doting Daddy is not the same as a loving Mama. Typically, men like to pick up their child once in a while (when they have nothing better to do), but even when men do touch their children, it is not like a woman's touch. It isn't possible to be the same. So, when the child looks at Mama and feels, "That's God," that doesn't happen on a level of self-reflective conscious awareness. That imprint is one of pure, primal, organic instinct.

If the child is female, she instinctually feels, "I've got the same imprint. When I grow up I'm going to have to be god ... Damn, that is a heavy responsibility." And it is! The imprint says: "I'm god—serve, serve, serve, and serve some more." The imprint says to take care of the whole damn world. It's a hell of a job to be god! Who in their right mind would want that responsibility? Nobody. Yet, the little eight-, nine-, or ten-month-old girl already knows, "One day I'm going to have to be responsible for being god because I am, in my essence, WOMAN."

Most grown men, as we all know, are still children (or at best adolescents) at the emotional level. Somehow the little girl knows that, and feels the profound woundedness of the society—a woundedness that only God can heal. Such an awesome responsibility! And woman grows up with that imprint very, very deep. It is an implicit, unspoken, usually unconscious drive that is foundational in all activity.

What happens to a male child? At the point when he's starting to realize duality he gets an imprint from God/Mama that says, "I'm a boy. I don't have the same imprint as Mama. I'm not sure I like that. I wanna be god. I wanna be. I wanna be. I wanna be."

The lack of education in relationship to this issue has caused untold misery and violence, not to mention the unconscionable moral, social, psychological, psychic and spiritual imbalances in our contemporary world. Based on this lack, men are trained to be god as the patriarchal reaction to the undeniable and organic fact that woman is god.

Paradoxically though, men grow up trained to be god while inside they say: "I'm not god. Woman is god." What kind of psychological reaction do you think that causes? Anger, frustration, guilt, self-doubt, fear, defensiveness, and more. And what do these internal conflicts cause? Corresponding pain, violence, abuse and blindness. Men put women down by demeaning, hurting, brutalizing, and taking advantage of them. These are men's ways of trying to ignore or forget what they know to be true, bodily. Adolescent reactivity against the goddess takes the form of denying the truth of her.

Certainly there are some more sensitive men around than the ones I've just described. Yet even so, many are unaware of all the subtle psychological recoil that leaks out of the cracks. The whole male psychological dynamic is a reaction against the conflict of being trained to be god and yet knowing that he is not.

Rhetorically, of course, and speaking non-dualistically, we are all God: men, women, all of creation. And rhetoric is all well and good, but what about the organic reality that moves us? What about those twenty-five or fifty years' worth of denial and other unconscious ego strategies that have literally formed the body, mind, health, and all of our reactions and beliefs? A man can't just say, "Yes, we're all God," and expect to be healed, although that would be nice and delightful. But it doesn't work that way. We've got to root out the unconscious motivations and transcend them in clarity and through the disintegration of life-negative habits. That is a lifetime operation.

The child lives and grows as a result of food that it receives from Mama, and that is obviously not going to change. Men can't nurture with physical milk, with nutritional sustenance from their own bodies, as women can, even if men can give an infant a bottle. (Maybe it's different on some other planet, but on Earth, as long as Homo sapiens are around, children will get suckled by Mama.) The imprint of the sustainer, of where life comes from, is still going to be woman.

The Divine Mother has been seen in the great spiritual traditions as the nurturer of the world, and in a limited sense as the nurturer of humankind. In Sanskrit they even call the woman goddess, Ma. For Ramakrishna, Kali Ma (a form of the Divine Mother) was his favorite deity.[2] Ramakrishna so loved Kali that he even became a woman in practice and consciousness for a time. He wore woman's clothing, lived among the women, and acted like a woman. The women, in turn, really loved and accepted him as one of them. He treated every woman like the Divine Mother. Even if dirty beggar women would come to the temple, Ramakrishna would bow down at their feet because they were the Mother, Kali. Every woman was Kali. It wasn't that he liked women as different from or polar opposites to men. It was that he loved the Goddess.

Wouldn't it be nice if men could grow up with the imprint of reverence for the Divine Mother—the reverence she deserves for being the sustainer of the world? If it were not for Shakti we would not be here. (If it were not for Shiva we would not be here either, but if there were only Shiva, and not Shakti—which is a purely hypothetical situation, a concept of there being only void—that would be a very dull existence.)[3]

Wouldn't it be interesting if men were so mature and natural in their maleness that an objective masculine imprint were passed on too? It is hard to imagine such a society because it is not in our middle-class experience. We don't yet know what it would be like if men and women honored women as Woman, as Shakti, and honored men as who they are, essentially. I'd like to see a group of people living together with genuine recognition of that, without regard for the psychological mechanisms that prompt men to belittle women, and women to respond through either fear or anger. Yes, I would.

THE PROBLEM TODAY

A lot of instinctive mothering has become buried in the modern world in the last fifty years due to the overwhelming technological obsession that most people have in their homes. Microwaves, television, videos, and two parents working ... all of that has led to almost the complete burial of a woman's instinctual, archetypal mothering responses with her child. Women today still have these mothering responses of course (they have to have them), but they don't have reliable access to them, in the sense of being able and willing to give what it is that children need from mother. They have become unwilling to put aside their usual gross self-indulgences and fascination with technological gadgetry and wizardry, and the seductions of a life of shopping, entertainment and social absorption, and just be *Mother* with their children. This is a shocking, sad and even profound loss to modern generations. What is required to be Mother is an almost zealously singular attention on the child (and obviously an ability to get done what needs to be done practically, i.e., cooking, care of the home, etc.). This means that the distractions of the usual worldly obsessions—such as taking two hours in the morning to rise, bathe, do hair and put on make-up, and so on—must be dropped.

A mother has to *be there* first of all. If the child is in front of the television all day, there's no mother. Even if the mother is in the kitchen, there is no mother present with the child to express tenderness, satiety and pleasure, and that child is missing out on what mothering is organically meant to be. Soap opera "heroines," or Bugs Bunny, or some super-hero are hardly role models or replacements for Mother.

All of the negative social behavior we are experiencing as epidemic in the Western world is because none of these people, as children, had tenderness, satiety and pleasure expressed in relationship to them. When a mother runs into the bedroom, whips the kid up, runs out, throws the kid in a car seat, whips the kid out of the car, runs into the supermarket, whizzes around the supermarket without paying any attention to the child at all ... stops to chat with a neighbor while the child is screaming, and just looks at the child and says, "I'm talking to my friend, do you mind?" and then goes back to talking to the friend, it's no wonder that epidemic, negative social behavior is showing up in our world.

Since most of what a child learns is in the first two years, if a woman is *really* giving herself to mothering, her attention for these first two years, especially, should be dramatically focused on the child and his needs, even to the exclusion of some of her own comforts. It is my recommendation that for two years a mother basically has no life of her own, but belongs to her child.

Sometimes just five minutes of adult conversation is like treasure from God to the mother of a young child, so a lot of times what happens is that a woman will miss adult conversation so much, no matter how much she loves her child (that's never an issue), she will be willing to compromise her attention on the child in order to have a nice ten- or fifteen-minute uninterrupted adult conversation. Nevertheless, we recommend that for two years one forego their own preferences and their own kind of joy from that sort of input, and focus their receptivity and their joy on their child's growing, developing and expanding. Such focusing is good practice for serving selflessly, in any case. The basic needs of life—food, rest (maybe not as much as the mother wants or is habitually used to, but enough) and so on, will naturally fall in place, in sync with the new patterns of motherhood.

SMOTHERING OUR BOYS

These days, the tendency for boys to be more aggressive than girls is common, to a large degree, because most boys have been "smothered" instead of mothered. They have been controlled so that they weren't allowed to be themselves. Not that little boys should be wild animals any more than little girls should necessarily be always delicate, contained and polite. But, little boys have long been confined to a certain cage of conventionality, the old "children should be seen and not heard" edict, and they blame their mothers for that. They also blame women for that, because Mother is all women, is Woman, to a child.

I've been asked if men inherently hate women, and whether there is something to be expected about boys in terms of their relentless teasing of girls. On some cultural level, all men tend to be afraid of women, and therefore seek to dominate and control them, often through violence and subjugation. However, boys don't necessarily have to grow up with that influence. In fact, they shouldn't. With the right kind of parenting, they won't grow up with it to the same degree most of us guys have. A boy's predominant male role models should be conscious enough not to animate these antiquated behavior modalities; and a child's predominant female role models should not be overly sensitive, to the degree that they see mountains where there are molehills, and evil men—demon male chauvinist pigs—behind every blade of grass, or every longing stare. Of course, this whole dynamic happens so early in life that, by the time we are adults, this hatred of the imagined "constraining force of woman" is deeply ingrained.

Men also *enjoy* feminine company and do develop a kind of social consciousness. Men and women learn to be socially acceptable with one another. Certainly men still experience the conquest of the hunt (this primal mood), and they definitely seek the company of women so they can show off their hunter's prowess. But also, there is a level at which men enjoy feminine energy, the soft and receptive comfort of feminine nature. They want to be embraced with love and true affection. This is what little boys need from their mothers: boundaries, of course, but out of a context of soft, accepting, loving nurturance.

The minute I was divorced, my mother said, "Come live with me." (I mean, she would give me everything I wanted: "I'll do your laundry. Come live with me, you can have your old room.") And a lot of us would like to be taken care of that way. Sure we want to be adult men or women, but since we were never taken care of, never mothered properly (not smothered but mothered properly), we want that. And our mother is always our mother, no matter how old we get (although I did maintain an independent living situation in spite of the temptation to become "little" again!).

THE IMPORTANCE OF FEEDBACK

When we in our community feel that there's a certain relationship to being a mother that has escaped a woman who is a mother, we share our input with her. Now "out in the world" of course, one couldn't get away with saying anything that is too true, too real, too threatening to someone who is insecure, shame-based, prideful, and in denial about their true state of psyche and personality. A friend who had just had her first child might ask a woman with three children (all healthy, happy and holy): "How do you sterilize the bottle, and how do you get rid of the jaundice ... ," and all that stuff. But if the experienced mother really sits her friend down and says, "I think you need to look at this, your avoidance of affection and intimacy with your child," the friend will nail the other mother to the wall and never want to play *mah jong* with her again. It is *very* unusual for a mother to be open enough to ask another mother, "How am I doing?" and really *mean* it. Yet, this is something we must do if we are going to raise our children in line with the principles of childraising that we have discussed.

Fathers are included in this, obviously. We must ask input and help of other parents who are sane, wise and experienced—perhaps we could even say "successful" in the domain of conscious parenting. To ask other parents, "How am I doing?" is very threatening, however. If we are smother-mothering our child, but we simply think we are loving them up, and that we are just giving our child genuine affection, touch and understanding, if we ask another parent, and that parent says, "It's like you are smothering; your affection is artificial. What you are doing is giving your child what you felt *you* never got; what *you* want. And it's overdone—it's empty, it's dramatic, it's not real, it's not clean, it's motivated by impurities," we will be shattered, and angry as hell at the advice-giver.

No new mother, especially a first-time mother (it's different the second time around) who is aglow in the beauty of this new experience, wants to be told that she is psychologically crippling her child from day #1. No new mother wants even any hint of that, anywhere within a thousand miles of her. But if we are going to be raising our children truly in line with these principles, we must be willing to take feedback.

ADVICE FROM COMMUNITY WOMEN

With childraising in our community, it is very much a dialogue and not a formula. We are constantly asking questions and working out details.

Where does one go to find the vision and what the vision is really rooted in? Where does one find the underlying principles that one can check into and then work out the details from? All the spiritual practices that one does, whatever path it is that we have, can provide that. Each women should take into herself the deepest guidance that she has in her own tradition.

For us, it's turning to our Teacher and our tradition and to our practice, and having that come first, in terms of the embodied wisdom in those resources. If that is in place, if that is consciously being turned to, it's a wellspring. Mistakes will be made (and they will be made), but they will be workable, and there will be inner guidance. Through one's love for God and love for her child and her mate, she will find the foundation of everything that she does.

For a woman, we can't overemphasize the need to have women's culture and to have supportive woman friends who one can go to; because we each have "moments," like every other mother, where it is hell, and we are tearing our hair out and feeling like if we can't get away we are just going to flip. Parenting is a tremendous demand. If we are coming at it from the place of really wanting our childraising to be an integral part of our life and practice, it's going to be a thousand times more demanding than it is for one who

158

ascribes to the values of the "conventional world" in which childraising (or parenting) is at best a secondary affair. Parenting is going to be a lot more demanding, and it is going to tap into those places in us that have not been met yet.

Mothering is really going to stir the fire, stir our own consciousness in a way that we just can't perceive of ahead of time. So, we need to have the support of other women whom we can talk to and be with. Mothers need to be mothered; mothers need other women who can hold them in their arms sometimes.

Don't be discouraged, though. Women will be surprised at how fast "mother" is going to come up in her body. Who we are instinctually, organically as a mother, is going to be there!

If a woman is uncompromisingly self-honest that clears away all the layers of stuff that keep her out of touch from what is instinctual. She will always know what to do, creatively. She won't have to struggle with it. So that kind of practice in general—uncompromising self honesty—opens the door to instinct and will be a natural wellspring bubbling up all the time as a mother cares for her child.

THE FATHER'S ROLE

A child must adapt to two forces in order to grow. One force, generally represented by the mother, is the pleasurable force of love and intimacy. But the other force to which the child must adapt, if he or she is to grow, is the force of obligation, or the demand for further learning, adaptation and change of behavior. That force is generally represented by the father.

Unfortunately, bonding to the male parent is rarely present for girls or boys in modern families. Maybe Daddy will hold the kid a little bit, but it's more common for men to be helpless with children—not knowing how to change a diaper, and too busy with other projects, in any case. (Certainly that was true for most of *our* parents.)

That is why, when a child is young, he or she should have a lot of masculine attention. When a baby is born, the father should hold the baby often. Otherwise the infant gets entirely bonded to the mother. This creates imbalance internally that frequently gets expressed in some psychological aberration later on. Once a child is bonded to the masculine as well as the feminine, they have an opportunity, boy or girl, to deal with their masculine nature—an opportunity that is almost unheard of under other circumstances. Part of the health of the culture has to do with how children bond.

A child is automatically bonded to mother because of having been carried and nurtured, fed, kept alive in her body for nine months. Mother needs only a minimal amount of effort to continue to deepen and broaden this bonding, but Daddy must work at it—he must actively engage the child in order to bond deeply. Just that one-celled sperm that is his part in this miraculous creative process isn't enough to maintain the bonding process when the child is born.

In our community, as backward as it may seem, most of the fathers here help essentially equally, taking care of a baby when it's sick, for instance. (When did our fathers take care of us when we were infants and we were sick? By God, when a baby was feverish, diarrhea-ish and throwing up, that was a woman's work!)

Ideally, the bonding process begins with bonding to both parents, and then continues with male company in a natural way through friends, role-models and so on as the child grows. It shouldn't be that as soon as children can make their own way and walk, then we just let the women take care of them. There should be a continuation of male company, male play, male influence. Obviously we are assuming in this whole discussion that the available male company for any child, boy or girl, will be completely healthy, life-positive and nurturing, and a mature presence. The man who fondles little girls (or boys) instead of offering loving affection, or the father who demands that his children "perform" (whether it is certain forced social *personas*, or a son who is a great football player at three years old, or so on), is not the kind of male role-model who raises children who are confident and mature in relationship to their own masculinity or masculine sides, or in relationship to other men. There are men who want their little boys to be warriors, and believe that there's only one way to make them be "men" and that is through pain. This kind of parenting is a way to devastate innocence and joy. I've seen people out in public who, if their kids cry, they smack them and say, "You cry again, I'm gonna hit you harder," and that's how they stop their children from crying—by fear. That's not the kind of parenting that produces unconflicted, productive adults. On the other hand, if a child is going to get a healthy male dynamic we can't have a bunch of sentimentally sappy men walking around, or men sashaying around flirting with women all the time. We have got to have men who are confident in their masculinity; men who are solidly with their partner, satisfied, working in the relationship and being men. And women have got to be mothers, not simpering, overprotective ogres. If the father's relationship to a child is deeply loving and bonded enough, the father can repair the damage done if there is a lack of mother's bonding and love.

With couples, we recommend that fathers "be there" as close to fifty percent of the time as possible. Again, for fathers too, we recommend that they sacrifice for a couple of years. For the rare individuals, attentive presence to their child is not a sacrifice; for rare individuals it is great—the wonder of their growing child is so brilliant it eclipses all the other stuff. That is the ideal, of course. Ideally, the father will want to be with his child, for the child will certainly want to be with the father in either case.

What is needed for both men and women is that we be real, solid, understanding, kind, generous and loving from a context of wisdom and sanity. Not too soft and insecure, and not too tough and unfeeling either.

──── 6 ────

DRAWING A LINE:
The Challenge Of Responsible Boundaries

THE NEED

If we love our children, we have to be responsible for
them beyond simply being role models or teachers of
sorts. Of course children need to see men and women
with virtues like patience, honesty, justice, gentleness,
and so on, but at least as a corollary to that, the basic
responsibility with children is to be reliable with discipline—not punitive discipline, necessarily, but discipline in terms of being able to set firm, just boundaries.
Children need to learn the definitions, limits and
extents of both their world and *the* world. A child raised
without reliable boundaries is a child who will grow up
confused, unsure of themselves and their behavior, and
often acting out negatively as a desperate attempt to
have boundaries imposed upon them.

The primary boundaries are those that are
inalienable, such as boundaries surrounding basic
physical health, like, "You can't drink Draino®; you
can't run into the busy street without stopping to look
for cars; you cannot jump in the fire ...," etc. Secondary
boundaries have to do with circumstantial things, and
may vary (or not) depending on the situation. These

secondary boundaries may also change as the child grows older and develops a greater competance and skill level.

Without the proper boundaries the best education is useless. Some of my closest friends (and I'm sure some of the people you know) are extremely well-educated, refined and well-informed adults, yet are completely psychologically or emotionally messed up, almost incapable of relationship and barely human, it sometimes seems. So, education is important, but not even secondary. First come proper boundaries; secondarily is our presence with our children, i.e., our being with them; and thirdly come the formal elements of education—the data so to speak.

Author and educator John Holt held a view similar to Jean Liedloff's "continuum concept" view,[1] which is that if we just let children develop and be who they are, without expectations and fears, they will grow up innocent. (*Wise innocence* will be the fruit of that approach, as we would say.) This view is contested by those who feel that children need to be controlled and closely directed and monitored.

My view is between those two. Giving a child space that comes from the domain of neglect, from the parents' being too busy, for example, develops a very neurotic child. And, "sitting on a child" based on the need to dominate, control and manipulate shatters innocence very quickly and is psychologically damaging.

Conscious parents need to define limits, ones that make sense; limits that they can explain to the child. We might think that people do that, but actually many do not discipline their children in a way that is rational. The bottom line is to keep honest, sensible, explainable limits, but at the same time pay attention and direct gently, in ways that are needed.

* * *

Children need and want boundaries. Every child knows what it feels like to be happy and what it feels like to be miserable, which is why they ask for limits. They will push the limits as a way to discover for themselves what the limits are, but a child who knows their limts, and for whom the limits are trustworthy and reliable, is a child who will be happy and confident.

Between ages two and four, an immediate response to the circumstance and fair, non-arbitrary discipline is crucial because that's when children get their major teaching about boundaries. Setting consequences for breaking boundaries is an important consideration here. We need to know *what* to do and *when* to do it, and quickly. To set consequences a week after something happened is useless for a young child — after a week it is a different universe for them. Consequences should fit the disobedience, and be directly in time with the event, so the child knows what the consequence is for.

We want so much to be gentle and loving with our children and not shame them in any way, shape or form, that we often miss the boat in terms of providing a kind of loving discipline that they're craving. Kids at the ages of two to four start acting out in often negative ways if they're not getting the boundaries that they need. And they will let us know that they need reassurance that our love for them is responsible and wise in terms of firm but loving boundaries.

Often, when one child, perhaps a sibling, sees another child breaking the rules, and if they feel that the disciplinary consequences for the child who broke the rules was not harsh enough, they will ask the parent, "Aren't you going to punish her?" What they are saying is, "If I did that I would want you to punish me more strongly." They are saying, very clearly, "I want you to maintain limits for me." There is no consciousness involved in that process at all. It is an unconscious request for a reliable world.

Another example of children craving boundaries: if we have ever made a boundary for a child who does not have them (a child whose parents don't know how to make boundaries), that child literally becomes instantly affectionate, even trailing us around and clinging to us because they are so grateful. It's such a relief for them to finally have an adult putting his or her foot down, so to speak. Beyond a certain age, of course, all that changes. After that age, if they've been trained that anger is the only response, they might not respond to boundaries with elegance and affection. And, it may be a little too late to try to put one's foot down with a teenager.

WILL AND AUTOMONY

DEVELOPING THE MASCULINE

In the beginning it's all maternal—all of our perceptions and our makeup are feminine. Then, at a certain point in our ego development, in order for the developmental process to fulfill itself and for the dictates of humanness to evolve and blossom, we begin to develop the masculine within each of us. This may show up like a resistance to maternal demand—fighting with mother, or wandering off alone without looking to make sure the mother is there ... all those kinds of things. That's very healthy under ordinary circumstances. (Of course it is assumed that a mother will be attentive enough to her child to watch him when he wanders off so he doesn't get lost.)

The tendency in most parents—mothers and fathers—is to take every minor developmental expression and react as if this manifestation is defining the child for the rest of his or her life. Which is why, often, parents will see a child becoming independent and will lament, "What have we done wrong? Why aren't they listening to us? Why don't they come back when we call their names? They just keep running ...," when this is simply the natural course of things. Obviously boundaries are necessary, but there is a point in every child's development, boy and girl, when it is natural for them to develop more independence. And children go through countless stages (the intensity of which comes and often goes quickly) in their growing-up process. Often they will experiment with some manifestation for a few days, and then either drop it (and we never see it again) or integrate it in some way into their "repertoire." And sometimes, an organic developmental stage (contrasted with behavioral) may last weeks or months.

If the mother is too freaked out by every little change and attempts to maternally smother the child's urges to separate and distinguish him- or herself as an individual being, that can have very adverse affects. It can stunt the natural, personal and psychological evolution of the child. These changes have nothing to do with the child not loving the mother or not wanting the mother's company, attention and affection. Simply that, at a certain point in human development, it is evolutionarily appropriate for greater individualization.

To make matters worse, there are many therapists who know nothing about children (since they were trained in psychopathology). They will see some minor manifestation in the child—a little experiment or part of a one- or two-month developmental stage—and will start treating it like a symptom, when it is nothing but a natural affect of a developmental stage which will pass in its own time and place.

SURRENDERING TO A HIGHER POWER

Children need the ability to surrender gracefully, to concede their wishes or preferences to a superior power, and that is another thing that they learn, or don't learn, by watching how the adults around them handle their own "superior power," and how the adults relate to God or to the dictates of social and political necessities. So, for instance, whether we like it or not, there are certain tolerable speed limits to each driving situation. Whether adults respect these limits, or moan and complain and break them, has a very impactful effect on children observing this behavior. This is another aspect of right role-modeling. Another example: when we take our child to a restuarant, it is obviously not in our control how the food will taste, how efficient the waiter will be, and so on. We can choose, however, to be elegant about it all, very matter of fact; or we can whine and make a gross and inappropriate "scene." Children learn to accept unchangeable or inalienable situations, and they also learn to effectively make efforts in relationship to things that are flexible, or in situations in which there are options.

Since adults are going to be making boundaries for the child for awhile, if the child is not able to easefully surrender to a superior power (not necessarily on the outer level, where the child will argue and cry a little bit, but inside, in the child's being), the possibility is that every enforced demand on the child could be a struggle, even if the boundary is for the child's own good. If the child cannot surrender to a superior force—from parents, to the laws of their state and country—he or she will be very unhappy as an adult.

Lack of trust is the main factor that would create this inability in a child. A lack of trust is caused by a negative primal relationship, which is simply a parent-child relationship that is unloving, unreliable and unresponsive on the adult's part, or one that gives the child the impression of being unloved.

PUSHING AND STRESSING

Even though children recognize the importance of limits, and the comfort, security and love communicated within those limits, they will keep trying to "push" them. That need for limits may be simultaneous with a kind of panic, because once a limit is imposed "the game is changed." Well, to a child it is not a game, it's survival! So, the appreciation of the limit doesn't necessarily take effect right away. A three-year-old may not, in one day, change an established habit and start treating Mom differently, or speaking to her in a less demanding or critical tone of voice.

One woman told me about a problem she was having with her child pushing limits all the time. It would be time to go to school and the child would not want to get dressed. So the mother would keep coming back and trying out all these different strategies to get the child dressed, and the child always refused. My advice to her was, "If you are clear and firm about your limits, and about consequences for not following them, your child will follow suit. It is difficult, but you have to do it."

In growing, children seek to and need to define their limits: the limits of their environment, the definitions of who they are and what they're doing, the limits of peers and adults. That often shows up as testing or disobedience. It is nothing personal. They don't like to manipulate their parents—they learn to by necessity. They are taught to manipulate by parents who cannot be reliable adults with their children. If we listen to everything our three-year-old says, they end up being the parent and we end up being the child, which is devastating for a child. (And even though they might complain about it, when they leave home as a young adult they will be immensely grateful to us for not letting them manipulate us.)

Discipline can put stress on a child, which can actually be a healthy thing. The right kind of stress allows strength and clarity to be present in our lives. Most of us were very lucky that we grew up in stressful situations, because unknowingly it allowed us to come to necessary decisions and integral functioning. The world is stressful. It is a great gift to be able to deal with stress with dignity and equanimity.

In our community, the way we parent our children ostensibly aims at little to no stress. We attempt to give our children a great deal of freedom. This practice has been called *permissiveness*, but that's not really the right word to use. It's not the "hippie kind" of childraising lifestyle. We should not be permissive parents, although many parents who are insecure about boundary-making actually become over-permissive, in the sense of being afraid to step in, make firm limits and maintain those limits.

Proper boundaries do create stress for the child. Even though the child longs for proper boundaries and is incredibly grateful to anyone who gives them, it is the healthy *being* of the child, not the child's psychology or personality, who wants and is grateful for these boundaries. Young children don't yet understand, intellectually, why a certain boundary is drawn, even though essentially they want it, need it and are grateful for it.

If we simply provide proper boundaries, not arbitrary boundaries, but proper boundaries in a proper way, that will create a natural and unavoidable stress on the child, but also allow their deeper instincts to be exposed and active during those periods of stress. Proper boundaries are a necessary training ground for successful living, both during childhood and adulthood.

Unhealthy stress might be: as soon as the child shows an inclination for something, whether it be sports, music or anything, we send them to a special school for little geniuses ... train them to be a musical prodigy, for example. That's indulging the parents' projections and manipulations of the child for their (the parents') satisfaction. Clearly, that creates a different kind of stress. Some young children are even uprooted from their homes and sent away to schools of special education, ripping the child-parent fabric to shreds. Of course we want to provide both exposure to and education and training in something that a child has a strong inclination for, but the circumstances under which this is done are crucial to the health of the child.

There is also a fair amount of constructive stress for children caused by interacting with and being around other children. Having to work in any kind of group process, any kind of cooperative effort, will involve dealing with many different types of boundaries, and will be stressful, but extremely valuable.

HOW TO SET BOUNDARIES

I. KEEP IT SIMPLE

My belief is, the less boundaries the better. As I've noted in terms of primary and inalienable boundaries, one might say, "Stoves are hot and you can get seriously burned," or, "That pot is full of boiling water; you can't jangle it around and play with it." I would not let a child play with razors ... that kind of thing. In terms of noise and the energetic level of play, however, I make very few boundaries, except in the domain of physical safety and cruelty towards others.

If a child grows up with little outright discipline, but the parent is essentially a person who is completely friendly with who they are, and lives a life of impeccable integrity, the child does not need much discipline. The parents' role-modeling is communicated and transmitted. All children need, basically, is to know that cars run you over if you run in front of them. Very simple. Or, if you jump into a fire you'll get burned. That's all. But they don't need to be told, "That's fire, it's hot." Let them stick their finger in it, and before their whole hand is burned, believe me, they will retract their finger quickly and will know from then on that fire is hot.

A lot of adults have this idea that children are so lacking in intelligence that if we didn't tell them, they would go up and stick their hand in the flame and sit there in excruciating pain deciding whether fire was hot or not. They won't! It will take them a fraction of a second to realize that fires are hot, and then the lesson is well learned.

Another example: If we take the child to the seashore we will definitely want to pay attention to them, because the undertow of even moderate waves has more force than a year-and-a-half-old child has. We should just pay attention to them. That is all. We don't have to run up every time a big wave comes and shout, "Oh my God! That wave almost got you and could have dragged you out into the middle of the ocean ... and you would have drowned dead ... and I love you so much, where would I have been without you if you drowned and they never would have found your body, and a shark would have eaten you ...," and that kind of stuff, which I have heard at the seashore. None of that is necessary. Just keep it simple.

II. "IT ALL DEPENDS"

We were travelling in the car one time. The window was open and one of the children was playing with her ball and talking about throwing it out the window and "over the mountains." Her mother explained, "If you throw the ball out the window it's going to go down the mountains, and we won't be able to get it."

The child said, "We'll climb down and get it," to which her mother replied, "No, we won't be able to; it'll be lost." But I said, "Besides, there is another reason."

In fact, we could have stopped the car, climbed down the mountain, spent two or three hours and found the ball, and that wasn't the reason, to me, that she shouldn't throw the ball out the window. I said, "The reason is that we're going from one point to another point, and we have a certain amount of time for doing that because I have an important appointment to make. We would not stop the car because it is extremely bad manners to be late for an appointment."

My reason had nothing to do with whether we could get the ball or not get it, although to go after the ball would be totally unrealistic given how much work it would be, and how easy it would be to get another ball, as well.

I continued: "So you have to understand, on this particular ride today, from point A to point B, the given criteria is: I'm not going to stop the car. If you throw the ball out the window, it's gone; that's all. If we were riding through our neighborhood, we might stop the car and get the ball."

That boundary was true for that particular circumstance. One does not know what is true till each time one gets in the car and goes. Everything depends! We take it day by day. One day we might say, "If you throw the ball out the window, I am not going to help you find it. But I'll stop the car and you can find it, okay?"

Of course a child will usually say, "I want *you* to get it," and we might say yes or no ... depending. It is important also, for children, that they know both the extent to which their parents will do things for them— it's a sign of reliable care to them—and the extent to which they have to be personally responsible for their actions. Obviously this changes, even dramatically, as they grow. When a one-year-old is sitting in a high chair and throwing something (like a spoon) on to the floor over and over, it gives them great security to know that the parent will pick it up every time. This proves the parent's reliability. But if a ten-year-old does something similar you've got a problem! A two-year-old shouldn't be expected to do their own laundry or prepare their own meals, but a fourteen-year-old might, again depending on circumstances.

The principle that children need to learn is that every circumstance has its given factors, and sometimes the given factors are designed by other people. So a child might have one clear boundary in their own house and a completely different one in someone else's house, where the house rules were different. In fact, even within their own home there might well be different boundaries between their own room and the rest of the house. At twelve-years-old, for example, they might be allowed to keep their room as messy as they want to, but this wouldn't likely be the case for the living room or the kitchen.

We tend, all too easily, out of our desire to pay less attention to our children (or actually to pay attention elsewhere), or out of some unconscious desire for them to grow up quickly, to relax boundaries and assume that a two-year-old can manage food, for example, the same as a twelve-year-old. That is simply not so. On the other hand, parents need to maintain responsibility for the growth that is taking place. So, a lot of adults make a rule for a two-year-old, and then when the child is four and the rule becomes absurd, they will still maintain it because they made it, and because they don't know how to explain to their child that the rules change. Or, because they are themselves so rigid that they want to completely dominate and manipulate their children, and "rules" is one of their weapons.

Really, it is very simple. One of the things that we might say to children when they say, "I want to cut my own steak with a sharp knife," is, "You can when you are older. That knife is too sharp for a three-year-old to handle." It is important that children know that as they get older many rules change because they become capable of doing more. Essentially it is common sense. Obviously some rules, the "commandments," don't change—rules regarding not to lie, cheat, steal or hurt, among others. At the same time, when a child begins to learn to use a sharp knife, don't expect them to cut their food exactly the way that suits your sense of esthetics.

In terms of our overall childraising practices, this acknowlegement of age differences and skill levels is a very important consideration. Simply put, do not give children more territory than they are literally capable of managing effectively. It is also true that different children develop at different rates of speed, and develop different skills, so one rule or boundary for one three-year-old might not apply to another.

III. DON'T BE ARBITRARY

Often I find myself incapable of knowing how to talk to children—I'm not very creative; but I will *never* be arbitrary in terms of a boundary or a discipline. I think this is a vital issue. When we make a boundary for a child we should always be able to explain why we made the boundary—why it is important—in language that the child can understand. Answers like: "It's good vibes ... " or, "That's the way my Dad always did it ... " or, "Because I'm the parent, that's why ..." are totally unacceptable, even ludicrous.

One of the most enlightening things that ever happened to me with children was with my first daughter. I decided I wanted to take her on a vacation to Disneyworld, in Florida, for maybe a week; just her and I. She was four or five years old.

When I took my kids out they would occasionally cry and fuss, and I never thought that children did not need to cry and fuss once in a while. But, on this vacation we went and we had no fights, no disagreements, no tensions at all. She didn't cry, she didn't whine, she didn't frown. Nothing upsetting happened for her or me. Before we left I had said to her: "You know, we're going to be together a long time. Your mother is a thousand miles away. I'm not always patient, and I love you very much, and I want this to be a nice vacation. But you have to understand one thing—I'm not trying to be a tough guy, but I mean what I say." I knew that she knew that I meant what I said—that my boundaries were fair and firm. There was no problem, whatsoever! It was a complete revelation! And, she had a fabulous time and so did I.

I wouldn't, with a child, the first three times they break a limit, keep repeating: "You know I mean what I say." I would give one clear warning and then enforce the limit, but not violently, angrily, too abruptly or with undue consequences. Just firmly and matter-of-factly. I would wait until the child gave me their nod of agreement that they had heard what I had said, even if I knew that they heard. I would still give them the respect of a conscious eye-to-eye recognition. So, don't mumble some rule to a child and expect them to get it. Speak clearly and make eye contact and ask them if they have heard you and if they have understood the boundary.

Do not make assumptions for a child! Let him or her make the decision, even if it is our definition of the agreement they are making. If, as I was speaking to them, they turned their head away, or covered their ears, I would turn around and look at them and say, "We're going to keep doing this until you let me finish. It's only going to take a few seconds." Then, when they looked, I would say, "I mean what I say, and I'll try not to be arbitrary; and I want to hear what you have to say about the matter. But, I have more experience than you in these things, so I have the final say." (No child has ever asked me what "arbitrary" meant. They know what it means.)

I would also tell them, "Once in awhile I may make a mistake, and if I do, I will do my best to correct it; but I'm still the one who defines the boundaries." That's the understanding I want with a child. If I make a mistake and get too heavy, I will definitely apologize. But, I also explain, "You're my responsibility, and as long as you are that's the deal. I mean what I say. I'm the manager of the environment. As soon as you are able to take care of yourself, believe me, you have my blessings. But as long as you're my responsibility, this is the understanding we have to have."

* * *

Some of you have probably noticed that when you are used to maintaining discipline with your child *no matter what*, and they are used to it, then one day you realize that you are really being arbitrary about something, and so you bend the discipline a little bit. Then the child asks, "Why did you do that?" They want to know, "Why did you let me get away with that?" And you need to be very clear about your stand.

A good response might be something like, "Because I felt that the discipline was arbitrary under these particular circumstances, and I felt that you were old enough and capable enough to do such and such without my sitting on you," or whatever. Not just, "Oh, I'm in a good mood." For example, if you have a certain dietary restriction, like being basically vegetarian, and when you go out you occasionally let the children have a hot dog, as we do, and they say, "How come?" the answer we would give is, "This is a celebratory event, and on celebratory events there are times in which we relax our dietary restrictions." But, you would generally hold to the boundary at other times.

Children want to be an integral and functioning part of the environment. When they ask such questions they are not trying to "get one up" on us. They really want to know how best to be a working part of the environment. They want to know what the rules are so they don't overstep their boundaries. A bright child is going to start asking as soon as they have language; even before—they will ask with their eyes and they will want to know what's going on. But, once again, not because they are questioning our authority, but because that is how they learn about their world. They want to know why certain things are denied to them and why other things are not. A cardinal rule in this is: Avoid hypocrisy.

* * *

One of the things that we find as the child grows is that different people do things differently. For instance, a child will come back from a play group, they will do something, and we will say, "Oh, you can't do that." And they'll stand back and get really self-important and say, "Well, Mary lets me do it."

My response is: "Different adults have different senses of boundaries, different rules. You have to listen to the responsible adult of the moment." And that's true. Rather than, "Well, I think Mary is a little loose, and I'm going to have a talk with her."

If the child says, "Well, how come they let me do it there and I can't do it here?"... which they will—they will ask .... Then, if I have made a boundary for a child that is not arbitrary, and I have a specific reason, and I believe in that boundary and that reason, I will say: "This is my belief, and obviously the other person feels differently, and that is their prerogative. That's the way it goes. But, you need to be responsive to the authority of the space."

Another thing to keep in mind is not to counter the other parent's discipline towards a child. It is really good to agree ahead of time (when the child is not present) on certain boundaries for a child, so the child doesn't come to one parent and say, "Can I have a piece of chocolate?" when they know the other parent would disagree. We should always do our best to support our mate, and especially not alter one parent's discipline in front of that parent and the child. From that, a child will only learn to polarize the parents to get what he or she wants.

So, if a child says: "Can I have a piece of chocolate?" and we ask, "Well, did you ask Mommy?"

"Yea-ah."

"Well, what did Mommy say?"

"She said no."

Then it is a good idea to say, "Well the answer is no," rather than to look around sheepishly and say, "Well, I suppose it's okay this time." That sets up a very unhealthy dynamic, as one can imagine. So, I suggest that parents (and others, if possible) try to agree ahead of time, if they think of it, and work to maintain consistency and unity as parents, as a family, in their boundaries for children.

IV. MAKE IMPORTANT DISTINCTIONS
FOR A CHILD

Some adults are a little too liberal in terms of the behavior that they, by their silence, support. You don't always have to be moralizing to a child, but you might give them some important distinctions to help them understand why you are drawing certain boundaries. You can say, "Windows are not something to throw blocks at." That's the way I like to use language. Or, "There is a difference between a toy and an antique chair." That's a fact. It *is* lots of fun to jump on chairs, and sometimes it's okay for children to do that. But the fact is, a chair is not a toy. A chair is a piece of furniture. And a lot of adults, I've noticed, simply cannot or will not say to a child, "The blender is not a toy. So throwing rocks in and turning it on really doesn't work." If an adult does say this, the children will always say, "But I'm having fun. I like to do this." And the truthful response then is: "Well, we can't always do what we like."

They don't need to hear us say, "That's not appropriate," eighty times a day. Simply make clear distinctions for them: "This is a toy and this is not a toy," or "This is not a toy but you can play with it," or, "This is not a toy and it is not for this kind of play." Or whatever.

They may ask, "Well, what kind of play is it for?" And then you need to explain, for instance: "You can take the pillows off the chair and make a fort. But when you take the pillow off, and the bottom of the chair is just canvas straps, and you jump up and down for a long time, you're going to rip the chair." Not "maybe"—there's no question about it, they are going to rip the chair if they play with it like they play with a toy. And if a three-year-old is doing that, then pretty soon the seven-year-olds are going to be doing that too, and the chair is going to be broken very quickly. So, simply define reality in a way for them: "This is not a toy. A chair is a piece of furniture. It has a different purpose than a toy."

V. MEAN WHAT YOU SAY—BE TRUSTWORTHY

With children it is wise not to threaten things that you are not willing to carry out, and to make sure that the consequence fits the situation. If we were going to go to Disneyland, for example, I would never say, "If you don't stop teasing your sister we're not going to go." A trip to Disneyland should not be held over a child's head as a prize for good behavior. It should be inviolate. But I might use things like, "You can't have ice cream; you can't have french fries; you can't have coke ...," something little that means something to the child, never something so big that it is devastating. The really important things I would never use as threats, because if they make us carry the threat out, we had better be ready to. And besides, children don't do things so dramatically offensive or wrong as to warrant taking away the big trips! That isn't discipline, it's cruelty.

Still, we need to be reliable—good for our word; for once we lose credibility with our child, we have lost it permanently. And in order to live a life of clear and tender relationship with our children, it is helpful if they don't think we are hypocrites. If we kill a trip to Disneyland, they will remember that as long as they live. We can kill ice cream twenty times, they will not remember it in the same way. Nonetheless, in the moment, the little things are just as important as the trip to Disneyland, so denying the ice cream could be an effective disciplinary consequence.

If there is something *I* am really looking forward to, I won't use that as a threat either. I have a good time when we go to the zoo because the children have such a good time, so I will never use that as a threat— if they call me on it I am going to follow through, and no use punishing myself when the need is to make a consequence for the child.

If we are going on a trip that they have been anticipating excitedly for weeks, and they are stalling and fussing and can't get dressed, I'll never say, "Do you want to go or don't you want to go?" Never! Because, what if the kid says, in a moment of petulance, "I don't want to go." Then, what are we going to do? The suitcases are packed, the car is turned on ... are we going to tell them we didn't mean it? If so, we have lost credibility. However, I might say, "We won't go" if the trip is just for myself, to do an hour of non-crucial errands and their "payoff" for going with me is a brownie or a chocolate chip cookie (neither of which we have as a regular daily part of our diet, so these are big treats!). If I have to, I will break precedent—I'll pick them up and I'll carry them, screaming and kicking, into the car. Because usually, after three minutes on the road they are willing to get dressed and are happy as can be. I will do that over and against saying, "Do you want to go to California? If you don't want to go, don't get dressed." Because a major trip is not something easily readjusted.

If the trip is not so important and you are willing to cancel it, then say to the child, "Look, we don't have to go, you know. If you really don't want to go, let's stay home." Of course we can always tempt them into going with ice cream or a new toy, but then we teach the child to hold out for bribes, in a sense to blackmail us, hold us for ransom. ("All right Mom, gimme the new skateboard or Dad gets it.")

Don't say no unless you're going to enforce it. If you know you are not going to enforce it, don't say it, equivocate! Because once you have made a firm boundary and they have weasled their way around it, for some children one time is enough so that they will never trust you again. They will respect your authority because they have to—you are bigger and stronger than they, and you can withhold things that they want. But they won't trust you. So, when you've set a boundary maintain the boundary.

Even if you've sort of said no *impulsively*, you should stick to it so that children learn that they can trust you—that you are trustworthy and reliable, and that your word is reliable. Because before you know it they will be dating, and driving, and going to the mall with friends, and it would be helpful at that point if they trusted your word.

I think that if we threaten a child with punishment, we should do it when they really overstep their bounds. But we should make very sure that the threat is just for the circumstance. Of course, it is best to effect discipline without using threats and carrying them out. Especially since sometimes it is tremendously complex to carry out the threats we've made. But if we threaten, we should follow through. Surely we could apologize if we make a threat in a moment of anger and in another moment decide it isn't appropriate. But better not to make the threat in the first place. So, think these things out. Don't act impulsively or blindly without being aware of implications or consequences.

Don't make long-term threats, like, "No ice cream for a month." We can't even *remember* for a week, let alone a month. We can't maintain consistency for a month. If we say, "No swimming for a day ..." or two days ... or three days, okay. But if we say, "Okay, no *whatever it is* for a month," we will forget and then get loose, and we'll feel sorry for the child; and then we may say to ourselves, "Oh, I was angry at him. It was too harsh a punishment ..." and then we will break our word.

Discipline should be immediate (if possible) so the child knows what it is for. Two weeks after an event, if some punishment is effected then, the child has no idea what they are being punished for, so it is just confusing. Clearly, I am speaking here of young children. An eighteen- or nineteen-year-old does have a different sense of time than a three-year-old.

Also, never say, "I'm leaving and if you don't come with me, you can stay here." Never walk away like that from a child. Never! Because that is a threat that you are going to have to back down on, and every time you back down, you are not serving that child. You are giving them a neurotic hold on you. You should keep your word with your children. Obviously, if you are in your own home and talking about leaving them in the bedroom while you go to the kitchen, the situation is different than if you say something like that in a store, at the mall, in a park far from home, or whatever. Really, little children are terrified of being left, abandoned by their parents. You can walk away a certain distance and then say, "Come on," and almost always they will run like hell to catch up with you. Sometimes they will be stubborn, of course—they want to see how far you will go. If a child wants to see how far I'll go, I will come back and say, "Okay, I'd really like you to walk because you are too big to carry everywhere," and they will usually cooperate. If they are two or three years old I will just pick them up and carry them.

If the adult is patient and calm, non-abusive and loving, however, even in a moment of telling a child of a consequence for disobeying a boundary, such follow-through is rarely, rarely needed. But *never*, I repeat, *never* walk off as if you are really going to leave them.

* * *

185

If we can, it is advisable to always give children a way out. For instance, if they say, "Carry me," we can say, "Well, you walk to there, and then I'll carry you from there." It helps to know how to bargain with children.

Give them a chance to save face, to adjust to a parental demand. If we don't, we are either going to have a lot of fights on our hands, or a very neurotically and unhappily adaptive child. We can make a bargain with them, but we should not go against our word. Give children training so that they can get out of things that they don't really mean, gracefully. Often a young child, whose attention span is mere moments, will make some show of stubborn defiance, but in a minute or two will be ready for completely different behavior. So, we should give them a chance to get out of their impulsive yet momentary act in a way that doesn't make them "bad" for it or "wrong" for it, or in a way that won't get them severely punished for it.

VI. DRAW BOUNDARIES WITHOUT JUDGING THINGS AS GOOD OR BAD

It can be difficult to tell children what is appropriate and what is not without phrasing it in terms of right and wrong, good and bad, and saddling them with righteous morality instead of common sense and thoughtfulness. There are ways to do it, however. Suppose a child is manifesting a nasty mood at the dinner table and we know that they are just mimicking. We can say, "The dinner table is not an appropriate place in which to do that."

"Why?" they will certainly ask.

"Because the dinner table is a place in which everybody comes to eat together and enjoy one another's company, and that manifestation disturbs a lot of people. If you are alone at the dinner table with me, maybe you could do it; maybe it would be fine. But you're not alone, you are with other people. You have to consider every circumstance, and who you are with."

I wouldn't actually use this language with children, it's a little "adult" and a bit too preachy, but the important point is that we can always make our language suit the circumstance, never make it a function of good or bad, of telling the child *they* are good or bad. We are, after all, addressing their behavior, not who they are as essential human beings.

In a similar vein, some people, men and women, make pretty good discipline with children, but their tone of voice is worse than the value of the discipline they are making. They belittle the children, demean and shame them. What I encourage is not using a tone of voice that makes the children feel that they are "bad" or wrong. Some people say nothing, which is probably one of the better things to do, but with discipline it's often necessary to say *something*.

BOUNDARIES BASED ON PROTOCOL

Children need to learn to be responsive to the given elements of any space or environment, including rules, of whatever circumstance they are in. One of the ways that we work with children, at least I do, is to consider the protocol of the situation. A lot of adults are just terrified of saying no to their child, terrified that their child is going to be deprived in some way. Once a child learns how easy it is to dominate their parents they will proceed to do so, not because they like to act this way, but because in their experiments with boundaries they assume that what they can do is right. A child will never assume that the parent is weak or at fault. Of course, later on this will be obvious to them, but by then it's too late, they are already dominating and manipulating by habit. For instance, if a child in a formal dining situation goes up to the food table or the food trays and starts popping little goodies into their mouth, a lot of parents don't know how to say no, because at home the child can eat anything, at anytime they want. One would not act the same at a formal wedding party as one would act at a hotdog vendor on the street (at least I hope not).

A better example might be: If there is a defined discussion going on in a space and a child comes in, if they can be in the space without disrupting the discussion, that's fine. If not, we would tell the child, "This is a space in which the discussion takes priority, and if you can respect that, you can stay in the space. If not, then let's go play in a space you can play in, where you can yell and it's perfectly all right. I don't want to be here and keep restraining and restricting you if you want to be free to play. So, if you want to be in this space, these are the rules. If you don't, well, let's go play. Let's go outside and run around." Frequently, the child, for various reasons, would rather stay *in* the space and will learn to respect the boundaries of that space. We can also say something like, "This is not our home and we don't make the rules here. It is very important in life to understand that many times you need to respect others' rules."

Generally, however, when it comes to teaching children a sensitivity to spaces, our expectation would be that children learn to relate to spaces based on observing us, rather than based on a verbal or rhetori-

cal definition of spaces. In the beginning, of course, setting appropriate boundaries is a way to initiate the
learning process. Once they get the limits down, however, then if we obey the limits, they generally will also.

[What follows are some specific examples of
boundaries for a number of different spaces. The
author does not mean this to be an exhaustive or exclusive coverage, but only to indicate how one might apply
some of the general principles that have been drawn
thus far.—*Editor*]

BOUNDARIES AT THE DINNER TABLE

For the first couple of years of a child's life, if
they don't want to be at the table, one parent or adult
should leave the table with them and not force them to
stay. Once they have fluent conversational language—
at two or two-and-a-half, or so—then we can tell them,
"I'd like to sit at the table with everybody for a few minutes, and it is reasonable that you sit with me, *or* you
can play in the kitchen where I can watch you, *or* you
can bring your box of toys in here and play ..., but I
want to visit with the family (or I want to visit with my
friends), since I haven't seen them all day. I've been
with you all morning, and you can let me sit at the
table ...," or words to that effect to suit the exact circumstance. I wouldn't keep jumping up from the table,
but a lot depends on the child and the particular situation.

When I was young, whenever we went visiting,
the minute dinner was over I was gone. I would not sit
at the table, literally, for sixty seconds, and I was
allowed to do that. (I was never social, at all.) But now,
as I learned from my parents' role-modeling, that is
totally reversed. I enjoy mealtime communion and con-

versation, even long after the food is finished. The socialness of the dinner hour tends to be a cultural thing in many families—dinner time, the social enjoyment of the company and so on, is something very special. I am of the opinion that dinner should be a time of soft and intimate communion with one another, and that children should be allowed to come to their own appreciation that "where it's happening" is at the table. If they choose to stay at the table, I don't think children should be shushed up all the time. If they are engaging in the social scence, let them engage at their level of energy.

When they are little they just usually prefer play, and if they are disrupting things there is no need to keep them at the table. If the table is where it's happening, however, to be asked to leave the table is to be asked to leave the source of nurturing, basically. They may jump at the opportunity to go play, but after a while they get to see that the source of nurturing is at the table. We can't explain these things to children, and they certainly don't want to be lectured all the time. But they are quite sensitive, after all, and will come to their own feeling conclusions.

Leaving the table could be a type of necessary discipline with a child who gets too wild or disruptive as a way to capture everyone's attention. One might say, "If you can't be at the table with everybody in a way that is pleasant to be with, you can leave the table." Not, "Shut up or leave." A child's natural exhuberance should *not* be squashed, but if they are animating that in a disruptive way, allow them to be exhuberant in a different place. The tack I always like to use is one of a simple statement of the way things are—*not* making the child a bad person because he or she has to leave the table. The issue is about the protocol of the space, very clearly. Instead of accusing the child of being bad, tell them that people enjoy conversation at the table; that's all. (This is certainly a much more "pleasant" way to communicate than accusing a child of something harsher than a little unpleasantness.) If a child is being "grumpy" that can also be included in the "unpleasant" category. Just don't accuse a child of being nasty or horrible. Be careful of the language you use. After all, we get grumpy and we aren't bad, just in a bad mood temporarily.

An important part of this issue of children sitting at the table has to do with treating them like adults. If they are *made* to stay at the table, they will never *want* to stay. They should be included in the conversation because they are at the table and because they have interesting things to say. All children have interesting things to say. If we don't find their conversation interesting, it is usually us who has the difficulty. If we are talking, instead of looking only at another parent or adult, we should look at the children too, and include them in the conversation so they feel welcome at the table.

In terms of who disciplines a child at the table (a parent or another adult), it is really a matter of what is needed. Patience in our engagement with children should always be present, even when we are feeling impatient. Yet, everybody has to use their own judgement of what types of behavior are "too much," of when a situation has gone beyond the point where one should simply be patient, talk quietly to the child, or try to be reasonable and "make a deal." Sometimes, however, we will discipline our children a little too quickly, and sometimes not quickly enough; but, that is how we learn, basically.

When there are several children at the table, siblings or friends, and one child is dominating the conversation, either by "louding-out" or over-shouting the other children or by talking non-stop, we can say something like, "Johnnie would like to say something also. You can continue after others have a word."

Children are going to follow the models of the adults, no matter what. If we are reaching across the table at mealtimes, yelling to the other side of the table and talking with our mouths full of food, that is what they are going to get and mimic. And once a habit is in, it usually sticks for a lifetime, creating great stress if it has to be suppressed later on.

BOUNDARIES FOR BEDTIME

Typically, children will learn habits of sleep very easily. What we usually do is begin with an eight or nine o'clock bedtime, and they will generally maintain that for several years except when they get too wired from adult parties that they participate in. (They will occassionally stay up until one or two in the morning after something like that—they plug into the energy and ride on it!) They will tend to be pretty consistent, with occasional natural exceptions, once they have learned a certain bedtime.

As they get older, if a child can play by themselves, then I would let them stay up alone if they can't sleep. We went to India a number of years ago, and three of the girls on the trip were five years old. A couple of times they just couldn't sleep, but we were exhausted from a day of walking ten to fifteen miles and doing all the stuff we did. I just let them stay up in the room and play, until they wanted to go to sleep. They would stay up until eleven, twelve ... sometimes one o'clock, and then just go to sleep by themselves.

Then the only boundary was, "You can't leave the room alone." It worked out beautifully. Children are quite responsible when they are empowered, and trusted in this empowerment (obviously with something that falls within their capacity). It helps when the adult does a bedtime ritual with their child, like telling stories, reading to them or playing a game. But keep the ritual to the actual bedtime, don't extend it way later even if it's a good story; *and* be willing to make the random exception!

SOCIAL PROTOCOL IN PUBLIC SPACES

In the usual consciousness of self-conscious and insecure adults, one attitude about how to deal with children is that anything they do (except within limits, and people's limits vary) except, "Sit down and be quiet," is "bothering" other people. The old adage: "Children should be seen, not heard" is the result of a terribly archaic and rigid patriarchal, child-negative culture. This is not an appropriate guideline for conscious childraising.

My opinion is that there is precious little "real culture" in the world these days, so it needs to begin here, with our children. If we go to the movies with a small child, for instance, we can let them quietly ask us questions about the things they don't understand, and if the people in front of us are so offended by such caring attention to our child, they will move their seats. I have been in lots of movie theatres where children have cried and talked, and if it bothers me enough, I move away. Because children are children! They can't be expected not to be children, and should not be made to act like little adults.

Of course, many people go out to have a little

time to themselves, without their children, and it may not seem fair to impose our children on somebody else. Generally, movies are for adults. Still, it depends on whether the child is being genuine, or is making noise to get attention or playing a game called "I'm going to control my parents," even if it is already an unconscious habit. If they really have a question, we answer the question, whether they whisper it, or speak it. If they yell it, that's unnecessary. And we can ask them to whisper. But, as we know, how long do they remember something like that? Thirty seconds? So, we can ask them each time: "Please ask me, but whisper so other people aren't disturbed." But to panic and say, "Don't talk!" in a derogatory tone of voice doesn't serve, although the people in the row in front of us might appreciate it.

If you think your children are being genuine, that, is innocent, then let them be genuine. But if it is not appreciated that way by the people sitting in front of you, then another option is to move to seats where the child is not looked upon as a little spoiled brat. What is more important—the child's development, or whether somebody who is unconscious can handle a little behavior that is natural to a child? Of course, sometimes it can be more appropriate to take the child outside, talk to them and let them talk. As always, it is a matter of circumstances. The mature and responsible form of activity is to recognize that other people exist in the space that we are in; to recognize that the circumstances deserve a certain kind of respect. I am certainly not suggesting that we be totally insensitive and not care about anybody else's preferences, and be as totally selfish as they are, like: "This is my child and she can do whatever she wants." I am hardly suggesting that! Of course, if the child gets bored and does not want to see the rest of the movie and starts fidgeting and making noise out of their boredom, it is always the appropriate thing to do to sacrifice your own desire to see the movie and go out with the child to play. There was a spiritual Master from India in the mid-1900's who would take his students to movies and would always get up and leave (taking the students with him) just when everyone got involved in the movie (and attached to seeing the rest).

It's okay to let children make a little noise in restaurants, after all they should be excited by a special event! Some people get upset if a child makes a peep at a dinner table across the hall at a restaurant. And that kind of person can stay in their own swamp of negativity and self-hatred; and will, with or without our "help." Such people are to be pitied (with compassion of course). We have to understand that what we are frequently dealing with in public spaces is a total lack of child-consciousness. We go along and kick rocks, and we don't think anything of it, do we? Well, to most of the people we sit next to in a restaurant, children are just rocks. One can't reason with such people. It is best not to subject our children to the wrath and intolerance of these types. At the same time, there is no need to disturb people out of hand. No child should be so unrestrainedly wild that they disrupt or destroy whatever circumstance we are in. (And remember, home meals are not restaurant or public meals; there is a significant difference between one's home culture and a more formal culture.)

We should give our children room for enthusiasm and a bit of behavior that suits their age. (After all, what a waiter or waitress gets a tip for is to wipe the table off when the child accidentally spills juice.) A four-year-old may be able to act like an adult in a fine restuarant, but they can only do it by totally repressing their "four-year-oldness." Don't take them where they are expected or required to be what they are not. It is not worth the price that they have to pay.

If we are in any given space, we have a basic social responsibility to that space. If we take our child into a grocery store, our basic responsibility is to make sure that he or she doesn't run down the aisles pulling everything they can grab off the shelves. That's all. It is not our responsibility, necessarily, to shut them up and keep our hand over their mouth so they don't speak in a way that might disturb somebody. After all, people are strange (as Jim Morrison said), and no matter where we go there is bound to be somebody offended by something! We have to protect our child's integrity, and as someone once said, "You can please some of the people all of the time, and all of the people some of the time, but you can't please all of the people all of the time." We should not expect our children to please all the people all the time. After all, it should be obvious that *we* don't, even if we try due to our twisted psychology.

Children naturally squeal and sing and cry, so if people go into a public space in which they are liable to find children, it is *their* responsibility to understand that children will be children. No adult should go to a place in which children can be found if they are not willing to be delighted by the noise that the children are making. (I mean *reasonable* noise.) Children will be energetic, and it is not our responsibility to try to make of our child a little doll that only squeaks when we tell it to. But it is our responsibility to keep our child from wrecking the grocery store.

Also, there is a certain responsibility for an adult to define a child's responsibility towards the space they are in, and to help the child with that. There should be a time in which children can make all the noise they want, and a time in which quiet is relevant to the space. It is not a matter of children being told to be quiet; it is a matter of children learning to recognize the principle of circumstance and response to space. The broader a range of manifestation a child learns, and the more deeply they learn how to "shift gears" quickly and with ease, the more relaxed and skillfully they will handle life as an adult. But, if Daddy is whacking the kid and saying, "If you make one more sound I'll beat the shit out of you," and the kid is wailing away, that is not a reasonable form of responsibility to the space or to the child.

How many of us, if we look at our own lives, were taught certain forms of politic—certain forms of manners? Yet we were rarely taught anything having to do with objective discrimination. So we learned that men always treat women a certain way, or women always treat their husbands a certain way. Or, "little girls always ...," "little boys always ...," you know, the "sugar and spice and everything nice" routine. Everything is circumstantial. When we are in the house, and children are making too much noise, we can say, "That's outside noise," and they understand that. We have to understand when to say, "This is a circumstance in which *such and such* doesn't apply, but if you want to do this outside ... if you want to go out of the room ...," etc. That is how they will learn, besides watching us, of course, which is the more impactful teaching.

In Ritual or Sacred Spaces

In very formal spaces the bottom line is: is the child creating a disturbance? Not, do we think he or she is creating a disturbance, or do we think other people are bothered? It is very common for a parent to have their entire identity wrapped up in how their child appears. In such circumstances the adult is usually so paranoid that any insignificant behavioral twitch on the part of their child will reflect negatively on them that they guard their child's behavior like a hawk. This usually produces a situation of wild projection on the environment, almost always untrue, and extreme tension in relationship to the child. Don't make your children wrong or implicate them in your own insecurities, fantasies and neuroses.

What is the *actual* situation? If the child is rolling around or climbing on the parent, that may require a great effort and a lot of energy from the parent to be the one who is being rolled around on, but that is not necessarily creating a disturbance in the space. That is something I would allow. Basically the issue is: what *really creates* a disturbance in the space, not just in our suspicious minds? That is what needs attention.

In a formal space I would certainly keep suggesting to the child, "Maybe it would be nice to pay attention while this recital is going on," or whatever. I would not force it, however, as long as the child is not rolling over six people, kicking someone who doesn't want to be kicked, yet is not objectively disturbing the whole space. Obviously, if I bring a child to a highly formal or ritualized space, I would sit in a place that is somewhat out of the way, certainly not at the center of attention in the space. The safety considerations and the sacred space considerations are relevant to limits. If a child is likely to be restless, then sit in the back or at an aisle seat so you can easily leave the space.

Children want to be where the action is, and

many levels of their being or consciousness are touched by objective ritual, but not the level that wants to play and express their level of child-energy. If we say, "We're going to go out if you don't settle down," they almost always want to stay. But *wanting* to stay and actually *settling down* to stay are two different things.

I think it is asking a lot for a child to be totally still. It will get to a point where even though he or she wants to stay in some ways, still they would prefer to be out playing, and they will make that clear. At this point I would not try to argue (or threaten, obviously) the child into staying. Of course, if adults in general were more child-conscious, more child-advocates, they would be perfectly willing to have children impinge upon their sacred space a little bit. Most adults are much too selfish to be willing to grant a child leeway for a little wiggling or a little whispering, so I don't think that it is to the child's benefit to psychically or verbally fight over unimportant territory on their behalf. They just take it personally. I would take them out to play and leave the offended adults to rot in their own misery (whether they are conscious of that or not).

* * *

Responsibility means recognizing in any given circumstance what is required, and surrendering our own uptight preference in order to do what is required by the larger circumstance. And that is a principle that holds across all boundaries. It is extremely helpful for children to learn to respect spaces, to learn that every space has its own definition and its own purpose, and that to be a wise person, a wise adult, is to respect and have sensitivity to spaces, to "be unto any space as that space is designed to be unto you."

Everything is a matter of circumstance in a culture in which whatever arises is seen for exactly what it is, without subjective expectations and projections. If whatever arises is seen not for what it is, but as identical to every other circumstance, regardless of the texture of it, then, no matter where we are, under what circumstances, everything is always treated in the same way. And this is simply not what is true. This teaches children to have no sensitivity, no discrimination, no refinement of tastes and diffferences. Boundaries and discipline have to be a function of our recognition of the truth of whatever circumstance is present. They cannot be an across-the-board affair!

DEALING WITH CHILDREN'S DISSATISFACTION

Most children are dissatisfied about something—with their living situation, for instance, no matter what it is ... the old "grass is greener" scenario. (There is some truth to the old clichés.)

When children complain about having to live in an environment that is less than totally immersed in video games, TV, greed and competition, and have to listen to adults talk about "consciousness," they are not doing anything different than we all did. Most of us complained about our home environments even though we lived the way our children are saying they would like to. I was an only child, fairly well spoiled, and I did exactly the same thing—I argued as much as anybody. Even though, looking back, I had a very enviable family situation—my parents were very gentle; I rarely got yelled at, and there were demands, but they were quite fair considering the demands most of my friends' families made on them. Still, I argued, and wanted other things, like chocolate and Coca-Cola all the time, which I was only allowed randomly as treats.

Parents often have their heartstrings pulled when their kids say, "Why do we have to live here?" or "Why can't I be like all the other kids?" But, no matter where we lived, no matter what we were doing they would say the same thing—"Why can't I have a dog?" or whatever it is they don't have and feel deprived about.

"Well, we live in an apartment and this is the only apartment we can afford and the rules are no pets."

"Why don't we move somewhere else?"

It may be difficult to draw intelligent boundaries and really stick to our principles when there is bedlam and decadence all around, but for our child's sake— their sanity, health and personal integrity—we should "hold that line," as the cheerleaders sang to the football team defense when I was in high school.

It is vitally important that we show our children that we care enough about them to sustain an alternative to the usual horror and abuse that passes for family life in the modern world. Even if they would rather be living anyway else (because of the social scene or whatever the gross self-indulgence that is possible), there is something about caring enough to sustain an alternative that has an effect, whether when they are growing up they agree with it or not consciously.

Something is transmitted to them at a feeling level that is also, I think, very important in terms of going against the tide. A lot of our children will see us going against the tide of the acceptance of abusive and demeaning childraising practices and self-destructive, toxic life situations, and even those circumstances may

201

seem attractive at some point. But, when they are old enough to realize what they have gotten from us, they will be profoundly grateful. In fifteen years they will be thanking us, lauding us for raising them with some degree of consciousness, of justice, of real relationship, clarity and honesty.

7

NO EXCUSE!
ON CHILD ABUSE

THE EPIDEMIC

Alice Miller's writing should be considered necessary reading for anyone wishing to engage conscious childraising. We must honestly deal with our own psychological labyrinth if we want to be clear enough to raise our children properly. When her ideas are fresh in my mind and I go out into the ordinary flow of society it is like I am hallucinating—I can actually see people who abuse their children in so many ways, as she has so brilliantly and passionately articulated; and it is grotesque, bizarre, other worldy. This was an eye-opener for me. I had no idea how pervasive child abuse in one form or another is in our society. It is really unbelievable and unconscionable.

Have you seen these parents out in the store who abuse their children? The kid starts crying, and they whack him and say, "Stop crying or I'll *really* hit you." The kid starts wailing, so they whack him again. Pretty soon the child is cowering, shaking and whimpering like a beaten dog. Fear is not a healthy threat to hold over a child.

Once, a woman turned to her little boy, he must

have been two years old, and started screaming at him and calling him a "little shit." And then she looked at me and smiled as if another adult would understand her behavior and condone it, or as if another adult would understand her view that all children are total drags. This is the state of ignorance we have come to! It is no wonder the world is so full of violence, crime and depravity—an abused child grown up must unconsciously see all adults as the abusers he once lived in fear of.

It is actually starting to be uncomfortable to be in ordinary social circumstances because of the way people in general treat their children. The incidents of child abuse are so pervasive it is a grotesque sign of a society-wide malaise in a world gone mad. Most of us are either naive, or the horror of this extensive dynamic has caused us to close our eyes in shame or self-protective desperation. In some way, shape or form—through verbal shame, or emotional or physical abuse, or neglect—very few of us escaped being abused in childhood. And very few of us want to realize that child abuse—or one could call it child ignorance or self-blindness—is probably the single most pervasive disease in our entire culture.

It is time we pulled our heads out of the sand. We must commit not to perpetuate these abuses in our own families, not to do what was done to us. The literal survival of our race may depend on it.

For mature adults, whose hearts are already opened, when they have their first children, they are or should be pretty safe in terms of having the wisdom to treat children decently, non-abusively. But often, as young selfish adults, our hearts aren't open; they're closed tight and sealed. For such immature adults, children are just another feather in their cap, just another

achievement. Another *something* that can be manipulated and dominated, shown-off and exhibited. And
nobody else can tell such adults what to do with their
children, because Hubby goes off to work all day and
Mom can do whatever she wants to with those little
kids ... and there's nobody going to say anything to her;
or Mom can go out with the girls and Dad can push the
kid around, and she'll never know. Many adults have a
secret life of a dark, perverse or negative sort with their
children, and it leads to tragic results.

So, for women, a child can be the ultimate
manipulative toy, the cutest object for praise, a real living doll; and for men, a child is often just another feather in their cap of masculinity, of power. When a man
says: "It's *my* kid," what he means is, "I've got a dick."
(As if that isn't already obvious, *ya know*. That should
have been obvious from the first ten years spent practically ripping it off with his hand. It's a good thing it's
well attached, I'll tell you that!)

Some of us got away pretty healthy as children,
but a lot (most of us in fact) didn't. We are walking
examples of the formalization and even acceptance of
child abuse. I believe the adage that says, "If you're not
part of the solution you're part of the problem." (This is
a statement you may have seen surrounded with flowers or attractive birds on one of the posters that are in
all the new age stores.) And, it is true! To not be dealing with the extensive pervasiveness of child abuse as
an accepted form of life in our culture is a serious sin of
omission. Not to participate in dismantling it, essentially, is to support its continuation. This must stop if
we want to avoid destroying our civilized culture
entirely.

Most people never even bother with doing something about the mistakes and the child abuse they have

inflicted on their children. Either they are in complete denial or they assume, "Well, what's done is done; it's too late. Let's just go on ...," and pretend everything is fine ... hoping it all stays nicely hidden in the closet and doesn't pop out to disturb their drugged sleep.

That's not good enough. It is not good enough to neglect what we do to our children by refusing to confront what was done to us. If we don't confront what was done to us, we *will* do it to our children in the vast majority of cases. Perhaps we will perpetrate such crimes against our own children with less overt violence (it will be subtler in many cases), but we *will* do it. Under the "right" circumstances, the "right" amount of pressure, the "right" time of breakdown, some of us might very well become serious child-abusers. We may! A fair number of us would have been abusers already (if we now are not), except that we had abortions when we were fourteen, fifteen, nineteen, twenty-three, or out of pure luck, because we failed to make pregnant or get pregnant before we were mature enough to handle the consequences.

Conscious life, to me, is not just about a kind of lovey sentimental, romantic and blind relationship to the realities of our neurotic motives. It means that from the ground up—in our personality, psychology, sensitivities—we need to become ultimately elegant and wise human beings, on every level of our being, full of dignity and compassion for ourselves and others.

When a fetus is several months in existence, before birth, it is already learning cruelty or kindness—that is how early abuse can start. A mother's viewpoint towards the fetus can be the start of it ... or the sound of the father's voice screaming derogatorily at the mother. Therefore, it is never too soon to begin to re-assess our clarity or self-awareness and get on with the work of a real shift of context.

HOW CHILDREN SEE ABUSE

In the psychology or mind of an abused child, they assume the abuse is their fault. A child can't conceive of someone arbitrarily torturing them, so they assume that they deserve it, that they are somehow essentially bad, or that they have done something terrible. This is the beginning of a lifetime self-image of shame, insecurity and self-loathing or self-hatred.

A mother or father beats a child. When that first happens, the child panics—he or she goes into survival, actually fearing for their literal existence. If the child accepts the abuse as being something that they caused, as their fault, they reason (in their child way) that they will still be allowed to be their parent's child; they will still be allowed to stay in the family. That is the mechanism. It is not in a child's intuitive consciousness that someone they love could be doing to them what is being done to them, unless they (the child) were at fault. That is the only option, the only conclusion possible for a young child. However, if physical abuse began at twelve years of age (from a new step-parent or a vicious teacher, for example), once a child's psychological viewpoint was already quite formed, the child usually has the reasoning skills at that level of development to understand it is the adult's dynamic, not theirs that is at cause.

Children don't judge behavior in terms of good and bad, they don't make moral delineations like that. To infants, there is no good or bad. If an infant gets hit, there is just pain; they don't reason, "Daddy's bad," or "Mommy's bad." But they do feel at cause or at source for the experience they feel.

We have all probably read stories of terribly

207

neglected, abused children who don't want to be taken away from the people who abused them. They love their Mom and Dad! There are examples of children who are beaten all the time, treated really awfully, and the social worker comes along and says, "Well, we're going to send you to a nice home," but the children don't want to leave. They may be abused, but their home is what they know as reality, and they are very attached to it, feeling like they belong where they are— no matter how bad it is.

As we grow up, sometimes we don't even remember the abuse that happened to us as children. We just have this vague feeling of "dis-ease." If somebody mentions our father, we may immediately leap to his defense: "Oh, he was very good to me, he loved me. He only did what was best for me." Yet, something inside still niggles away; there is "something else" there, but we only remember how "loving" it all was, even if we have to fantasize, to whitewash it all, even to make it all up. Why bother remembering the rest? It is just too horrible.

Even in the worst families nice things happened randomly—like when we got the lead role in the fourth grade play. Boy, our parents were just so proud of us. It was great! "Hey, that's my kid!" we heard our father say to the person next to him in the fourth row. So, no matter what else went on within the family, there were some things that convinced us that this was a loving family, a loving environment. There was a payoff there: we could *pretend* we were confident, useful, strong, contented, positive and wanted individuals, and that we contributed in some way. That is what is called blind ignorance, which forms the central part of the mandala of psychological denial. Where does it begin? Right at the primal levels. This blind ignorance is at the heart of ego; and is the center of the mandala—the mandala of illusion.

Our lack of self-worth today is not because we aren't some Nobel-prize winner. It is because we think we are essentially bad, essentially flawed as human beings. Poor self-worth is not because we lack some creative genius; it has nothing to do with that. It is because our parents' outright abuse, or their unconscious neglect, *taught* us that we were unwanted and un-needed in the family unit. We sometimes even believed that we were simply in the wrong place, in the wrong family; that the stork (or God) made a big mistake.

DENIAL OF CHILDHOOD ABUSE

My ex-wife is a nurse. One time, during her on-the-job training (she was training in a hospital in Westchester County, NY that received a lot of people who had no insurance and couldn't pay—i.e., indigents), this very large woman, about three hundred and fifty pounds, came in complaining of cramps. She was screaming and yelling and giving all the doctors a hard time, being extremely difficult. One of the doctors who was going to examine her asked her to take her clothes off. Just as she got her skirt off, a baby came out. The cramps stopped; she looked at the baby and said, "Where did this come from?" She refused to acknowledge any complicity whatsoever in the act of having that child. She said she didn't know where it came from, and she was close to hysterical.

A couple of things about the story strike me. One is that such weight is not only a buffer against the world, but it also numbs one's own senses—or can, depending on whether the reason for carrying that much and putting it on in the first place is psychological. That woman was buffered against not just pain but reality, by her weight. Probably during the previous nine months she felt like she was having some digestive discomfort. Considering that she drove to the hospital simply with a minor complaint, she must not have been in any great amount of pain ... she was just having some "cramps." Obviously, the whole process of labor did not touch her; she could not even feel *that*!

Secondly, that story struck me as a metaphor for what a lot of people do. Probably this large woman—who claimed she didn't know how the baby got there, beyond even not feeling into the labor—was probably in some way seriously violated as a child; probably beaten physically frequently. Who knows? But it seems a pretty straightforward scenario, a "good bet." And she probably buffered not only her body but her mind from reality, and from the awareness of the childhood abuse, to such a severe degree that she was even in denial about where babies came from. A very severe case.

To a lot of people, pain is so antagonistic to their worldview, so anathema, that even small amounts of pain create a decision, at some point in their lives, to buffer themselves from a certain intensity. In order not to feel pain they will also sacrifice pleasures of similar intensity, or experiences of similar intensity on the other end of the spectrum to pain.

Typically, all of us have a threshold that we buffer ourselves against due to the terrible fear of extinction, of obliteration, caused by childhood abuse. Beneath the threshold we feel pain, and above the threshold we buffer ourselves. In severe cases of childhood abuse, many people will buffer themselves almost totally, so that they feel nothing. They become blank, totally sealed-off from *any* intrustion—not only pain, but love, affection and tenderness as well. From a clear perspective we could look at the faces of such people and we could realize what incredible suffering they had endured once (and are still enduring inside), but which they are totally closed down to, totally insulated against feeling or even acknowledging. Such suffering can't be kept from affecting their physical appearance, facial expression, health, tone of voice and behavioral manifestations. Of course, such people always excuse any noticeable elements as coming from other causes. Observing them, we may say to ourselves, "My God, they're in pain." And we imagine that they are feeling it, that they *must* feel it—but they aren't. If they were feeling it, they would look differently. They have buffered themselves against the conscious association or connection to the pain that we see them in.

Many of us, in our adult lives, rationalize the abuse we received as children. Haven't we all heard people say, "My father beat me and it didn't hurt me any. I learned discipline and strength. If I put my elbows on the table, my mother spanked the hell out of me, but I've got good manners. It doesn't hurt. We need to have good manners." Why do we need good manners? Look at American culture—what do we need good manners beaten into us for? We are such crude and inelegant creatures compared to most of the rest of the world, including Third World countries. Culture? We don't even know what culture is! A little genuine culture wouldn't hurt, but we aren't going to get it by being abused in the name of teaching us to be polite.

NEVER, NEVER, NEVER

There is a difference between taking out frustrations or anger on a child and just being a passionate or intensely fiery, but basically kind, person. It is never appropriate to take out our angers and frustrations on a child as if they were the cause. That is not to say that we don't cry in front of a child or get angry. Simply that we don't blame them for what is clearly not their fault. Have you seen the example of the child who feels powerless and helpless in the face of an older sibling or a parent who hits or beats them, so they don't fight back; but, after awhile, they find someone or something, like a cat or dog, who won't or can't fight back to them, and they pass on the beating? We should not refrain from expressing very intense emotions or feelings, but we should just not make the child the object of it, that's all.

* * *

Okay, today I am going to do something very different, very unusual. I am going to complain, to bitch, to gripe, to sour grape you. I know you find this unusual, given the tone of the previous couple of months but yes, something has finally pushed me over the edge. You may even find it shocking that a so-called self-proclaimed expert has so little self-composure, so few patients, I mean so little patience, that he is dumping all this bile on you, gentle readers, but yes I must confess, indeed it is so.

What really riles me, as if I needed to say that after the first paragraph, is when adults have an issue, a problem, a cramp or a knot in relation to another adult and when the party of the first part either cannot for some unimaginable reason, or will not, for any number of imaginable reasons deal directly, openly, and honestly with the party of the second part and when the aforementioned party of the first part, in frustration and unable to manage their toxicity maturely, takes their conflicts with the party of the second part out on the innocent and certainly unwilling children of the party of the second part. I am sure, to take a small excursion, I mean diversion here, you can well understand why I ended up in the personal transformation field instead of in legal practice. To return to the issue at hand and to restate it for the sake of repetition and clarity: when one person uses another's children as the brunt of their abuse based on a disagreement or a conflict with the child's parent(s), I think it is unconscionable and despicable. I think such people are due for a cold dose of reality, and I wish they would get it soon.

Parents blame their own children for enough bullshit of their own (the parents') without the children having to be subjected to more blame and shaming for their parents' real or imagined failures of relationship. In fact, parents who blame their own children for their (the parents') failings should also, and quickly if you don't mind, be given a good cold dose of reality.

In any case, particularly the one we are currently discussing so passionately (at least I am discussing it passionately and I hope you are interacting with it or considering it passionately, whether you agree or disagree), it would benefit any adults who consider themselves open, mature, and conscious, to be willing, and able properly, to take their problems with another adult up with that person directly and not to gossip to others or poison the innocence and happiness of children just because most children won't fight back, or can't clarify the attacker's (or is it abuser's) cramp or problem at issue or because they are little and easy to beat up, unlike their parents. That is the way of a mature, sane adult to deal with disagreements directly with the one who the disagreement is with. To pick on the children of someone as the easy way, and the safe way, to vent impotent frustration and to avoid one's own part in the disagreement is to be a coward and a dastardly excuse for a human being.

Well, that's the bad news. Now for the good news. It is also true that sometimes an otherwise strong individual, who would never consider dumping their own problems on a child, just has a weak moment and loses their sense of clarity. If that is the case, one will know it's the case by seeing clearly what they have just done and allowing the manifestation of remorse to dramatically increase the probability of such a thing happening again to almost zero. Ah, now I feel so much better.

—Journal, July 9, 1990

THE RESULTS

Abuse as children leads to all kinds of inappropriate behavior as adults. It is commonly stated that physical abuse, particularly of a sexual nature, can and often does lead to prostitution (or it's opposite, frigidity). I am not just talking about prostitution for pay, but also prostitution of ideals, of integrity or personal responsibility. Usually, it is physical abuse, but emotional abuse is easily powerful enough to create such inappropriate behavior—you know, like: "Jesus, I wish I never *had* you. Leave me alone, will you? I just got home from work; give me a chance to relax. I go to work all day for you, and the minute I come home you're crawling all over me. Get the hell out of my face." That kind of emotional abuse is developmentally shattering to the healthy self-image of a young child who needs mother's (and father's) loving attention, support and affection. All children are weak in the sense of smaller and more easily dominated, and therefore easily victimized by unconscious and hateful adults.

Have you ever seen a little child, a one- or two-year-old, being thrown up in the air, giggling and squealing with delight and always asking for more? They have no fear. (Unless they are not inclined—by born, biological disposition—to sailing through the air and being spun around. In that case, when an abusive father, uncle or big brother does it, because they suppose that a child who doesn't like such intense activity must be weak and a "scaredy-cat" and needs to be toughened up, the child will scream with terror. Some little children are inclined to wild movement and some aren't. In children that are, there is no fear.) Some of you have probably noticed this with amazement and thought, "Gosh, aren't they trusting?"

Of course they are. Why would they not trust? After all, to them they are in the arms of God! Trust comes quite naturally to a child, until they are taught not to trust. A child's dominant psychological habits— the personality features that they form based on the conditioning of their environment; the manifestations that act as a primary relationship to life—are not fully crystallized yet at a year-and-a-half or two years old. These personality features are beginning to show, but are not completely in place. It is this personality network that develops fear. (When a child is two years old we hear people say, "All of a sudden little Bobby has gotten such personality," and they will puff their chests out, like, "Isn't it wonderful." They don't know that little Bobby has just stopped growing. Life almost stops at that point, for an individual, because he or she stops living to the full extent that they are "designed" for.)

Children trust implicitly. They will eat anything we give them to eat—at least taste it—when they are a year-and-a-half old. Some adults find that so unbelievable (because no one that they can remember has ever trusted them) that they cripple their child out of pure spite ... they just keep testing the child—by beating it, by throwing it in the closet and locking the door; by screaming at it, lying to it or by purposely feeding the child cayenne and lemon juice and hot mustard. Some of you have probably been in a Chinese restaurant where someone (fathers tend to do this quite frequently) will take some hot mustard and give it to a baby, and when the baby starts to scream, they laugh. The adult's abusive behavior forms their child into not just a neurotic individual, but an absolutely psychopathological one who still loves them, usually, and even shows it. Can you imagine? Of course there are those rare individuals who are so in touch with their hatred of being abused that they react, even to the point of great violence, towards their abusers; but that is not the usual case. Usually, the abuser is inviolate, and the rage goes outwards toward others, or inwards towards self-hatred and self-destruction. A child may unconsciously come to the conclusion that if they are bad enough or unwanted enough for their beloved parent to treat them so viciously, they might as well not be here (i.e., die), so they go about trying to accomplish the job themselves, often through severe addictions and dangerous occupations, as well as through psychosomatically-induced illness, and obviously in extreme cases by suicide.

If a girl child grows up being sexually abused by her father, or for that matter by her mother (who likes to stick things in her child's orafices), she will tend to look for mates who will do the same thing to her, but in adult terms. No matter how badly we are treated, we still love that parent. And that parent translates to that gender.

If a woman has a father who sexually abuses her, her relationship to the masculine polarity is being twisted, aberated, and she will have a very hard time living with someone who is not like that. Every once in a while, though, a woman who has been sexually abused will get into a relationship with a man who doesn't abuse her, verbally or physically. And, for this woman, it becomes very difficult to live with a man like that. So she tends to become abusive. Such a woman will say to her partner, "Get angry sometimes!" because she can't understand how someone can love her and not abuse her, not duplicate her childhood environment or circumstance. She feels, "He can't love me if he doesn't abuse me, because Daddy loved me and he abused me. How could a Daddy not love his children?"

So it's like that.

A RADICALLY DISTURBED RELATIONSHIP

A radically disturbed primal relationship, full of neurosis or psychosis, is chiefly experienced as un-lovedness. An example of such a radically disturbed primal relationship would be when a mother is so "coked-out" or "heroined-out" that she can't take care of her infant. It is not so much the drug itself that is doing the damage, as it is the mother's inability to love her child in a way that the child can instinctually relate to as being loved. Of course, within the psychology of sur-vival we often twist situations of abuse into some unconscious image of love—as if being beaten was being loved. At the same time, there is an essential knowing element of our make-up—whether that is con-sciousness, soul, being, or whatever—that feels the reality of love and the reality of the lack of love, or abuse. So, radically disturbed primal relationships would be common in drug addicts and alcoholics with children, especially among severe users. For an alco-holic who still had enough consciousness to give gen-uine attentive love to their child, the adult's addiction might go relatively unnoticed until the child was old enough to have consciousness of such things.

Another example of a radically disturbed primal relationship would be when the mother has a severe ill-ness during the child's first couple of years, and the child has to be cared for by relatives who really don't want to care for him or her. Obviously this would also be true in a situation of constant physical abuse which the mother either supports, or makes no attempt to comfort and protect the child in relationship to.

The primal impression of not being loved, which when a child grows older is usually imbedded in the unconscious, is often accompanied by some insatiable and ungraspable longing. This can be (and is) the basis for many neuroses. For instance, most psychologists and psychiatrists say there is no such thing as nymphomania," but that all forms of what is mistakenly or popularly called nymphomania is simply this—an attempt to compensate for the feelings of lack of love and attention as an infant.

There are people who have to have everyone they know constantly complimenting them or they feel despondent, depressed, worthless. That kind of dynamic also points to this basic lack. I am sure most of you at some point have been in a relationship, and not necessarily when you were fifteen years old, where the person constantly asked, "Do you love me? Tell me you love me?" No matter how much you told them you loved them, it was never enough, because their need was far deeper in their unconscious than all the feedback of love that they perceived through their senses and their intellect. (Those primal feelings are usually inaccessible to any form of ordinary input.) These people needed constant feedback just to feel minimally functional. It was compensatory, and of course it never really compensated, so the wound never healed.

Fortunately, such a wound can be healed in other ways—ways that address the deep place from which the feelings of un-love arise and reside. [Some of these ways will be considered in the upcoming section called *Hope For The Abused*.]

TAKING IT TOO FAR

These days, with all the accusations and fear surrounding sexual abuse in preschools and such, more and more schools are demanding that teachers do not touch the children at all. That, in my opinion, is taking it too far. The decent teachers are totally handicapped by the few who should not be teachers at all.

There was an article in *Playboy* about this guy who was an outstanding father and an incredible child advocate. He was in a very bitter divorce-custody battle, and his wife accused him of sexual abuse of their five-year-old daughter. Literally the week that happened, the courts turned against him and refused joint custody, saying he could not be in the presence of his daughter except with a court-appointed social worker. He was battling that. He took a lie detector test, and had three social workers stay with him while he was with his daughter, and everyone gave him a clean bill of health; but his ex-wife would not relent. Then, one day, he went to pick up his daughter, and his ex-wife's father shot him, dead ... while the five-year-old was in the house!

We as a society are going insane. We have gone from total non-involvement and legal child abuse, as in beatings admininstered routintely to children as recommended in disciplinary regulations a hundred years ago, to total paranoia and fear connected with traumatizing a child around sexual abuse simply from honest, non-intrusive, and desperately needed affection. Even people who should be teaching in schools and nurturing the children are walking on eggshells, because anybody can accuse someone else of child abuse on the flimsiest of grounds. Have you heard of the McMartin case? In California, at a childcare facility or grade school ... something like that ... one of the children went home and said something that the parents thought had to do with sexual molestation. They eventually accused the primary male teacher of sexually abusing many of the children in class ... making the children do things together .... It was an immense scandal in which, after the first parent said something, twenty or thirty other parents literally jumped on the bandwagon. The FBI came in, and the kids—some of them three and four years old—were subjected to exhaustive cross-examination, with bright lights and two guys standing over them, questioning them. You can't believe what they did to these kids ... talking about abuse!

Eventually the guy was found innocent. (I don't know what all the details were.) And even after he was found innocent the parents did not let the case die. They wanted to nail this guy to the cross for what *they've* done to their children, justifying all their own children's problems because of *him*.

Who knows whether there was child abuse or not in this case? But the way it was handled showed such gross negligence towards the sensitivity of the children that it was a nightmare. Witch hunters are never concerned with the accused witch's children. They only want "justice" (meaning blood).

HELP FOR THE ABUSED

MINIMIZING THE RISK

In an abusive environment, the priorities of a non-abusive adult should be clear. If the father comes in drunk and starts looking around for the first person to smack around, it is imperative that the mother pick up the baby and get out of the way, and not start in on the father: "Christ! Ron, do you have to come home drunk again? You always do that. I can't even afford lettuce and you're out drinking up your pay check every week ...." *Smack, smack, smack*, and the baby lies on the couch crying while the mother gets beaten up.

If the mother won't protect her child, and another adult is in the space, that adult should just keep the child from witnessing or participating in the combat. It is the parent's responsibility to take a child out of an abusive, violent environment to minimize the negative effects, *whatever* the circumstance might be! When a little girl gets practically beaten senseless by her father, and goes to her mother and says, "Daddy did this to me," no way should Mommy ever condone or justify such treatment. And, it is her responsibility to give the child a lot of affection, a lot of touch, a lot of cuddling, a lot of kind and soft reassurance, for balance. Not: "Oh baby, oh you poor thing, oh I'm so sorry, but Daddy's under a lot of pressure you know." That's the worst kind of senseless drivel. That is *not* support. But a lot of affection—cuddling and touch—is one of the most important factors in minimizing a child's traumatization based on major negative influences in his or her life.

The right thing to do, of course, the first time that abuse shows up, is to get out of there and stay out. Anyone with their eyes open will see such things coming, and either get major counseling or therapy with their mate, or end the relationship before children are involved. One of the worst (and stupidest) things a woman can do is get pregnant as a way to try to soften or repair damage within a relationhship due to an abusive, cruel and violent man.

Because this issue of child abuse and its dangers is getting more public, more women are willing to leave their husbands to save their children, and more husbands are asking for custody of their children to save them from abusive mothers. In our generation, a lot of your mothers put up with very severe shit, and would never publicly support their children against their husbands—it wasn't acceptable social behavoir for a "dependent woman." Thank God that has changed, and continues to change.

BREAKING THE CYCLE

One of the singularly most important things that Alice Miller speaks about in her books is that if a parent comes to terms with their own childhood abuse, or with the way they have abused their child, their child will automatically begin to be less affected by the parent's conditioning on them.

This is a crucial point, because if (as some suggest) the only way psychological health can be attained is to redo or re-animate and re-program, in a sane way, every single insanity of infancy and childhood, then the realistic expectation of psychological help is patently absurd. It would be impossible to achieve successful psychological help, because the vast amount of infancy and childhood experience would be impossible to both completely discover and rework or redo. It is too vast. Some people do primal therapy, and they regress to infancy and to the womb, and they have "primal" after "primal" after "primal." (And you can't get any deeper than re-experiencing your birth, or re-experiencing yourself at several months in the womb; that is about as far back as you can go.) When they get tired of doing "primals," they go on to Transactional Analysis or some other kind of transpersonal therapy, due to still feeling this wound of un-love. It is an endless process, because there is endless data to remember, re-live and re-condition.

So, to reiterate: If a parent who has abused his

223

or her child (the way Alice Miller describes abuse) comes to terms with their part in that, their responsibility for that, the child will immediately cease to be limited by the psychological and pathological dynamic between child and parent—that dynamic by which parents condition the child in a certain way, and by which the child continues to function at the effect of that conditioning (whether it makes sense or not) even when he or she is fifty years old and the parents are long dead! This parental revelation—the owning, so to speak, of their own abusive dynamic, and more deeply of the abuse they have suffered that they have repressed as a child—gives some space, some possibility, to their own children to not be at the mercy of the old worldview, but to begin to live free of the chains and bonds of the old chronic habits.

So, in my work with students, a lot of psychological work *is* done, but incidentally, in the context of a broader commitment to health, healing and true sanity, rather than as a solution to a specific problem or difficulty. Basically, in intimate relationships, some psychological work can make it easier for people to live with one another very simply. Just to relieve certain elements of resentfulness, greed, possessiveness, territorialism and so on, can make living infinitely more graceful. Our opportunity to do the work of personal transformation, free of the drag of psychological problems or conflicts, has to do with an absolutely uncompromising and clear vision of the psychological dynamics that disempower us.

If we follow the cleansing and purifying principles of Alice Miller's brilliant considerations, then we can take our past, burn it and then forget about it. What good is it? What does it remind us of? All the fun we had at our birthday parties? Yes. But it also reminds us of all the times our father beat us (except we often don't remember that part consciously; but that part moves us more than the happy birthday parties). To keep dragging the same old issues out of the basement again and again is not only boring and a total waste of time, energy and resources, but can also keep something alive that deserves to be dead and buried. Our past is history and belongs to the world of academia, not to the world of creative, juicy, exciting, ongoing life and its infinite potentiality and possibility.

8

SPEAKING THE TRUTH:
Language and Honesty

LANGUAGE

Children don't relate to stimuli the way adults do. Since they are not intellectually mature or life-experienced, they can't make the kind of judgmental leaps that adults make. For instance, if we meet a friend and, joking around, look at the friend's shirt and say, "That's a really ugly shirt ... Whadidjya do, pick it up in the street?" An adult knows that this is a kind of play, of good-natured teasing, but children take things literally. Adults don't understand that a child can be prejudiced for life by an innocent comment. There was a guy I used to spend time with many years ago whose way of greeting a friend was, "Hey, you look like shit today!" He would say it with a smile on his face, with warmth in his heart, and he would embrace people. He was a really friendly, bubbly, just give-you-the-shirt-off-his-back kind of guy. But his language was deadly, and his children showed the effects of it. His teenagers demonstrated unmistakable behavioral manifestations clearly linked to his use of language.

Another example: When their child turns three or four and starts to speak, many people will say, "Oh,

I like three-years-olds much better than babies. They are really like people now." That is not an innocent remark to the child. Many children spend the first six or nine months of their lives being treated as if they were not human beings; and believe it or not, they are sensitive to these things. They hear every word spoken in their presence—whether spoken directly to them or not. It is imperative, therefore, that we be very clear about what we are saying when children are present, for often they won't ask us to explain something they hear, but will draw their own conclusions and file them away. By the time they bring these conclusions back out and we might hear their wild idea and try to correct it, it is too late—the idea is already deeply ingrained in their behavior and consciousness. I have often had a four- or five-year-old tell me some piece of data that they heard from another child as if it were a fact. When or if I tried to convey the accurate information, they were so sure that I was misinformed that there was little possibility of "adjustment."

Children hear *everything*—a child can be playing in one corner of the dining room, and adults are in the other corner talking about something that should not be talked about in front of a child, and of course the child will hear it. Even though he or she may make no acknowledgment at the time, two or three days later when somebody's name is mentioned, the child will pass on some gossip, or make a comment that they obviously heard when we thought they were not listening. Then if we ask, "Where did you hear that?" the child might look dumbfounded, like, "I don't know." Adults, therefore, need to be cognizant about their own language—about their own backbiting and pettiness, especially when children are anywhere in the vicinity.

Basic Do's And Don'ts

The first things to keep in mind when talking to children is to consider them, at every age, to be fully cognizant, and deserving of the kind of respect that we would want to get as adults, and that we would advance towards other adults whom we respect. Therefore, I strongly discourage the use of baby language, *"goo goo ga,"* an affected tone of voice, and all of the usual things that first-time parents tend to say and do. I guess we have seen this approach to children on TV so commonly, that we assume it is the way we are supposed to be with them.

I recommend that even when a child is in the womb one should talk to the child in adult language. The concepts behind the words used will translate *literally* to the child, and so he or she will get used to associating language with feeling, even in the womb. As I've mentioned previously, the kind of "conversation" to have with a child in the womb may be to tell the child how excited we are to be welcoming them. Don't say things like: "If you're a boy, I know just what we're going to do—we're going to go out there and play football." Just tell the child: "We want to be the best parents we can be. We're really looking forward to welcoming you out into this world," and like that.

In tone of voice and inflection in words, we should talk to children like they are adults, but not talk down to them. If we want them to go with us we can just say, "Okay, let's go." Not, "Mommy's going to store now, do you want to go, little one?" in some kind of a sing-song, birdlike voice. Regardless of how cute the child is and how much we tend to want to coo and fuss and primp on them, we should not belittle them with incomprehensible gibberish.

One of the boys here was into a habit of talking to himself in baby talk. One day we were preparing a meal and he asked if he could come in and help cook. He was using that baby voice with me and I said, "How old are you?" He said, "I'm eight," and I said, "Would you use an eight-year-old voice when you speak with me?" (That was a different approach than saying, "Knock off that voice, will ya?" Or, "Stop acting like a baby." One would think that this distinction was common sense, but unfortunately adults with children often seem to have little.) He said, "Sure," and he has never spoken in that way since. I checked myself the next time I was in his company to see if he seemed inhibited or felt that I was going to be angry with him, and he didn't. That one short encounter was a strong enough reminder. He evidently felt that with me he would be heard as an eight-year-old, so he didn't need to get little and cutesy to get attention and acknowledgment.

I would never use threats like, "I'm going to smack you, I'm going to knock your head off, I'm gonna ... etc, etc." Never in kidding, and never out of anger or frustration! I don't think I have used such threats once in my life, and there have been times when I have been really angry at a child for something. I don't believe one should ever use the threat of violence. Some parents do that for fun, as their way of playing around with their kids. That is their idea of humor. Some Dads are always doing that to their kids, and knocking them on the side of the head, lightly boxing their ears. I guess that's okay to some people, but I would *never* suggest it. My fury lasts about ten seconds, but that is enough to say some heavy stuff. We can really say some bad shit in ten seconds—but we must not. We must always be bigger than our anger, especially with children.

Don't talk about the child as if he or she were a lump of inanimate matter, or as if the child were not there. For instance, when an infant is laying in a crib just looking around: "Is there anybody there? How come he isn't smiling?" Or, when three-year-old Jimmy is standing next to us: "What should we do about Jimmy's habits?" I've heard all of these things said to children, and noticed or felt the child's reactions.

Never criticize one of the child's parents (or both of them) with the child present or in hearing range. My assumption is that, all the time, from conception on, there is consciousness that is cognizant of the environment, within the full range of the senses.

Don't call children "dirty" when they shit in their pants, or indulge the whole kind of derogatory commentary that people think is cute. Like, when the child farts: "God, does that stink!" or "Say, you should consider joining an orchestra." Some so-called "mature" or intelligent people don't have enough brains even to know that!

In terms of language, I would apply the same rules around a seven-year-old as around an infant—this goes for whether they are sleeping or not. It is common psychology that the sleeping mind still actively picks up sensory data in its environment. So, one should not fight over the child in their room when they are sleeping.

Don't be a wise guy with the kid. The child is not going to know how smart Daddy and Mommy are for a long time, so we don't have to show off in front of our child, which is essentially what all that strutting, shouting and joking is about. People are so full of inflated pride, due to basic insecurity and immaturity. Out of two billion men on the planet, all of them except a very small percentage can have children. But every man who has a child thinks and acts as if he has done something special. Of course such behavior is epitomized in Western cultures, the so-called *civilized* cultures. So, when men are full of pride they show off by saying dumb things to their child, often calling the child ridiculous names.

Even when we recognize that something is required and that our input is appropriate, if we are talking down to the child instead of simply providing a boundary in a natural, unaffected way, the communication has a really uncomfortable feel, and the child can't miss the "off-ness" of it. Men especially tend to talk down to children, to be really condescending. There is a quality to many fathers' voices which says, in effect: "You better not sass me because you're a little kid and I can just force you to do what I want, so do it!"

Anybody can shame a child, and most anybody can berate and beat a child into submission. We can shame and behaviorally modify a child into just being a good little boy or girl ("good" by our idea of the word). Even if we draw the line in the "right" place, but with the wrong attitude or with too much force, that's just patently wrong.

We don't recommend any kind of funny nicknames, like "my little monkey" or "my little peanut." Recognize that children take things we say literally. This is not some deep esoteric principle, it is basic psychology. Don't make jokes about their bodily smells or excretions, like: "Oh man, your vomit stinks," or "Wow, what a shit for such a little thing!" For children, what comes out of their bodies is a part of themselves, so "Vomit stinks" literally means, "You stink ... and that is bad. Therefore, you're bad." So, be very, very sensitive in the use of language.

Instead of saying, "Don't close the door," one

might say, "Why don't you leave the door open?" Try always to make positive suggestions to the child instead of negative commands. If we are not creative, it is often hard to think of those things on the spot. However, we should do as much as possible, in any case.

Let children be eight when they are eight, and let them be ten when they are ten; and when they are twelve and they want to be fourteen really badly, okay, let them reach a bit. But, joking with a nine-year-old boy about dating is inappropriate. For example, if the kid has gone to some event at the local high school, and he comes back and we say, "Hey, meet any hot chicks?" It is horrible to talk to a nine-year-old like that. Joking with kids about what is way beyond their present developmental experience is inappropriate. Don't joke provocatively with a thirteen-year-old about dating. Believe me, when they are ready to date, and dating, it won't be funny. It will be really serious, as some of us must remember. Don't make complexion jokes or breast jokes with pre-teens or young teens. Treat children— even when they are fully grown and have children of their own—with honor, respect, dignity and camaraderie.

LANGUAGE CAN DESTROY INNOCENCE

Children learn to get separated from their innocence at a very early age by the language that we use around them, just as they separate from innocence due to physical abuse. As I've discussed previously, supposedly innocuous little comments like, "Oh, isn't he sweet," and "You are just so cute," can make the child aware of how sweetness and cuteness are ways of manipulating adults and getting a certain type of attention. The tendency is then for the child to dramatize those behavior manifestations and become quite affected.

For a long time we have considered the negative effect of comparisons like: "Oh, your brother didn't walk till he was three years old, but you, I'll bet you are going to be walking at nine months," or "Gosh you're so skinny. You look like your mother must starve you to death," or "Your cousin gets all A's in school. Why can't you be smarter?" All these types of comments are liable to be commonly made by unthinking adults.

I am sure all of us with small children have brought them to the supermarket or a busy public space and had people make negative comments to them, in one form or another. It is extremely important to negate those comments. One friend, a first time father, said he had no idea how bad it was—how constant the negativity was—until he took his child back home for a visit to the grandparents. Not just once in a while, but *every minute* that his mother's mouth was open, she made critical and disparaging remarks, such as, "Why don't you dress that poor child. Heavens, he'll catch his death of cold." I think many families are somewhat like that—well meaning, but simply uneducated and unconscious.

So, we recommend speaking to the child quietly and discreetly and canceling out all of that negativity. For instance, if someone in the supermarket says: "Oh, she is a chubby one isn't she?" we might say to the child, softly without needing to provoke the unconscious commentator: "That person doesn't know what she is talking about. She doesn't understand children much. She is just unconscious. You don't need to pay any attention to her. You are perfectly fine," or something like that. Another common example: if a child just fusses a little, some adult in the environment will say: "Ohhh, are you sick?" And we always recommend that a responsible adult say to the child, "This person doesn't understand sickness," and not wait to say this until later, because children are very much in the moment, and later they will not relate to what one is saying. The way one uses the word "sick" can commit a child to a lifetime of hypochondria and self-indulgence, or can make a child think, "Ah, it's nothing."

Many things that appear to be very benign to adults can actually be quite disturbing or confusing to a child. When we nickname children, as mentioned earlier, children don't understand the double meanings. When they learn a word, they learn what it literally means. When we use words that mean something other than the literal meaning (words that are common idioms), they still hear it literally and will often take on behavior that is a function of what they hear, not what we mean. A one-month-old or a four-month-old child might not understand the language, but they definitely understand the intention, the feeling and the mood. Most children understand language far earlier than they can actually speak it—even at six or seven months we would be amazed how much a child will understand if we speak properly, clearly, to them.

It is almost impossible to eliminate all dissonant elements from any environment, not that we would want to anyway, but we certainly do want to establish life-positive, sane, healthy and conscious habits that will serve our children for a lifetime.

CAREFUL CHOICE OF WORDS

To choose our words carefully around children does not mean that we should take all of the color out of language ... all the poetry. Actually, children respond to metaphor; they instinctively understand real metaphor and poetry. What I am talking about is not just using a word that has a different meaning, but rather using the language in a way that is not metaphorical. For instance, adults commonly say, "I'm starving!" That is *not* metaphor; that is saying something that is not true, basically. We want language to empower, so we want to say what is true. "I'm very hungry, and this food tastes really good," is a communication that has life to it. "I'm starving," or "I'm famished," when I'm really not, is deadening because it is not true, and it teaches children to exaggerate in a way that divorces them from the truth of their own experience.

Our language, in general, is so sloppy that it is horrific, nothing less. When one of my friends was trying to organize a basketball game between his company and the men from one of the other local businesses, he said, in the presence of some of the children: "We haven't heard from these guys yet; they're chickens." That kind of language can be not only confusing to children, but also demonstrates an aggressive competitive bias and a "put-down" of friends, which children don't understand even if the adults are meaning it in fun.

If we observe people's responses to inane comments like that, we will find that they automatically and unthinkingly laugh at such remarks. In fact, the majority of us did laugh, at the time, and that gives a double message to the children. They wonder: "Are those people on the other team friends or enemies?"

Another example: A man was speaking with another adult about work, and he said, "The Republicans are killing us." Immediately, one of the children asked, "Killing what? Killing who?" in a very scared tone of voice. Later, this man asked me if that was an inappropriate use of language, and I said absolutely, it was very misleading. There are a whole litany of phrases in common usage in the language which children will respond to, and which can be disturbing and confusing, even when the tone of our voice is not directly threatening or shaming.

In my early teaching work I used to give a lecture about how our language creates psychosomatic illness. For instance, if we have the habit of always saying that things are "a pain in the ass," it disposes us towards hemorrhoids, literally. That goes for any kind of language that refers to the body. "My feet are killing me"—that, in the ultimate sense of things, would dispose one towards slipping and breaking their neck, or slipping down a mountain. I try not to even use the word "sick." To me a cold is not "sick." When we have a cold and we say, "I'm sick," and we feel the need to be laid up in bed for days with this "cold," I find that a disgraceful indulgence. You know why we do that? Because we *learn* that we are "sick" when we have a cold—it's all behavioral conditioning and wrong thinking. To me, sick is *sick* — the mumps, or a 105-degree fever, or food-poisoning ... something that really makes us unable to function! Not a cold. We get a cold and we *make* ourselves sick. We learn associations as children, and often incapacitate ourselves purely on expectation.

The great thing about such examples is that we get to see how unconsciously mechanical we are. Seeing that becomes a way to turn the circumstance to our advantage. If we can see that enough, if we can be shocked by it enough, we will stop being so mechanical. Or we will be mechanical less and less. We might even talk less, and that would not be such a terrible outcome.

* * *

"Mean" is a word to watch out for. Even among aware, "child-sensitive" people, there can be a tendency to talk about the behavior of some children who are acting out rather aggressively saying that these children are "being mean." Children, especially young children, are not malicious. Instead of holding the idea that "the kids are being mean," we can approach it by simply observing this certain activity which is showing up in the children, and then asking ourselves, "What is the best response to this?" Sometimes children are just bored. Or, perhaps they are acting out their parents' violence, or unconsciously reacting to being demeaningly or abusively treated. We should try our best not to categorize their actions or set them in a mold that we have in our own minds. Rather, we can attempt to see what is behind what they do, and determine what they are needing in order to be different.

It is crucial that our language be elegant. "Dirty" is another word that is really misused. "Dirty" is like tar—tar is dirty. Oil paint that dries on the skin is dirty. Earth, pus, bug gook—that's not dirty. Dirty is something that we really *have* to clean. If we are tarred and feathered we are dirty, but if we are covered from head to foot in mud we are not dirty, because all we have to do is jump in water and the mud is gone. "Dirty" on a piece of clothing is a stain that won't come out. Something that will come out as soon as we throw the blouse or the pants in the wash ... that is not dirty. So to call a child "dirty" is often to imply, again in the child's logic, that they themselves are essentially unclean.

Children are extremely sensitive to name-calling. Recently, a child I know called an adult by a name, and the adult said to him, "That's not okay with me. I don't call you names." But the child replied, "Yes you do." When she asked the child about it, he said she had called him a "smooch," and the child felt this was some negative inference. What we can understood from that interaction was that we should call children by their names, because that is who they know themselves to be, and that is how they want to be referred to.

At the same time, I think there is a place for terms of endearment. Every person has to "feel into" this issue, and not just have a black and white, letter-of-the-law attitude. The spirit of the principle needs to animate what we do, from a heartful place, not from a rigid set of laws. We can resolve this issue, of course, by always only calling children by their given names; and then not have to worry about it. But to me that leaves out a dimension of relationship. One of the ways humans show love to each other is through language. So, to call a child "sweetheart" or "honey" from a clear place—unpretentious, unaffected and unbiased (not unconscious)—can be a warm and affectionate form of address. Whereas to constantly call a child "lovey," or whatever, from a place of sentimental hypocrisy is not recommended.

Be aware with children, depending upon their ages, to say what they can understand, something that means something to them, not just what means something to us. Adults find it easy to read between the lines, but children don't. For instance, if we are going someplace and we say to an adult, "We'll eat when we get there," and they ask how far it is, and we tell them two hundred miles, an adult has a pretty good sense that two hundred miles means three hours or so. If we say to a child, "We're going to eat when we get there," and they say, "How long is it?" and we say, two hundred miles ... to a child that is meaningless. Even if we say, "Three hours," that is meaningless too if the children are under a certain age, because their attention span is fifteen minutes, and when they are hungry they want to eat *now*! If we say, "It's going to be a long time," that is different than three hours, but we still may have to give them lots of reminders and support for it being okay for them to be hungry. We certainly don't want to make them *wrong* for being hungry just because *we* are annoyed by them asking, "When are we going to get there?" every ten minutes. After all, we are the adults, aren't we? We should be able to hold the space with patience, love and even security. Imagine that!

How They Learn

Children learn how to speak properly by listening and paying attention when people speak, not by being corrected for their speech patterns. When one child was first learning to talk she couldn't pronounce Y's, so when she learned the color yellow she used to say "lellow." I just let her say whatever she wanted, and she learned as she grew. Why make a child wrong for her innocence? I never corrected her or leaned on her to say it "properly," and everyone who heard "lellow" knew what it meant. I mean, if everybody else in the room is saying "yellow" and our child is the only person saying "lellow," he or she will start saying "yellow" as soon as they are ready—the difference will not be lost on them. They don't need anybody to point it out, or mock them for their speech idiosyncrasies. My opinion is, as children are learning to speak we should not correct them unnecessarily. They will learn to speak by listening.

When I think about how I learned to speak and

how I learned my mannerisms and so forth, it was just by copying the people around me. Whatever their *intention* was, came through as strongly as whatever they did. Whether they were carefully trying to correct themselves as they spoke to me, or whether they were just "full tilt" into whatever they were doing and saying, that came through as strongly as anything else.

If we relax a little bit about whether we are doing everything exactly right, children will get our intention both to speak articulately, and to speak and act out of our hearts. Children sense true sincerity and genuineness even if the actions are a bit bumbling or eccentric. Moreover, we can't judge their reception of our intention in anything like the short term. That comes out *years* down the road.

BE NATURAL WITH COMPLIMENTS

Although this is probably obvious to many, acknowledgment of children's accomplishments should be done without being overly sugary or redundant. Many parents get into this idea of complimenting their child, but they go so far overboard that it actually becomes a negative input rather than a positive one. When a child brings us some scribbles, for example, we should try not to gush: "Oh, you are such a little artist. I'm going to hang this up ... this is so fantastic. My little Picasso." Because, as they get older they will know we are being hypocritical, false or patronizing. They may have done their best, but they know they're not Picasso or Chagall. They simply want us to be grateful for what they've brought us because of the love that we share, but we don't have to overly dramatize how fantastic every little flower they paint is. Give them full attention when they bring something—give them a smile, a touch, tell them you like it ... and that's it! Going over the same praise again and again and again doesn't give them more confidence; actually it diminishes the joy and spontaneity of the whole exchange. So, avoid such errors of judgment.

It also depends on *how* we compliment children, as to the effect of such feedback to them. Certainly we would not want to praise them a hundred times a day, complimenting every tiny little thing they do! If the compliment is made because it is true, rather than because we are trying to bolster their self-confidence, then of course it's a perfect response. If they just climb up on a stool, we wouldn't say, "Oh, you climbed up on a stool so well." When everything a child does is rewarded, then the habit that tends to develop is to do everything for the rewards. The child may become totally lost, suppressing their own uniqueness in order to be whatever a key adult wants them to be, so they can get the prize of reward or praise. They become totally adaptive, to use the popular psychological term.

Some educators have said that even complimenting a child's artwork can be detrimental, because then the child will adjust their natural creativity—i.e., draw the tree the same way every time—in order to get the teacher's ongoing approval. If our compliment is true to who we are, and we are not being false to who we are, then it should not have that effect. If, normally, we are not very effusive, but we become tremendously effusive when complimenting our children, that will affect them—in terms of their looking for that, and, at the same time, wondering why we are being so different with them than we usually are.

It should go without saying that children's creative efforts, the ones they are so proud of, should never be called "trash," "lousy," "terrible," and so on. Of course, if who we are is a neurotic mass of torturous insecurities, frustrations and confessions, perhaps the kind of extensive education that this book hopefully will initiate is a key element in being natural with our children.

So, before we speak, we should stop for an instant and then speak consciously. That alone is usually enough to get a sense of what would serve a child in the optimal way.

HONESTY

DON'T TRY TO BE PERFECT WITH THEM (NOBODY IS)

It is very healthy to let children know that adults are human. After all, we are. We can only fool a child so long before they won't buy adults' misguided attempts at trying to appear infallible. They see, soon enough, that we make mistakes ... errors of judgment, for instance ... and if we try to behave otherwise they will just distrust us. Such acting perfect doesn't create confusion for them—they aren't confused, they will simply distrust us. If, however, they know we are doing the best we can, that we are older and we have had more experience and some wisdom because of that (wisdom that we want to share with them), then they will trust that we are in charge of the space, and they will watch how we handle things, learning both from our successes and our failures. Otherwise they close off to all of it.

When a child is throwing a tantrum, for instance, we may say to them, "You know, I get angry too, sometimes, and boy it's really difficult. I understand your feelings" ... we can sympathize with them. Of course, this response rests on the fact that we must *actually* sympathize—to pretend we do just doesn't communicate. We must really understand them. Then, they will look at us like they never thought we could experience the same things they are experiencing. At that point we might say: "I know just how you feel. Sometimes I get that way too, and when I disturb everything it's as hard for me as it is for you when you disturb everything. I'm working with it and I'm trying to manage it." Because children are upset with themselves for interrupting the flow; they just don't know how to handle their upset.

I expressed myself in this way a few times with my two older kids, and they always stopped what they were doing and listened. If my son would say, "This is a real gyp, this toy just broke," I would respond, "Yeah, it really doesn't feel fair does it?" and he would stop and listen. Once we have a child's ear, we can explain things to them. I would never say, "Oh cut it out, grow up, that's life"; rather, "Sometimes I don't feel things are fair either, but there are some situations that are beyond our ability to do anything about," or words like that. I would not say: "Well I *told* you not to play with it so hard."

We should try to get out of the way of our own processes and be objective with children. If we "lose it" around children, after we recover we can just say, "Oh, I lost it that time. I'll do better next time," or something to indicate that we aren't trying to pretend we're something that we're not. And they will say, "Okay." Or sometimes they just pat you on the back and say, "That's okay Dad. It's really all right."

* * *

If we have a child who is "pushing all our buttons," it's fine to break down in tears if we need to. Sometimes that's the best way to get a child to look at things in a different way. If a four-year-old is already manipulating the entire environment out of habit, they really have no idea that it disturbs people in the ways it does. To them it is just usual behavior. Such manipulation is their relationship strategy, and it is already unconscious. Seeing their mother crying they will say, "What's the matter Mommy, why are you crying?" They really mean it. They *feel* for us and want to make things better. Nothing much shocks a child more than when they do or say something and then see that a grown up cries over what they did or said. Nothing we could ever say would give them that kind of reflection on what their actions or words mean. When they find out that we take such things seriously, and how deeply affected we are, it gives them pause to reflect as much as they are able to at their ages. It is so painful to them to think they could make their mother cry that it may shock them into change. I have literally seen behavior turn around, ostensibly permanently, by just that one time when the mother couldn't handle it anymore and began to sob. But don't make it a habit, and don't blame them for your own limits of tolerance. Of course, as children get older, they do learn how much power they have to wound or heal others. But for the little ones it is just learned behavior. We would not want to fake crying or upset (they would know it), but there are times when crying arises out of our own feelings of inadequacy, frustration, helplessness, or whatever.

AN HONEST APOLOGY

Suppose we are conditioned, habitual beings at the effect of our own mechanicalness. And suppose our child pushes all our buttons and we can't control ourselves, so we whack them around. Then, what should we do when we are done ... when we come back to our senses again?

We should take them and hold them and tell them we love them, and apologize. We can say, "Mommy (or Daddy) lost control, and it wasn't right to hit you. I have some bad habits, and sometimes I can't control my habits." We explain to them that we made a mistake, and we give them lots of affection ... that's what we do. And, we don't *ever* justify hitting them again based on the fact that we still love them!

A key to this giving of affection is not to force ourselves on them—even a hug can be a form of subtle abuse if we are restraining them while they are pushing to get away. To give a child affection is to give them caring and hugs that *they* allow and nestle into. If we grab our child unexpectedly, and start roughing them up in the name of affection, while they are screaming to be let go, that just compounds the problems. Children crave and enjoy affection between themselves and adults and other children; but affection freely given, not forced and oppressive.

After we lose control and yell or hit, we need to apologize—right after, not the next day, because the next day is a whole other universe to children, especially to young children. Right after, when they are cowering in the corner not wanting to be hit again, we need to walk over, take a deep breath, pick them up, hold them, give them our attention and apologize. We can say something like, "Adults aren't perfect. I'm very sorry. Adults aren't perfect."

TELLING THE TRUTH TO CHILDREN

I am very much in favor of telling children the truth, but not in using the truth as an ax over their heads, or as a weapon to keep them in line. For example, if we give a child a toy that is easily breakable—something made out of porcelain, for example—and we say to the child, "This is very delicate. If you drop it on the floor or hit it against something hard it may break," the child will register what we have said, but in a moment of exuberance may knock the toy against the wall. When it breaks, the child will start to cry, "Mommy, fix it." In this situation the truth is: "I told you that was breakable, and when you knock something breakable against the wall, it breaks." That's the truth ... and, we can add, "But let's get some glue and see what we can do." Of course you wouldn't blame them for forgetting the truth, you would just state an obvious fact about the physics of things.

What we tend to do, however, is distract the child and try to interest them in something else, and tell them, "Well, we can always get another one," if to us it looked like an accident. We certainly don't want to imagine that our child just whaled the thing against the wall to see if it really was breakable. A lot of times, though, I think parents act with their children as if something was an accident when it clearly wasn't. Not only subconsciously, but consciously it wasn't an accident. The child knows it wasn't an accident, and if we try to make it seem like it was, we acquit them of the responsibility for their intentional actions if we say, "Well, we can get another one. We are going into town to the fair on Saturday, and maybe we will see something there that you like." Or, "Well, I didn't like that toy anyway." It is fine to try to comfort the child, but also it is important to tell children the truth. Whatever the truth is! Very simply, directly, unsentimentally or unapologetically And remember that children often don't want "another one"; they want that one back, and only that one. So we should be understanding and patient.

Basically, some children don't need to be told the truth very much, and some need to be told the truth pretty regularly, like for instance: "If you hit Tommy, this will happen ...." Little children forgive and forget very easily, so when one child doesn't want to play with another child it is always because of a reason. If we say to our child, "Oh, maybe Tommy was in a bad mood today," that is not really telling the truth to the child, which is: "You know, for the last two years every time you've seen Tommy you've been tripping him, hitting him, punching him. That's why he doesn't want to play with you." Simple as can be. Then they cry and they say, "Well I didn't mean it," and then the truth is, "It's wonderful that you have a good, sweet heart and that after you hit somebody you feel bad, but if you *really* don't mean it you have to learn to not hit him to begin with."

If the child says, "Well I don't know how to stop," then we have to get into a situation with helping them learn how to stop. We don't want to reject children or isolate them because we are telling them "how it is."

Sometimes we try to protect our children as if the truth will hurt them. If we tell them the truth properly, however, it will never hurt them, although in the moment they might be upset to hear it. A child who has to be told the truth is usually in a situation where conditioned psychology is already absolutely in control, running the show, so the truth will upset them and create stress. But, at the same time, they may still have

248

some volition to be more relational.

If a child is functioning innocently, they don't need to be told the truth as often or in the same way. One of the ideas of proper boundary setting is to help children live non-manipulatively, as much as possible. No child (or adult) lives this way *all* the time, but we can certainly help their dominant activity remain on the side of innocence and right relationship to others and the environment.

* * *

Then there are cases of a child's imaginal grandiosity. For example, a boy having ideas about how he is a better basketball player than Michael Jordan, and can do amazing feats. Some parents feel that to tell kids the truth about these things could harm their self-esteem, since it is often very healthy for children to exercise their imaginal skills. I think that in such cases the truth is subjective. Maybe this child *will* be that good in twenty years. If a child wants to stand in front of a car and stop it because they think they are strong enough, like Superman, then we have to handle it one way; but if a child is thinking of themselves in a fantastic way in relationship to their interests or passions, personally I would not say anything about it. I would just let it go. This is an important distinction to make. Children do live in the imaginal world a lot, and it is really up to parental common sense where to decide to set a context, and when to let them live in a magical and imaginal world without comment or with our support and participation. If we tell the child there is no Santa Claus at the wrong time, that can be harmful—even though it is the truth in one way, it is not the truth in another way. In talking about the imaginal realm, it is vital to have a sensitivity to their relationship to fantasy and so on. A lot of what we think is the truth in those realms is just *our* rational truth, which is not necessarily *the* truth. Where would we be if C.S. Lewis and J.R.R. Tolkien had been told that their imaginal worlds were ridiculous illusions?

It seems like with Santa Claus, for instance, we were the ones who introduced the concept first. Santa was not something they came up with—like an imaginary playmate—that we can be supportive of. We gave them the idea, so we need to be open-minded—not too literal or zealous—about bringing our children to an adult, critical view of reality.

* * *

Don't be resigned with children. If a child wants to play outside, but you don't really want to play with them or want to take them outside, then to sigh and moan, roll your eyes and agree anyway is not the best response. Hey! You shouldn't have children if you're going to resign yourself to being bummed out by them all the time. You should tie your tubes, get a vasectomy, do something! If you are too busy, you can tell the child straight: "I'm too busy right now, I've got to finish the project. I'll play with you later." And then you should play with them later. If you're *always* too busy then you have a big problem ... and you need to get a grip on your denial!

A PERSON OF ONE'S WORD

One should be a person of one's word. To other adults, such reliability may be neither here nor there, but children grow up learning a vital principle about life from living with trustworthy adults. They learn how to be persons of their word—reliable and clear. But, of course, we have to know what our word is! We have to "know who we are" in terms of knowing how to set boundaries that are realistic and keepable. As I've said before, I'm not going to break the child's arm ... I'm not going to abuse a child, so I'm not going to say: "Look, if you don't change, I'm going to box your ears ... I'm going to tweak your nose ... I'm going to smack your bottom, and you are going to be so sore you won't be able to sit down for a week, do you understand?" I know I'm not going to do those things, so I won't bluff, hoping that an intense-enough threat will scare the child into compliance.

We should not promise a child anything—from playing with them, to a sweet treat to eat, to a spanking—if we are not planning to or can't deliver. Why was it that every time our parents told us what they thought was good for us we never believed them? We knew it all, we were just so smart. We learned never to believe them because they didn't carry out their words, most of them. They were not reliable in the moment, nor consistent over time. If a child asks, "Can we go to the circus?" and we say "Sure," and they say "When?" and we say "Sometime," and they say "Okay," this creates great confusion. To a child there is no such thing as "sometime." So they will define "sometime" as next week, or whatever, and when we don't take them exactly then they will accuse us of lying, and no amount of explanation on our part will convince them that they didn't understand us. So, think ahead and watch your language, or even if you are sincere you may lose credibility.

* * *

If we are arranging something with children, something they are definitely planning on at a specific time, and we don't show up, our credibility drops dramatically. It is unfortunate, but sometimes people are wonderful when they finally get to do what they promise, but horrible about actually getting to do it.

There was a lady who taught horseback riding here, and I guess she had never seen the disappointment in an eager child's face who had been waiting all week for the lesson when she didn't show up. She had every kind of excuse: her car broke down, the brakes failed ... you wouldn't believe what happened to this woman so that she didn't show up to teach horseback riding lessons on a fairly regular basis. Eventually we had to stop using her completely, because the children were too deeply disappointed too many times. Too bad, because she was an exceptional teacher when she randomly showed up. It is crushing to children when they are disappointed like that!

Of course, there are those who are of the opinion that children must learn to be spontaneous, to take unavoidable situations calmly and philosophically. Such people say, "That's life ... and children need to learn to roll with it." But to shatter an innocent child's trust and anticipation around some activity they love is simply not acceptable to me. On one hand they need to learn to be spontaneous and graceful about unexpected changes of plans, but on the other it should be a responsible person's impeccability to be trustworthy—to children and other adults. It is more important for a child to learn to be reliable and have trustworthy integrity than to learn to subsume disappointments philosophically and unemotionally.

As adults, therefore, we should never promise or agree to do something for or with a child if we are not going to do it and be on time. Even when they are not anxiously looking forward to something, it is terrible to keep children waiting. We should simply not get involved if we are not going to follow through with our promises and agreements ... and on time!

As children get older we can be honest and say, "Well now, I didn't think before I said that, and there are circumstances I didn't foresee, so we may have to change the time or change the situation." But when they are young, children don't have that concept of an all-powerful adult not doing what they say they will do, or when they say they will do it. Children are inherently trusting until we prove to them that they should not be. It would be much more useful and helpful for the mature, even education and growth of a child if they could trust their parents, and if the way they learned that *all* people weren't trustworthy was by observing situations involving others—other children's lives and other children's friends, or with adults less intimate than Mom and Dad. That way the child would be essentially innocent—that is, trusting but not naive, and clear about the nature of human beings in general. But, they would not feel the need, or the unconscious demand, to be untrustworthy themselves as a way to survive amongst other untrustworthy adults. "A lie for a lie" (or hypocrisy for hypocrisy) is not a mature model to live by.

HONESTY WITH OURSELVES

Nobody I know is such a saint that they are never annoyed or angered in relation to their children once in a while. When a child gets on our nerves, if our mind is immature and unmanageable, we are going to think, maybe seriously, of punching them or screaming at them. People do get violent thoughts—everybody does sometimes, and there is nothing wrong with that.

But, if we walk around all the time saying in an airy voice, "My children are so sweet. I love them, they *never* bother me," and inside we are boiling with suppressed rage, that is not healthy for them and very unhealthy for us. Sometimes children *are* difficult, at times very trying. If we admit that when they are (both to ourselves, and at times and in the proper way to them), then it doesn't mean we don't love them, just that sometimes they are more intense than we can stay calm with. The most wonderful, beautiful, loving, perfect children fuss and try our patience sometimes.

Children need constant attention ... and they make noise ... and everything else. In fact, they *demand* constant attention, besides needing it. They don't know about *our* rules and *our* tolerance levels. So if we admit that they are getting to us, i.e., disturbing our usual peace of mind, but recognize that it has nothing to do with our loving them, but only has to do with our lack of patience, then we will not have a problem with it. It will come and it will go. That's all. And we won't get caught in thoughts like, "What a monster I am. I am a terrible person because I hate my child." No. When we tell the truth to ourselves about how our children are getting to us, we are simply willing to be responsible for our own self-centered mind games, and a lot of people aren't. You can see that some people really get bent out of shape over their kids, and yet they refuse to admit it, blaming everything on the child and taking no personal responsibility whatsoever for their own role in it.

It is much better to admit our impatience or frustration, but we don't need to tell the child about it unless we can do so in a loving, non-threatening way, because they will not understand. If we say, "I want to hit you right now," that would be quite out of line; but if we say, "I'm angry now because I don't think you should have torn the cover off my new book," that is non-threatening, but makes its point.

If we are *really* angry with a child we should never say, "I'm not angry with you." Say, "I'm really angry right now, and I love you anyway, but I don't want you to throw your milk on the floor again."

When I took the est course, the trainer covered the subject of children in about two minutes.[1] He said, "We're going to cover children," and everybody who had children sat up full of eager anticipation. Then he said, "You have to admit that children are a royal pain in the ass sometimes. Really."

A lot of people in that course—people who tried to love their children always, no matter what the circumstance; who tried to never get angry with them, and never be annoyed with them—recoiled and rebelled. They said things like, "That's Werner's solution to parenting? Two minutes? 'Sometimes children are really a pain in the ass. Really.' Just a pain in the ass? Nothing else? What about the joy, the beauty, the tenderness?" Well, we aren't in denial about joy, beauty and tenderness. We are only in denial about what we don't want to see, not about what we love to see. And nothing in life is totally one-sided. Nothing is *always* or *never* except this: life is *never* one-sided. Life *always* has two sides: pain and pleasure, ugliness and beauty, joy and sorrow.

If we could admit that there are times, as infrequent as they may be, when we do run out of patience, then the times when our children aren't doing something that upsets us (which is the overwhelming majority of the time), we can give them everything we have to give them, freely and without any restraint or tentativeness. If during the times when they are "a pain in the ass" we are obsessed with trying to pretend that everything is okay, and that we are perfectly serene and undisturbed (because they are our flesh and blood, after all), we will close ourselves off from them. We *make* the relationship false in those moments; and if it is false in those moments, it is false in other moments in which we try to make it "real" in other ways. We close ourselves off to our children because we equate annoying frustration with a lack of love on our part. And because we are so threatened to feel that we might not love our own children, we fail to find the clarity to make the necessary distinctions, which are: we *always* love them no matter what, *and* sometimes we lose patience with them and get angry or upset.

That is one reason there is so much child abuse. People "try to love" their children all the time, no matter what. When they can't live up to that, their own deep crises of self-hatred for imagining they don't love their children produce explosive violence, which then strikes out at the closest object, usually at the children themselves, since the children, in a twisted logic, actually cause the crisis of self-hatred. Such adults try to blame what (or in this case who) they think is the cause of their failure. Of course, this is a very simplistic explanation, and only one of the multitude of causes for child abuse—but one to consider in any case.

* * *

The need to pay attention to literally every element of our relationship to the child is an incredible practice, intention-wise. To provide for children the appropriate language, the appropriate emotional environment, the appropriate broad and deep range of stimuli are all responsibilities which will be of profound benefit during the child's growth into mature, happy and healthy adulthood.

9

EDUCATION FOR LIFE

LIFE IN CONTINUUM

[*Editor's note*: The term "continuum" is used in the sense that it was presented by Jean Liedloff in her groundbreaking book, *The Continuum Concept* (NY: Penguin, 1975), based on her life among the Yequana Indians of South America. One of the primary tenets of Liedloff's thesis is that children who are nursed on demand and allowed to remain "in-arms" with close bodily contact with parents and others until such time as they are ready to set off on their own to explore their environment, naturally receive the kinds of attention and establish the energetic bonding that assures their present joy and comfort, and their on-going healthy development. In the section that follows, Lee relies upon these principles to discuss the values of and practical means for integrating children into "life as it is" within the culture into which they are born, and as a means of enhancing their self-confidence and independence by encouraging their basic goodness and trust of their own instincts for safety and survival.]

A part of the key to making the "continuum concept" principles workable in our own lives is a thorough integration of children as full-fledged members of the culture. This can begin even before birth. As soon as a woman knows she is pregnant, she can begin to help this other full-fledged member of the culture to be integrated to varying degrees. Even in the womb the child is being integrated by the celebration of the joy of awaiting birth. There are a lot of details to this, but what I am expressing is the primary mood.

The principles in *The Continuum Concept* resonate instinctually to a sense of rightness and of innate justice, and they make a lot of sense as well, even though these childraising principles happen within a context that is very far from the context that we tend to live in. I haven't seen that these principles have been perfectly applied in even the best of situations in the West. Nonetheless, the most sincere and dedicated parents will definitely use these principles to the extraordinary advantage of their children, themselves, and all of society. We just need to intelligently make the necessary transpositions of these principles to our own culture.

Before a child is walking, it is quite healthy for him or her to witness all the things we ordinarily do in the course of our daily lives—that's the way they learn. It is healthy for the young child to have a parent carry and maintain body contact with them, while otherwise continuing to live without interruption. In native communities, this is much easier and more natural to do than it is in our modern technological, fast-paced Western civilization. In these native cultures a child's coming into the world is respected as a miraculous event—he or she is fully wanted and loved, tacitly and unquestioningly from the beginning. Therefore, "paying attention to the child," as we have discussed in a previous chapter and throughout this book, literally need not be considered, because it is already ingrained in the culture. Within these societies there is much more of a distinct community of women and children, and much more support for such bonded relationships. These cultures naturally have the orientation that the parent continue to live a normal and productive life, and that children need not interrupt that, except in organic and necessary ways—to be nursed, to be bathed, to play, etc. Children are then a witness to life in its natural pace and variety.

In alignment with these principles, during the "in-arms" stage—up until a child is two or three years old, depending on the child—our recommendation is to keep the child on one's body. (Body slings, Guatemalan slings, are really nice for this purpose, as long as the child is comfortable there.) Of course, when the child initiates movement out into the world of their environment, which is a natural developmental process, we allow them to explore as they will.

During this stage, parents should just go about their lives and do what they ordinarily do—write, work and whatever—while the child is just an observer to that. (Rather than carrying the baby on one's back, I always prefer front-of-the-body carriers or side carriers so that the child can be a witness to our lives and maintain eye contact with us if they wish.) Yet, as children get older, of course, they will assert themselves more in terms of polarizing the relationship to what *they* want to do, over and against what the adult wants to do. Then it's a matter not so much of having the adults compromise their lives, but of making adjustments to include the child's growing independence and need for different stimuli—i.e., more child-centered stimuli.

* * *

261

Whenever children can help in our ongoing daily environment, I think it is phenomenal. The more encouragement they get, the better. As soon as they can toddle they can certainly carry one piece of wet clothing out to the clothesline, or one dish to the sink. Children really love to help Mommy and Daddy. If we let them—give them freedom to learn without hovering over them and guiding every move with our dominance—they will continue to want to help. The little girls help cook and clean and do what women do, and take care of the smaller children, which they see adult women predominantly doing. And the little boys, at four or five, begin being integrated into the men's culture. They go out to the garage, they saw a piece of wood, they clean the car engine, and once in a while they help fix the sink. That's the way they learn, and then they grow up involved in a culture. In a healthy culture, of course, boys learn to cook, sew and be with smaller children, and girls learn how to use tools, etc., but there also seem to be certain areas of work that traditionally fall towards one or the other gender.

Much of what is described in *The Continuum Concept* is a really complete integration of children, not as dependents of adults, but as full and useful members of the culture. In a lot of cases in Western society, people who deal with children often view them as dependents, as if they have to take care of them until the children can hold up their part of the deal. And that actually interferes with them holding up their part of the deal. For example, if we don't give a three-year-old credit for who they are, and basically treat them like a six-month-old, they don't hold the responsibility in the family team that they could. If children are treated as dependents they will work with that dynamic subconsciously, and do what is expected of them, which in this case would be to be helpless and incompetent.

Joseph Chilton Pearce [author of *Magical Child* (N.Y.: E.P. Dutton, 1977), and other masterful books about child development] has a theory that *everything children do* is their work. Even when a child is playing with blocks and knocking them down, that is their work—in the sense of livelihood, the way an adult would do a salaried job as work, or fixing up the house as work. And children take their work very seriously. Taking the shoes out of the shoe rack and putting them somewhere else, one at a time, is very, very serious work—to them, it is not a game. We may say, "Oh, how cute," or we may get annoyed and tell them to stop, or put all the shoes back immediately, but to them this is their work, and they are very intent upon it, and we should acknowledge that. We should recognize that they are doing a good job even though we may have to take all the shoes and put them back and in order ourselves. Of course, with only a minimal amount of positive feedback and encouragement, they will put the shoes back themselves, because they too like completion.

* * *

I think aptitudes show up when children are very young. Almost from the time they are mobile they will indicate particular leanings toward different things. For instance, lots of children would like to cook, but adults need to realize that a child's liking to cook because it is *fun* is different from their being able to help in the kitchen to an adult's complete satisfaction, or with a skill level comparable for their age to an adult's. For a young child learning to cook, we have to make some leeway for some stuff getting on the floor. So, every carrot won't be exactly the way we want it, that's fine, and we will have to sweep up lots of flour and sugar! I would not expect a child to be able to keep his mind on chopping vegetables for hours. Basically, however, he should be able to listen to the adult, serve the adult, and participate for awhile—chopping, stirring, spicing, and making patties or shaping cookies. Any child who really shows an aptitude for cooking should be fully encouraged to be in the kitchen helping. On the other hand, if a child really doesn't want to help, and is going to be mischievous or stubbornly resistant, sabotaging the work effort, then to me it is not worth trying to force them to help. In that event the environment becomes centered on their battle with the adult.

Instead, I suggest that you let them play what *they* want to play, while you do what you need to do later, or as they play next to you or close to you. Unless you can't do what you need to do later, and then they need to understand that everybody has responsiblities and theirs is to play, but when they're with you, and you've got to get something done, their responsibility is to hang out with you until you get it done. The more easeful they make it for you to get done, the sooner you'll be able to play with them. Most children are quite easily brought into agreement with a little creativity on the part of the adult. But threats are not creative, by the way!

If an adult is cooking, and they are very particular and want things done a certain way, if their tension about how it is getting done is too great, I would not have a child help them cook, because the tension is less productive for the child than their gaining confidence by helping to cook.

* * *

There is a big debate among childraising experts: "Do you *make* children work or not?" Do you *make* them clean the table, do you *make* them shovel the snow, do you *make* them cut the grass and take a share in the other responsibilities or not? "You live here, you've got to share in the responsibilities!" I really don't know the answer, but I'm not into dragging the children around to get the wash done, or "chaining" them to the sink until the dishes are done. We need to be creative, of course, but being heavy-handed is often counterproductive.

The ideal is to have child-centered environments, in which fitting the children into our lives isn't unrealistic; environments in which play is available for the children while we do our necessary work. When the child can participate they should, but when they can't, then the child-centered environment would allow the children to be related to from a position of health, acknowledgment and love. Such environments would be based on clear definitions of what is play and what is not play, what is education and what is not education, what is sane and healthy and what is not. That's the way childraising should and can easily work.

I tend to think that if adults work hard and are responsible, and bring integrity to their lives, that even if a child is not made to work around the house and share the responsibilities, that child *will* work hard and bring integrity to his or her life. I don't think you can take a twelve-year-old, and have them, or you, be satisfied with the efforts.

Years ago we visited a Hare Krishna temple in West Virginia, and there were a bunch of children, including a thirteen-year-old, being required to do a heavy workload. One of the senior (Hare Krishna) students was having this heavy-duty fight with the teenager, and really overpowering the young man (or trying to). This boy was like any average thirteen-year-old, already formed with certain habits. He had come to the Hare Krishna's at ten or eleven with his parents, and he just didn't want to do this kind of work, because he hadn't before. But in that Hare Krishna system you work! You work or you chant, and for maybe an hour or two a day you go out in the fields and play. This young man didn't want to do that. He wanted to go on hikes and do what thirteen-year-olds get to do in the country in West Virginia, so he was always fighting with the swamis, going out and not doing his job. Whether the Hare Krishna's have a healthy culture is not the point. The point is about allowing role-modeling to be the dominant teaching, over and against heavy-handed adult judgmentalism, rhetoric or demands.

It's the same in any culture. To raise children, we have to raise them as part of the culture in order for them to do what the adults do. And we have a hard time doing that in our society at large. We are quite divorced, generally speaking, from a thoroughly integrated adult-child system. Adults in our technologically-advanced society are quite polarized from the youth. To be involved with children requires a tremendous amount of time, energy, patience and participation in their lives and interests. It's a team effort. We can't just plop a child in front of a TV, or leave them with baby-sitters all the time, and expect them not to be alienated in many ways from adults and adult culture.

Generally speaking, the first major stage of life is from ages one to seven. There are many minor stages within this period, but this first major period involves the development of the motor-center coordination, movement, the body, and feelings. The second major stage of life is from ages seven to fourteen or so. Again, there are many minor stages within this, but this major stage has to do with the emotional development and maturity of the child, a deeper relationship to others, the outside world, and relationships to everyone and everything. In every culture, twelve to fourteen years is the age of manhood or womanhood in which the young people go through rites of initiation into adulthood. Confirmation in the Christian church and Bar Mitzvah and Bas Mitzvah in the Jewish faith are all examples of rites of passage. Following this is the third major stage which encompasses the development of intellect, ideas, logic, all the thinking and analytic faculties.

By the time our children reach ages twelve to fourteen, we should not have to act in a jailor-like fashion, controlling, bossing and hovering over them. Of course we shouldn't ever act like a jailor, but some adults equate parenthood with control and a heavy-handed management style. Children should be mature enough to generally take care of themselves, to work in a responsible way with adults, understanding certain limitations of course, which is the limitation of not having grown through the third stage of life yet. But, they should be essentially mature in the first two stages. So, we need to educate and help children as they grow to become more and more integrated into the adult social culture, and to be a responsible part of that culture.

Therefore, the more we practice working, playing and really living fully *with* our children—the more we do and create *with* them—the more the children will get deeply integrated and be happy, dedicated and naturally committed. They will participate when they are ready; they will *want* to participate, actually enjoy doing it. But if we complain about our work and our lack of time and energy, they will never want to help. Why would they? Our children will get the messages we send out.

Right childraising resonates within us organically; we have an instinctual sense of what works and what doesn't work, and we should be able to weave in what works from the continuum concept ideas into the way we need to live our lives. Really, there are not any problems unless we make them ourselves.

EXPECTATIONS

Jean Liedloff describes the basic nature of expectations:

Expectation is founded deeply in man as his very design. His lungs not only have, but can be said to be an expectation of air, his eyes an expectation of light rays, his ears an expectation of vibrations caused by the events most likely to concern him, including the voices of other people and his own voice.[1]

Expectation, then, is the context in which our bodies are functioning. Perhaps we could also call this instinct.

In childraising, it does help tremendously to have an idea of what is "expected" so we know what we are aiming for (instead of having thirty adults in a community wandering around wondering who the children are and what they are doing here, and what the adults' responsibilities are, and all that). It is extremely important to have as clear a definition as possible of psychological and spiritual health and maturity, and of the various stages that a growing child will naturally pass through developmentally.

We, as adults, need to treat one another with grace and elegance so that the children will treat each other (and adults as well) with grace and elegance. I definitely want to emphasize that unless we apply this consideration in relationship to one another, children are not going to get it. They will know intuitively or instinctively the rightness of such behavior, but will surrender to the demands of their adult role models. And, the way we behave *is* a demand for all others to behave exactly that way. We can't force other adults to behave exactly as we do, but we have a much greater power, even if we don't know it and don't exercise it dictatorially, over children.

Children respond to the expectations of the adults around them. Jean Liedloff used the example of how the Yequana Indians let their children crawl around freely, yet they didn't crawl into the fire or fall into the river because they were expected to be able to take care of themselves in basic ways. The children were even allowed to play with razor sharp knives, and they didn't cut themselves, because they were expected to know how to handle such utensils, and they did.

Unlike the Yequana, most of us are trained to feel how many things are dangerous to our children instead of utile. To offset this tendency, we recommend, as a guideline for stepping in to protect children, that if a situation is not life-threatening or dangerous, parents and caregivers should not step in too quickly. Let children cut cucumbers or bananas for their cereal ... and in their own way, at their own skill level, from their own perspective. Let them help and let them feel the pride of helping out. So what if every slice of banana is different? It still tastes the same. On the other hand, I tend not to give children small things to play with that might be sharp or dangerous, or too easy to swallow; at least not until they get to the point where they are eating solid food well and efficiently, and can work their tongue skillfully so they can keep from swallowing things. We need to judge each circumstance on a very practical level—if the child swallows a small glass bead, nothing happens; it just goes through. A paper clip with sharp edges or a tack might be very different though.

If children are playing with other children and they start to whack one another around, we so want to protect our children and maintain their innocence that the tendency is to be much more protective than is necessary in actuality. We don't want them—or even their feelings—to get hurt. But that kind of interference isn't usually necessary. It's amazing how well children work things out amongst themselves if they are respected and acknowledged in their ability to do that. Just don't let them hurt another child—swinging a T-shirt at another child is very different from swinging a heavy metal toy train.

If an adult who is responsible for the care and safety of a child is confident and reliable in their physical care of the child, and confident in their own pragmatic common sense, then if something happens that is purely accidental—a little accident, nothing serious, with maybe some tears and a little blood—it won't make any difference to the child, because they understand that the adult is responsible, and they absorb that. They may cry from the surprise of an unexpected fall but they will still feel safe.

So, what is "getting hurt" anyway? Is a broken arm getting hurt? It could be that the worst kind of getting hurt is being taught prejudice, bigotry, cruelty and selfishness, not a broken bone or scratches. Those things heal quickly and don't leave deep scars. Getting hurt is walking through the rest of one's life polarized against others of a different religion, race or political belief. Those things don't heal easily and not only leave scars on the one wielding them, but on those at the effect of such small-mindedness. Teaching a child fear, paranoia and violence is the real hurt.

In our relationship with other people's children, where safety is concerned, we need to maintain our own integrity, instead of being worried about what their mothers would say. We should not be insensitive to the wishes and lifestyle ingredients of the child's family, but it is important to be responsible to and for the children in our care even if their parents might do things somewhat differently. For many of us parents, one of the biggest problems is dealing with other people's displeasure with the way we are doing things. I am talking here about the displeasure of our close friends, not just that of our family, grandparents and so forth, because we may not see these relatives that often. Whereas it is amazing how critical close friends can become when something touches a vital sore spot for them—a spot that is usually never touched. How one raises one's children, if it is different from how other people believe it should be, is a "big one" for these others to be gentle and accepting about.

* * *

Having expectations of such things as health, intelligence and skill development for children is the same as understanding that they *can* do whatever it is that we are expecting of them. In our minds, a lot of us associate their saying no with the idea that they can't do something. We need to hold the expectation that they can do it. Clearly, we need to hold that expectation when they are young. In their own time and place *they will do it,* if we hold the expectation that they can. A lot of us, when a child says no, think in terms of, "Oh, they're incapable," or we assume that they really don't want to do something. Sometimes, of course, that is exactly the case, but often it is completely subjective. Often what they mean is that they won't do it the way we want it done, but they would *love* to do it a different way. Their responses vary depending on who it is they are interacting with, and how the adult handles the relationship.

Overall, then, the context of our expectations is the important thing. Coming up with specifics is not the point. All the specifics are circumstantial, and bypass the issue. To deal with specifics is not addressing context, but content, and then we would need to take every twenty-four-hour period and make a schedule for it, and that is just unrealistic and impractical besides.

* * *

Generally, if a child is given the appropriate kind of attention early on in life—loving, gentle, supportive—they will be quite self-confident and feel good about themselves. Then, when they get to be four, five, six and older, they won't always be pulling insecurely on the adults in their lives for attention. These children will have their own integrity. Whereas if they don't get this attention that they need so badly for healthy growth, if they are neglected early on, they will just be pulling relentlessly (and the mother gets most of it, even when a father is integral in childraising).

Based on observation and direct experience, it is my opinion that the more one is able to practice these principles we have been discussing in this book, the more a child has self-confidence and positive self-acknowledgment. Then they don't have to always be guarded or monitored by either of their parents. Children raised in alignment with these basic continuum principles are very independent—sure of themselves and willing to experiment and explore, not to mention competent and reliable.

THE CONTEXT OF EDUCATION

Someone asked me once how many generations it would take to create a conscious culture that would last ... that would be maintained over a long period of time, maybe even centuries. We got into a discussion of education and what kind of education is necessary, i.e., do we educate children about ideas or philosophy or only about practical things? What kind of educational system do we design?

I keep referring back to Idries Shah's book *Learning How to Learn*,[2] because the greatest gift, if we can learn how to give it to a child, is to teach children discrimination in relationship to the process of learning itself, over and against volumes of mere facts. If a child can be taught how to learn, and then if data is provided over that contextual foundation, it will be very obvious to these children which data is useful and which is not. If they have a sense of discrimination, they can select the most optimum information for any given situation.

Little children always want to do more than they can do—their minds are way ahead of their bodies. Some of us have probably seen our own children or other children when they get to a point where they want to read, desperately, but they can't yet. This intense desire is the greatest aid to their learning what it is they want to be able to do. Almost every child I have ever seen wants to do mechanical or practical things with their hands that are far beyond them. But, they learn by trying, or by doing, even if the initial attempts can be frustrating. For that reason we need to give children plenty of opportunity to experiment and to even to try things that we may feel are a bit beyond them. However, we can use some common sense discretion in this. To allow a three-year-old to help slice bananas may produce uneven mushy banana pieces, but they will learn quickly to be efficient; to allow a three-year-old to try to take a watch apart and put it together again is so far beyond their comprehension and mechanical skill level that the inevitable frustration would be counterproductive, rather than useful as a goad towards learning the skill. Encouraging results spur them on, but total inability often turns them completely off to the learning task.

Children don't have to be paying attention to learn, whether at home or in school. Even with left-brained subjects such as math and grammar, a child can absorb much just by being in the learning environment. They may appear not to be engaging the material at all, and yet they learn. I've found this even with young children, with doing things in play with them. For instance, when they were bouncing off the walls, running and yelling while I was trying to tell a story, it would seem like they were completely ignoring it, were not hearing a word and wanted to be doing something else. Yet, as soon as we went outside to do something else, they would be telling the story word for word to each other and back to me. They had absorbed every bit of it, but in a completely non-linear way.

If we make things available, like classical music for example, even if children are not directly paying attention, even if they are saying, "I hate this," they are probably absorbing much more than we imagine. A child's unconscious or peripheral attention has amazing perceptive and retentive qualities. So we don't need to dominate or control their attention in all the direct ways that are so linearly important to adults. We can let them play and daydream, while we continue to demonstrate what we would like them to learn. They will absorb this input in their own way, and when they are ready to use it, they will. A lot of the work of education is to make lots of data available for their absorption. They are like dry sponges in a dish of water. They just soak up learning. It's their nature, after all. Along this line, let me emphasize that for anybody teaching children, even one hour a week, for anybody who has children, for anybody who ever wants children, and for anybody who ever expects to have anything to do with children at any level, reading certain basic level books by John Holt (*Why Children Fail, Escape From Childhood* and *How Children Learn*), and those of Joseph Chilton Pearce (*The Magical Child, The Magical Child Returns*) are as primary for being with children as any study material one might use to keep sharp in one's chosen profession or area of experience. (See recommended Reading.) For anyone to be in a schoolroom attempting to raise children consciously without studying John Holt as a foundation, would be akin to flying with no wings.

Unfortunately, everything in the general school systems these days is materialistically oriented. All of the educational processes are designed towards establishing success in material terms. After all, what is success for? To travel, to have a good home, to pay the heating bills, to have a car—all material "values." None of it is for the essential satisfaction of the emotions or the mind, or the deep feelings that are possible for us as human beings. So, except in very rare instances, we are not trained in aesthetic appreciation, nor in the use of our capacities for refined creative expression.

The feeling dimension is the first dimension that develops within the child. In school, in the early grades especially, the feeling dimension is where the learning and the teaching must happen to establish a foundation or basis for successful future learning. However, most teaching is done these days through mindless talk, through language and thought. While it is true that the whole field of thought and language must be developed so that children don't remain isolated in their feeling-body alone, still a balance and a perspective are necessary. When children who are only taught intellectually get older and more mature, then the judgments that they made in their earlier education will not be empowered, because they were intellectual decisions not feeling decisions. So, it's a matter of connecting their bodies with their education in the early period of development.

My idea of education for children is that the primary concern be for their health— emotionally, physically and perhaps spiritually—and that academics are entirely secondary. Academics are not irrelevant, they have their necessary time and place; but academics taught on a foundation of neurosis or psychopathology do not and cannot bear the same fruits as academics on a base of a happy, innocent and open-minded relationship to life. Teachers formally trained in purely academic subjects with no education themselves in the inner life, so to speak, often over-emphasize the teaching of facts and figures to the detriment of the real life needs of the children they are trying to communicate with and to. One of a good teacher's functions is to provide a contextual basis and guidelines of principles for education, so that the academics (the 3-R's) have a fertile field in which to grow. But that is a real point of frustration, because there are so few teachers trained in both arenas.

The gift of teaching academics, to me, is either natural or requires much training. Even so, not everyone has that particular skill. A lot of us can have great intention, yet just not know what to do. But teaching the foundation of healthy attitude, emotions and psyche comes naturally to anyone who lives in that foundation themselves. Conscious parents make a teacher's job infinitely easier.

* * *

I feel tremendous trepidation, sometimes, when adults who are uneducated in conscious childraising make decisions and rules about how to better teach their children. The problem is not needing more or better rules, the problem is adults who do not know what it is to be nine years old, thirteen years old, twelve years old, four years old.

If we *felt into* who children are, at any given age—their values, their worldview, their likes and dislikes—instead of who we think they *should be* as adults, the situation would be entirely different. Without a relationship to children's needs and states of mind, there is no way to effectively teach them. Let me repeat, that without a relationship to them (relationship in these terms being "understanding where they are at"), to expect them to follow our lead, even if the lead is very gentle and very just, is asking more than is reasonable. It is not that they won't do it, it's that they can't.

If children have some sense that we understand them, they may argue or disagree at times, but they will get our point of view and usually respect the boundaries we set for them, because the boundaries will make sense. If we do not understand their point of view, we are only making academic and empty rules—righteously defining protocol in every single space, and then muscularly or willfully enforcing it. That doesn't work except to make them obedient but dissatisfied, and often resentful and rebellious.

Children and their wants, needs and enthusiasm are not the problem. As adults, we need to be able to feel into their viewpoint in order to understand how best to define limits and such. For example, when a thirteen-year-old breaks up with her first boyfriend, to us it may not be a problem. We may even be quite relieved. We've had love affairs, and to us it's like, "You'll get over it. You're young. You'll have plenty more chances." We have perspective, but they don't. To them, breaking up is a *very* big deal. To them, their entire social life for the next six years depends upon this situation. If we can't feel into their position, we will fail them in being sympathetic and in dealing with their emotions satisfactorily. If a child needs something, we may not drop everything we are doing and run to them, but if we can't feel into their viewpoint we would be unlikely to handle their needs in a way that worked for both ourselves and them, and they are likely to become increasingly frustrated.

Have you ever gone out to a wedding or a funeral and seen a five-year-old boy in a suit and tie and a little hat, all dressed up like an adult ... and worse, being expected to *act* like an up-tight forty-year-old, while Mommy looks at him like, "Isn't that the cutest thing you've ever seen! He is *soooo* darling." I always want to take off his suit and rip the tie off and give him some torn sweat pants or something. Parents like that always say, "That's my little man." Talk about not feeling into the child's viewpoint! It's very unfair to expect children to be little adults, or anything else that they aren't, for that matter.

A certain formal training may be valuable for learning about social behavior—about elegance, protocol, the whole social, human politic. We do need a basic definition, a basic outline to build from. It's the same dynamic as reading an astrology chart or using tarot cards—the cards or the chart give a certain basic definition within which the freedom to perceive various information is present, but the actual imagery of the chart also triggers something. The same is true of formal training. To have a gentle and flexible, but formal, training about saying "Thank you" and "Please" and "You're welcome," and other minimum basics is a good place to start. To eat with a fork and not stuff food in our mouths, and slop all over our clothes, speaking and spitting while we speak, is a basic foundation for table manners.

I think there is a value to some definition of elegance in relationship to both formality and intimacy, and one principal (one of the areas of the essence of elegance) has to do with the respect that we show one another in various circumstances. Again, I think that respect is nothing that can be trained by force or demand, even though I imagine that in all forms of personal training and formal education about elegance, such respect would be a specific ingredient discussed. Those trainings would try to teach an essential respect, free of all those sorts of psychological subjectivities. Basically, however, that has to come through a kind of organic communication—a feeling sense of others, and of environments and spaces.

The way we should grow up treating tools, for instance, is that working with a hammer means putting it away in the proper place, in the condition we took it out in. Not, "First we learn to use the hammer functionally, and then there is also cleaning up." Rather, that using tools and taking care of them are one and the same thing, not separate. So it becomes automatic to put the tools away. There should be no distinction between using the tools and taking care of them. It is all part of the deal. That is the context of tools.

Well, every aspect of functional life—dressing, washing, cooking, studying, even playing—has its similar essential pattern or context. The appropriate way of being is, itself, part and parcel of living a human life.

With older children it is hard to show them this context, because we may have to start after they have already been trained a certain way, and they most likely are crystallized in that training. For the younger ones, however, growing up into that mood of resonance to the essence or overall quality of everything is much easier, as long as the primary adults in their lives model such understanding and function.

Cooking means caring for the pots, the pans, the stove. It means remembering to turn off the stove, and remembering not to set the flame too high that it burns the pot, not to let the oatmeal boil over so it gets all over the stove and somebody else has to clean it up, or not letting the egg you want soft-boiled boil too long. Cooking means a certain relationship to the equipment in the kitchen, and to the preparation and care of the food. Gymnastics means a certain relationship to the equipment in the gym, and to one's muscles, and to safety in that arena. And so on.

As children grow up learning to work in the kitchen, for instance, the context of cooking should include that food is a vital, living substance, and that how one cooks affects the cooked food at least as much as one's technical knowledge. The whole dynamic of the sanctity of food, and the combination of cooking substances, and the color, and how the food looks when it's put out on the plate—literally, all that is part of the context that can be passed on by conscious adults, part of the collective data that having an elegant relationship to food is. When children work in a kitchen helping to cook, all of that should be taken into consideration. And these considerations should be continued into the serving, eating and cleaning up of the meal. Otherwise they will most likely learn to gobble everything on the plate with no distinction, barely slowing down enough to taste anything, spitting all over the table, jumping up the second they are done and running off, hardly giving their bodies a chance to begin to digest.

If we just chop up carrots randomly in all different sizes, that is very different than if we dice the food with intention and attention. And that is the feeling children have to get for all things—so that all things are unitive and important to them.

We can begin doing this when the child is an infant, so the younger ones learn; with the older ones, those already stuck in habit patterns, we just do the best we can. We have to find a middle path—to experiment a little and find something that works. That is the attitude that everyone being a parent should have. Then we can be gentle and easeful with our children instead of zealous reformers, inflamed by a mission to right all wrongs, which is an approach of great violence, and usually full of hypocrisy and abuse.

If children learn to relate to everything with a full and thorough approach, they will grow up intellectually diverse, broadly-based, relaxed about life, elegant and well-cultured. One reason we all forget to do things, to complete things—the reason we forget to turn lights out when we leave a room, for example—is because we don't equate "living someplace" with "the totality" that living anywhere encompasses. We don't equate it with the electric bill, the water bill, the thought that when the sink overflows it creates a leak when it seeps through the floor. We don't consider where we live and how we live to be the unitive elements of Life itself. That is a very crucial part of education for children—for them to see things not in pieces, but from the holistic viewpoint. If we would learn to recognize that principle in all areas, children would get it from us.

If we had grown up that way, and that was the way we approached life, think what that would mean in relationship, including in sex. It would totally open a relationship; completely expand our life's experience.

KEEPING THE BIG PICTURE

When two young children are friends, or love one another, they can get into furious disagreements, yelling at one another, "I'm *never* going to play with you again." Yet in ten minutes (or even less) they are playing happily together. In their innocence they don't hold grudges; they have not distanced themselves from their instinctual or essential knowledge, so it is the underlying pattern, the love or friendship between them, that is always predominant. Adults, on the other hand, don't function this way, obviously. Adults are more likely to get involved in the content of things, rather than to hold the context, commonly identifying with less primal realities of their consciousness. In marriages, for instance, it is not uncommon for the entire structure to be weakened because one person, insecure and tentative about the other person's basic underlying and pervasive love for them, will constantly react to every little sign of displeasure, discomfort or annoyance in their partner, as if each of those events indicated a lack of love or a disturbance in the love of their partner, rather than simply being an inevitable little ripple of life, which in effect meant nothing about the deeper reality. Enough of that petty reactivity can actually chip away at the love the other person feels, and may eventually bring about the end of the relationship.

We are always reacting vitally to things that are temporary, i.e., to superficial things, because we aren't trained to see broader patterns and to see the deep principles of existence. If we were trained in such observations and distinctions as children, we would not suffer such sad fates as adults. People *do* have underlying cycles in their behavior, as well as more immediate mood swings, and we tend to be much more reactive to the content, the surface details of someone's mood, than to the dynamic of internal movement. When somebody is in a bad mood, the reality is that it will pass. We need to keep mindful of what the principle of our relationship with that person is.

In childraising, in all areas, it would serve for those educating children to develop the ability to communicate to them how to see universal patterns in life—how to get an overview of things—instead of being completely focused on specific or gross details. If we were all trained to observe the patterns of movement in things, life would be infinitely easier.

SUPPORT CHILDREN'S PASSIONS

How were we supported as children? In other words, when we had a passion, say for piano or drums or trumpet, did our parents ridicule us or say, "I don't want that noise here. Don't bother me, go somewhere else?" Or did they say, "That's a stupid thing to do, you'll never make a living doing that!" Or did our parents encourage and support us in whatever our passions were? Probably not, especially if our passion was a dirty or noisy one. But, one thing we need to understand about raising our children is that *we are not our parents,* even if we may act like them, talk like them and even think like them. We are not our parents! And when we apply conscious-childraising principles diligently and lovingly, our children feel loved despite all of our flaws. None of us will be perfect parents, but our children can still feel loved in a way that some of us didn't when we were young.

Our willingness to support our children's passions should be obvious to them, even if we draw the necessary boundaries based on their ages, skill levels, or other factors. Here are a couple of examples:

One of the girl children loves to ride horses—she's a natural horse person, at ease, no fear, and really loves these animals. For me, horses are big, dumb, stupid animals that basically should feed dogs. (I am definitely *not* a horse person.) But I don't impress my obvious bias on others. So, when she started riding, at three or four years old, we completely encouraged it. We got teachers to teach her how to ride, and every time she wanted to, we went out of our way to support that. We even got a couple of horses.

Many adults with my horse-neurosis would have said, "Horses? You want to ride those big, dumb, stupid things? They should be feeding dogs. Don't you want to do something delicate? Don't you want to paint; don't you want to write; don't you want to meditate?" But we let her do what she wanted, and we thank God she did not want to play bagpipes or drums; but if she did, we would have made that available too.

A teenage boy wanted to play guitar, so he would practice four or five hours a day. When he first started playing he could barely put three notes together that sounded on-key. He just banged away on the thing ... and for hours, every single day. Then he got tired of practicing on an acoustic, so he got a little amp—little in size, but LOUD in tone. And he just cranked the thing up as far as it would go. He got this fuzz pedal, you know, and it sounded like a hurricane in the house. The more noise he could make the better he liked it— and it was so healthy for him! Practicing for all those hours a day he learned it, all by himself. After a while he became, and still is, of course, an excellent guitarist and all-around musician, and he is so nurtured by his music. It is more than worth all the initial "noise."

It is worth it to put up with a lot of noise in order to allow such natural talent not to be crushed, but to blossom and flower. This is a young man's *life* that we are talking about. I'm willing to put up with as much noise as I have to put up with for a young man's life. That is what we do when we want to support some-body's freedom and expansion. Of course there can be reasonable boundaries—such as practicing during the day, rather than at night when everyone else needs to sleep. But, we can keep the boundaries realistic to the passion, not repressive and arbitrary so that we, the adults, can maintain dominance and control. We need not show our children "who the boss is" with heavy-handed authoritarianism, but with gentle guidance, love and common sense help them participate in the family in a way that works for everyone.

* * *

Children should be brought up, from as soon as they can understand, with the idea of seeking out masterful guides. In some way, they should learn the need for expert or mature guidance in their lives, in relationship to anything. If the child, for instance, has innate skills in some form of art, it is very difficult for them to master it without some kind of consistent input from someone who has already mastered that particular art form (even though there are those who have done it). While there are many very fine musicians who can't read music and who have learned to some degree on their own, most have also learned from others (and been willing to learn from others), especially in terms of greater refinement, such as the technologies of the field. We want our children to learn to handle their skills productively, wisely and efficiently, not to have rote behavior drilled into them, like most of us had to memorize some Shakespeare soliloquy or some poetry when we were in school, but to learn whatever they learn sensitively and deeply.

HOME-SCHOOLING—
CHALLENGE AND JOY

It is really an art for a mother or father to school their own children. It is difficult because if a non-related authority figure says, "This math needs to be done by tomorrow," the child does it, but if mother says, "This math needs to be done by tomorrow," the child has this arsenal of little habitual ways of getting out of doing what Mom says. If we are not absolutely clear, home-schooling is asking for non-stop bickering and struggle.

Of course, home-schooling can be a great joy too, if the parent is willing to embrace all the elements of it. We have to be able to make firm boundaries and maintain those boundaries with love and humor, and not lose perspective.

Home-schooling means that the children are fully integrated into what is happening at home—with the people in the household, with whatever is going on in the kitchen, whatever projects are going on, with work like washing, or fixing up the house—all in addition to creative projects around art, music and academics as well. Learning takes place on the child's schedule, more predominantly than the parent's schedule. Some children, for example, don't want to start doing math until eight or nine o'clock at night, or until they are nine or ten years old. In the mornings, they may want to do art, or conversely, at five years old they may have a thirst for math. The willingness to address each of these needs is one of the major differences between private schooling and true home-schooling. So a parent must be quite fluid, flexible in their willingness to schedule various projects ... subjects ... and so forth. A parent must be deeply responsive to a child's natural learning patterns and interests.

With brothers and sisters in a home school, all at different ages, different grade levels, and different levels of emotional and intellectual development, sometimes we may feel like we are not able to give all the children what they need and want. This can be quite a heavy load, and obviously very different from sending the children off every morning and welcoming them home after a day of school, with no involvement at all except to ask, "What did you learn at school today?" and hear, "Nothing." Home-schooling can be difficult, but it also has it's own immense rewards, both for parents and children.

When I was directing the home school, one of the children pretty much refused to do anything in any of the learning centers, in any academics, except for crafts, for two years. I fought bitterly with the situation, because I was so freaked out and so scared for this child's future. Now she is in public junior high school and she's an honor-roll student. There wasn't ever a problem, and her father kept telling me the whole way through, "All I care about is that she goes to school happy, and comes home from school happy. That's all I care about." And that was the case.

That's been one of the greatest lessons in my teaching of children, really, because I was a maniac, and I was sure I was really standing for the integrity of this child. And I was, in one way. I really got to see that everything that was going on in the learning environment had sunk in—

whether there was any active appearance of engagement or not. Every bit of what the other children were learning had gone in. Someone who appeared to be functioning at about a second grade level went into the seventh grade in a public school and had every skill they needed to have, getting all A's from the start. That was really a great thing for me to see. It really changed a lot for me.

—Home-school teacher

If one practices home-schooling I wouldn't simply attempt to take a public school schedule or format and lay it on top of one's own schedule, which for all intents and purposes may look like it is the easiest thing to do. Home-schooling is going to look very different given each of our unique surroundings. There are a lot of parents for whom the public school system is just a childcare situation. They are glad that they don't have to deal with the kids all day. For them, school is like a break, a small daily vacation. This is pretty common, and such a parent is often totally frustrated by any attempts to teach their children anything at home. So home-schooling is a very big job, and not to be considered lightly.

On the other hand, when I look at the parenting that typically happens in the usual unconscious family, I can't imagine the children having any major problems in public school that are any different from the problems at home. But for conscious parents, unconscious public schooling may not be desirable for their children. Of course it would be wonderful to see the building of stronger schools in the public domain both academically and also practically. I'd love to see hands-on programs, cooking, crafts, building, lots of stuff that they only get a small taste of now. At the same time, when a public school program isn't rich, I think the degree to which children feel encouraged, respected and acknowledged, both by teachers in school and at home, is the degree to which they will be willing to go out on their own and get what they want. If school is not providing something, I think that if children feel honored they will be willing to demand, "I want this ... I want books ..." and to do lots of extracurricular research themselves. Of course, that's a very healthy attitude.

CONCLUSION: AN EDUCATION FOR LIFE

Most parents educate their children by passing on the principles that they grew up with, all in the name of "what was good for me is good for my kids." These principles, however, give children such limitations, forcing them to feel and perceive in such a narrow channel that, as adults, they are completely lopsided, which is the common state of affairs today.

As long as we raise our children the same way we were raised, they are going to make the same mistakes we made, even if we try to protect them from making those mistakes. The way out of this loop is by educating them to avoid similar mistakes, rather than by trying to protect them. Educate them in a way that allows them to handle the problems and mistakes that we didn't—mistakes that we may still not be handling. Of course, this is assuming here that our upbringing and childhood environment was not conscious, not ideal, was in some (maybe many) ways abusive, diminishing, manipulative .... We might ask, "How can I educate my children differently if I am still a product of ... still chained by my own abusive upbringing?" If we are totally self-honest about the abuses we suffered— whether physical, sexual, psychic, emotional, psychological—then we have the chance to clearly and consciously demonstrate behavior that does not duplicate this training in our children. If we lie to ourselves, then the probability of treating our children differently than we were treated is minimal at best. We must make a concerted effort to be aware of our parents' failings in our case, and make a willful attempt to be different with our children and other children with whom we have relationships. This is the only way to break the cycle.

Our children are going to have breakdowns now and then. That's a part of life. We can prepare them for it, teach them and *show* them how to handle it when they run into unexpected difficulties and the natural stresses of growing up, finding their way through the minefield of puberty, intimate and business or work relationships and self-discovery.

I think that one of the most valuable things that we could give our children is just the willingness and easefulness to be able to pay attention when it's necessary, and to be able to learn how to learn, and be elegant and sensitive to situations, other people and environments. If they get that, they could succeed any place, with anything, and pick up right away anything they needed to learn.

——— 10 ———

CHILD'S PLAY:
Emotions, Energy Management and Fighting

EMOTIONS

I think this will probably be obvious, but we should try not to make emotionality in a child bad, but be very generous with allowing our children the expression of fear, sorrow, anger, frustration, pride, greed, whatever. These emotions are not wrong. They can be exaggerated, over-indulged and dramatized, but they can also be very natural manifestations of the child's relationship to his or her environment. If a child needs to cry they will cry, and it's very healthy. Why tell them, "You don't need to cry"? Maybe they *do*; how do we know?

Children will exhibit a wide variety of moods, some of them unhappy, and it is important to keep in mind that we can give a child *everything*, but unless he or she comes to the point of deciding to be in a different mood, we cannot do enough. We can be happy ourselves, and they may even know they can be happy, but unless they *decide* to be happy, it won't happen. If we suggest, "You can be happy," they may look back at us and say, "I don't want to be." But, *when* they want to be, they will. If children don't know they can be happy, then perhaps we can help with letting them know, through direct but gentle education and inference, that they have various degrees of control over their moods and states of mind.

A child may not know what they are feeling. In that case, an adult can sometimes objectively feel the emotion that the child is experiencing, but may be having trouble defining or dealing with. If necessary, then, it may serve the child to say, "It seems like you're feeling sad, is that right?" or, "It seems like you're feeling angry. Is that what you're feeling?" rather than saying "You *are* sad ...or angry," or whatever emotion the adult is observing. It is best not to tell a child what emotion we imagine they are having, but to have a dialogue with the child, if it is necessary or useful to speak about it at all.

Actually, there are two different ways of approaching this issue. If a child has gotten into a habit where they are easily triggered into an emotional response, and then become so consumed by it that they can't gain a moment of clarity, some feedback might be useful for them. Sometimes, if the child merely leaves the room, or shifts their attention, immediately they become calmer. Then it might be helpful to ask, "Are you feeling afraid of this ... ?" or, "Are you feeling angry about this ...?" or, "It seems like you're feeling sad about this; is there anything I can do?" They will usually say no, but also they will feel secure and gratified to know we are in tune with them, and are there for them if they want to reach out. However, we should not force them to reach out, either by hounding them intrusively to talk to us, or by grabbing them physically in a violent and overbearing way.

The questioning approach is very different from telling the child, in a really demanding tone of voice,

"You're angry because Katie took the toy, aren't you? I know you are!" Terrifying or extorting a confession out of a child is hardly a loving form of behavior. Basically, we should avoid telling children who they are. If we say something like, "It seems like you're feeling angry. Is there anything I can do?" Well, that gives them the option to say yes or no. And sometimes they say no, and we can reply, "Right, okay." And sometimes they say, "Yeah, I'm mad. Why else would I break three toys? I'm mad." And that's "Right, okay" also.

It is healthy to encourage children to be self-honest. We all know the dimensions of "denial," as it is popularly termed in the therapeutic community these days. The healthier our children are in relationship to being able to own and express their feelings, not dramatize or indulge them in manipulative ways, the healthier adults they will be.

MODELING EQUANIMITY

If a child falls down, unexpectedly surprising themselves, there are two approaches as to how to handle this. There is the "jump 'n grab them approach," moving so quickly that our intensity adds another unexpected surprise and provokes a doubly strong reaction, especially if our burst of energy is coincident with a shrill and fearful tone of voice. (Screeching at a child is a sure way to scare them to tears and exaggerated reaction, even if the words we are saying are simply something like, "Are you hurt?" or "Are you all right?") Or, we can calmly pick them up and perhaps say, "Are you hurt? You look fine to me," or, "Wasn't that a surprise?" Of course if they are really hurt—a bloody and scraped knee or elbow, or whatever—we certainly need to take care of that, but if it's just a slip or a minor scratch, often our response will determine whether the child goes on about their play easefully after a momentary comforting acknowledgment, or whether the whole scene is interrupted with a major upset.

I rely on my own sensitivity and experience, when I see a child fall, to know whether they are hurt or not. Once, as a child, a friend and I were playing—pushing on opposite sides of a door against one another, laughing and having fun. His hand slipped on the wood part and went up and right through the glass—the cut in his arm was probably a quarter of an inch deep. Brutal looking. As kids, we broke glass a lot of times and hadn't been seriously hurt, but the minute his hand went through that glass we both instinctually knew it was serious. The wound didn't start to bleed right away, and we looked at it and I said, "Get home, hurry up," instead of what I would usually do, which was to say, "Oh, it's okay," and keep playing. He ran home and his mother took care of it immediately and everything was fine; it healed up quickly and there was no major damage.

My opinion is that an approach that shows our own equanimity in various situations trains children to be equanimous. An approach that shows wild swings from panic to hysteria will often train children to be unsure and incapable of quick action in a calm and competent manner. So, we should ideally be the examples of equanimity for our children. As a practical example: don't panic or freak out at things like getting a bit messy—you know, as the children are eating and their hands get sticky, and they get food all over everything, including their clothes. We don't have to panic when their handful of strawberry juice goes for our shirt or blouse. I plan ahead if I'm going to take little kids out for ice cream—I wear clothes that can be stained. I don't wear my best pants so that when they have their chocolate ice cream cones I have to be dancing around moving their hand out of the way so they don't drip on me. It is valuable to plan ahead for ordinary things like this.

There are also ways of communicating delight—for instance, when our child shows us some precious toy or some treasure they have found—without wildly exaggerated emotionality. Aren't some of us delighted sometimes without expressing that delight in wild, overblown gestures and manifestations? I would assume that we are. Sometimes, someone else is experiencing some great happiness and we are truly delighted for them, resonant to them, and yet we don't jump up and hug them and kiss them and pound them on the back. We just sit there quietly, being delighted, beaming delight. Generally a nod of assent or a sound of recognition is perfectly adequate.

One way we can show equanimity is when a child says, "Don't forget to do ..." whatever, to just say, "Okay," instead of, "Okay, I won't forget, don't worry, I'll remember! Do I ever forget? You don't need to remind me!" And, we should not yell at them in an overly loud tone of voice. If we get used to communicating with a minimum amount of recognition, but clearly, firmly and confidently, they will trust our communication. Of course we must follow through reliably if their trust is to be sustained.

ABOUT TANTRUMS

"Infantile aggression" is a term that is often used in child behavioral fields to describe behavior that is seen as a problem. Having a baby or young child who screams and does a lot of flailing about is perfectly normal in a situation where the parents are not responsive to the child's needs. Perhaps we should attribute such behavior where it belongs and call the child's behavior "adult aggression." It doesn't mean we should not have a mature response to this behavior, or not do something about it, but it does mean that we do not psychically, emotionally or verbally condemn the child as being bad, or as having something wrong with them, because they are doing these manifestations. They might be screaming, flailing about, biting, pinching, kicking, spitting. (Although, usually, at the age at which children bite, pinch and spit, they are already beyond the age that most people would call "infantile.")

My recommendation with children who throw tantrums is to hold them closely to one's body with as much physical contact as possible. While holding them, continue to speak to them softly and lovingly. Hold them with tenderness but firm restraint. Tell them things like, "I love you very much. Breathe deeply. You can work this out differently." That is particularly important if their tantrum is either dangerous to them or to the environment. If it is not, just let them go with it, as you tell them you are there for them and that they can have your help, affection, hugs ... whatever, whenever they want it. The main thing is not to get angry at them and reject or isolate them for something that has often gotten beyond their ability to manage.

If we are holding the child and talking to them, often that, at some point, will create a small break in the tantrum, enough for them to get a grip on the whole process, to breathe deeply and to begin to relate differently to whatever triggered the tantrum. (Of course, when I say "tantrum" I don't mean simply an angry outburst. I mean a state of such overwhelming immersion that they really can't stem the tide of what is arising in the moment.)

If we have a sense that a tantrum is what the child is doing to try to get our attention, that somehow they have developed a habit of having tantrums and they are not aware of using such high-energy states in that way, we can just say something like, "I love you, and any time you need something from me just ask." A lot of children don't ask for what they want, either because they haven't learned to, or because they just don't know they can, or because they have been taught by an unconscious parent's behavior that it doesn't do any good to ask because the adult won't respond. If we explain to them and demonstrate that they *can* get what they want, they will understand it. (Obviously, I am talking about a parent who really wants what is optimal, developmentally, for their children. If one is just an angry, righteous, abusive parent one wouldn't be reading this anyway, I suppose.)

Sometimes a child throws a tantrum because he or she is frustrated. Often, children learn to cognize a long time before their motor skills have developed to the point of being able to do what they know they want to do. They try and try, but just can't functionally reach their conceptual image. It is understandable that they get so frustrated. If we think that such frustration is the cause of the tantrum, we can say, "It feels to me like you want to do more than your motor skills can manage just now. You're growing up, and you will be able to do it before you know it." Reassure them, and help them seek a creative way to accomplish what they want done. But try not to get in the habit of doing everything for them. Although we could easily do the job with our motor skills, that is not really what they want. They really want to know how to do it themselves.

There are other ways to deal with a tantrum

than saying, out of our own frustration, "Don't throw a tantrum," and expecting them to stop. As I've mentioned, the main thing is the physical aspect: they are on your body and you are talking to them lovingly and tenderly. Keep physical contact with as much constancy as you can. Of course, you need to restrain their arms and legs or they may really hurt you in their blind rage—kicking and clawing and so on. Even if they are pushing you away and screaming, hold them in a way that, for you, is truly comforting them. But, if they do happen to land a good one, don't retaliate or drop them out of your embrace, as meeting unconscious anger with anger of your own just doubles their feelings of helplessness and frustration. After all, their tantrum is not an aggressive act against you. You just happen to be in the way. So, don't blame them for something that has just gotten out of control. And don't hold them with a look on your face that tells them that you are their jailer or their torturer, but with an attitude of caressing them and caring for them.

Normally a child won't throw tantrums unless there is something in their upbringing that has been amiss to begin with, although, generally speaking, anger or sharp or intense reactions to things under ordinary conditions are healthy—just other examples of the vast spectrum of feelings and sensations. A young girl came to our community with her parents when she was two, and she threw unbelievable tantrums very regularly. The way both the men and the women would handle it was to pick her up, hold her and talk to her, and it made a substantial difference. Now she is grown up and is quite an exceptional young woman with a lot of self-control—strong, very self-confident and highly intelligent. She was very wise even at age two (extremely bright and insightful), and I think a lot of what was happening was that she was so aware of the subtle and not-so-subtle abuse and unconsciousness in so many of the adults in her familial environment, that this, coupled with the fact that adults just didn't understand her, drove her "wild."

ENERGY MANAGEMENT

All things have their polar opposites, and children can graphically exhibit almost contradictory behavior at various times—sometimes they have too much *yin* and sometimes too much *yang*.[1]

Once, when we visited a Hindu temple, we drove about three-hundred miles to get there. A pretty long drive. The youngest child didn't nap, so she was awake the whole time in the car. When we got to the temple she started running around in circles, as fast as she could run—bigger and bigger circles; really tearing around. The guy who was showing us the place was very sensitive, and said, "She probably had a long ride, let her get the steam out."

That was exactly what it was. She had been *yin* for six hours and she just had to balance, so she was being *yang* for a bit. She did that for ten minutes, and then she was a little winded, and ready to go get something to eat and to settle in. Sometimes that dynamic is present and it is perfectly appropriate, natural. It is best to recognize such polarities and allow, or even help, a balance to come.

As we move through situations, especially with children, we need to recognize the nature of polarity so that it can help us understand many dynamics that sometimes appear confusing or contradictory if we aren't cognizant of polarity principles.

* * *

When energy is allowed to "go wild" or unchanneled, it will. Children have so much energy—they have a direct channel to the universal generator, so to speak. If they get too cranked up and the energy gets out of control, they often can't wind down on their own. The way they will usually wind down, then, is by crying, fighting or fussing, getting exhausted and finally going to sleep. This can be because they are so excited about something that they just get totally infused, as in a party or a visit to Disneyland or even just a plain old amusement park, or for other reasons.

Our expectation is that children would learn by experience and non-threatening instruction, when unmanaged energy is leading to frustration, tears, a fight with one of the other children, or whatever. Based on our allowing them to learn those lessons for themselves, with gentle help and guidance, and very importantly by their observing how we manage our energy, we expect that they would come to recognize right or optimal energy management as a principle of their lives. This isn't something that can be taught rhetorically, it's a hands-on, experiential process, and also a subject of the hardest intricacy to develop a really effective program with. We have to maintain such a delicate balance between too much control and too little input. And while it's relatively easy for one or two parents to do that with one or two children, it's very difficult in a larger-scale educational situation—one teacher or childcare person with a roomful of children. Certainly children always respond to an authority figure (although not always positively!) who is terrifying or threatening enough, but that is *not* the way to do it.

Energy education can start at the verbal level with the youngest children, explaining the whole dynamic of energy management in a very simple, direct way. We could discuss breathing deeply, taking a pause every now and then—really basic relationships to being wound up and speeding around. Then, we can explain more in principle as they grow; explain and explain, and put energy management into practice in our own lives, of course. Role-modeling is always the foundation of any truly effective teaching or education. I don't mean that they would always learn silently, and that we would always look the other way. Our input is necessary—but input as feedback, not as preaching or suppressing innocent activity or behavior.

The way I would handle running and screaming in the house, for instance, is by explaining the principle of protocol in spaces, which we have discussed quite extensively in a previous section. Something like, "That level of noise is not appropriate in this space, but you can go outside and make even more noise." If a child is feeling a lot of aggressive energy, not even necessarily towards someone else, but just in general, it is useful to suggest to them some other thing to do (other than beating up on another kid), like going outside and smashing small rocks on bigger rocks, or building a fort.

Sometimes adults will instigate a kind of vigorous play, and some can maintain that without the noise level getting to a loud screech. We simply need to be able to hear when something is starting to get out of hand and then simply say, "Take a deep breath. We're getting a little too loud. Do you want to go outside and play? Play tag, or run?" or, "Let's play a softer game for awhile." We need to have some cognizance of the space ourselves, and not just get so lost in the children's escalating play intensity that we are oblivious of other people and the space.

FIGHTING AND OTHER FORMS OF "CHILD'S PLAY"

Ideally, kindness, generosity and compassion will be taught through the example of the adults in the child's environment(s). Yet, how much of that can be *expected* of school-age children, and how much they will actually *learn* eventually, is another question. As an overall mood, such kindness, etc., could be expected of them, but not necessarily in every interpersonal relationship. Children are much more likely to be kind, generous and compassionate in relationship to strangers and with children they don't know, than they are in relationship to intimates—friends and family, especially siblings, with whom they just "let it hang out." Fighting with each other, or picking on the little kids seems to be a universal thing. Pecking order isn't exclusively a chicken phenomenon, although it may be foul (laugh here).

In my naiveté I think there may actually be a culture in which the older children don't need to be "up on" the little children. Under ordinary circumstances it is a question of whether the children are close friends, and whether they play together well. And if they do, they are going to have some tough fights once in awhile, and be unkind to one another, especially if they want to impress a new kid, or if they are in competition or whatever. Overall, though, if children have a close

304

friendship with each other then we can overlook some stuff, because love or affection is the context of the child's relationships.

As the responsible adults in the situation we can keep presenting the "moral" gently, without forcing them into that mold, and they will hear us. Even if it takes their moving away and being on their own (in college or in a job in a different city), for them to be kind and generous and compassionate, as long as we do the job, that is the important thing. It may take distance from the family for them to bring out such behavior, but it will be a lesson well learned. It is more "natural" for a child to be essentially caring for others than isolated, insular and cruel.

When children are playing with each other we don't have to hover over them and see that they are being appropriate with and not mistreating each other. Every once in awhile a serious battle starts, but basically kids pretty much take care of it themselves if they feel they have the adults' support to do that, and if they have some personal confidence and integrity. One child might take the lead and "power trip" everybody, and have it their way all the time, but the rest of the children will stop listening to that child after awhile.

Children manage quite well. If we don't leave them space and give them support to work out disagreements on their own, they won't learn such interpersonal management. Obviously, if a child's physical safety is at issue we should step in immediately. I would not let the older ones whale away on younger kids. If the older one starts swinging the wooden train, then I would stop it quickly. If real physical harm is possible, I would interfere, but otherwise it is amazing how well kids work things out on their own initiative. Basically, they just need to know that an adult is available if needed, like when they can't take care of a situation themselves, and that if they yell for help we will be there.

With what could be psychologically harmful, like an older child calling a young child "ugly," "fat" or "stupid," I tend to step in, especially if it is the little ones who can't talk who are being yelled at. Then I might say to the older child, "If you want to talk to him like that, wait till he learns language and can talk back. Then you can work it out yourselves. Then, if you want to call him names, he'll call you names back, and you'll see how you like it. But now he is basically defenseless, so chill out for awhile."

It can be difficult not to unconsciously shame an aggressive child in a fight, especially if we are ostensibly protecting our child from the onslaughts of a child who isn't ours. What I often do when two kids are fighting is to put my body between them. Without words, I just stop the action for a momentary break. I might tell them, "People are not for hitting. Chairs are not for sawing the legs off," just that kind of thing, with no shaming. Children are tremendously sensitive to shaming, unless they are already so shut down and conditioned that it doesn't affect them, which they can be even by four years old. When a child is young and innocent their self-image is so delicate. When their self-image is still in its formative stages, we should be extremely careful about what to us might seem like totally ordinary language usage, but what to a child could be devastating.

I tend not to moralize, but to be very careful about the words and language I use to instruct or guide children. In speaking to children about themselves or others, as I've explained in the chapter on language usage, I don't use the word "mean," first of all. I would never say to one child, "Don't be mean." I might say, "You could be more patient ... or kinder ... or less demanding." I might say something like, "You will have to play separately if a fight starts." If their interaction is just a little pushing with each other I wait till it gets to the biting or scratching stage before I step in. More than half the time they will stop before that point. If it starts getting upscaled to biting, I'll say to the aggressor: "You can bite me." Which I have. And they may bite half-heartedly, but usually that just sends them on to something more interesting—to a more benign form of play. They really don't want to bite *me*, they want to bite the other child; so, after a couple of seconds they forget about it.

We have to look at who the children are, at what their ages are, and at what the disagreement is actually about. If a ten-year-old is picking on a five-year-old, more likely it is just innocent, yet still, adult intervention may be needed. If a nine-year-old is picking on an eight-year-old, it is much more likely that the children can work it out. If it looks like it is really escalating, we divert the attention, break it up, and creatively re-engage the play mode.

PEER GROUPS AND PECKING ORDER

Children both learn from their peer group and find it very important to be embraced by others in group situations. If they are nine years old and the leader of the peer group is eleven, they will sometimes join in unkind or violent behavior, although usually not more than once, as they will often have learned from the experience, being impacted by their natural conscience, later, when they have time to reflect on it. Of course, some children are so strong and idealistic that they will stand up to a group, be quite independent, if they feel the group is "off" or unjust. But, most often it takes a bad experience to convince someone of the need for the opposite behavior.

When I was young, perhaps ten or eleven, all my friends went hunting for little animals, with stones, sticks or bow and arrows. I had a child's bow and dull-tipped arrows. I remember, and always will, gleefully shooting at every small, four-legged, furry creature from mice to squirrels to cats. One time I actually hit a squirrel in the leg and watched as it lay still, stunned, and then limped off, obviously in pain. I was so stunned myself, never suspecting the reality of inflicting harm on a small animal I loved, that I swore an oath not to do so again. It was a very dramatic lesson in my naive young life. And whenever my peers went hunting, including later on as teenagers and older (with guns), I simply chose not to participate.

* * *

The smallest child, no matter how loving the children are, almost always gets to be at the bottom of the hierarchy. The larger children are more dominant, even when they love the little ones and protect them when they need it. The little ones get sent on all the dirty errands: "Go do this. Go do that. Bring me this. Bring me that." And they run off, usually as happy as anything, proud to have a job and thrilled to be included.

Some parents get very offended, believing everything should always be equal, or evenly distributed. But if our child is the youngest child in their group, or if we have several children of different ages, they are *not* going to be equal, and it is not a matter of cruelty—

it is the universal pecking order, just the animal thing! Even within a set of twins there is a subtle order. The youngest child serves the others ... and is the go-fer. The older ones get to set the rules and order the little ones around. This can be quite healthy. Of course even the healthiest of natural behavior can be subverted and become perverted, but this doesn't detract from the essential objective principle.

TEASING

A child whose integrity is intact, who has gone through childhood essentially loved and respected, will never instigate teasing; and they will be able to be in a situation where they may be being teased without being psychologically impaired by the teasing. Of course they are not likely to enjoy it, but they would be more understanding, more impervious to "taking it seriously." At the same time, a child who would not likely initiate teasing may, when in a group that is teasing another group, go along with it, usually silently. This is often due to the deep need to belong, to be accepted by peers, and because of the lack of experience in handling such events, i.e., knowing how to diplomatically defuse the teasing or to just get out of the situation gracefully, without becoming another one of the objects of the teasing.

Most teasing stems from the need to be right, over and against clear differences of appearance, behavior or opinion (each of which indicates unconsciously, to an insecure psyche, that the appearance, behavior or opinion, being so different, may be wrong). So, a secure child would not likely have such a weak motive.

MIMICRY

When we see how well children mimic we should encourage the talent, but not necessarily the tendency to do it all the time. Even the nasty things that children see and mimic, to many children these are just a game, a form of play and of discovery as well. For instance, they may see one of the other kids really being spiteful, and to them it's as much fun as being happy, because it's purely a game, like trying on "dress-ups." If we say to them, "That's not a pleasant manifestation," they look at us in surprise and ask why, because they are having as much fun doing that as they have doing anything else—it is pure mimicry; they are playing. When they are trying on Mommy's high-heeled shoes as play we are delighted, we smile and talk sweetly to them, but then when they are playing "bad boy" and we are getting annoyed, they don't understand it. They don't understand spitefulness; they have seen somebody else (an older child or another adult) do a manifestation that they haven't seen before, or aren't thoroughly familiar with, and they are acting it out to get to know it, to explore. It's really an adventure to them.

We have to explain to children, early on, the differences in the ways that manifestations affect people—how some manifestations affect people positively and some affect people negatively. But, we should always encourage their ability to do a variety of manifestations, to deepen their repertoire of knowledge, of feelings, of states of manifestation. So, we may say to them: "It's fine to act that way at certain times during a game, but the dinner table is not a place to express that. Still, it's great to be able to do it when you want to ... to pull it out of your bag of experiences. Wonderful!"

RESOLVING DIFFICULTIES

If there is a way that we work out our misunderstandings with one another, even if our children don't work out theirs that way, our example will not be lost on them, and they will follow our lead at some point; maybe not until they are out from under our physical support, or maybe not until they are thirty years old, but they will. Our example is primary.

If we routinely scream at our mate, we can hardly expect young children who observe this not to believe that this is normal and healthy. After all, we have to train our children to appreciate how neurotic we really are. In the beginning, they assume that we are perfectly, holistically sane and healthy, so it behooves us to actually be that way, so *they* will learn to be that way, and to keep our neurotic eccentricities to ourselves as much as we possibly can. All that should be our business, not theirs.

For me, the key element is always resolution, because all of us are not experts at mediation. The important thing for children to see is that we come to resolution with one another. Sometimes there are disagreements, and sometimes someone will storm out of the space, and sometimes we get loud too, but as long as the children can see that the next day we are walking arm and arm with the person that we were really aggressive and nasty towards—still in love with them, still friends with them—they will learn about resolution. Positive resolution makes the strongest impact. How we come to resolution, of course, has its effect, so certainly it would be a little bit more effective if we came to resolution without undue emotional or physical explosions.

To come to resolution is actually something we

311

can learn from children, if we don't do that ourselves. One moment a child is swearing they will never play with another child as long as they live, that they hate them, and the next moment there are no traces of that—they are just the best of friends, playing as if nothing happened. Most of us could use such a lesson! Children are like that because they are innocent, but they will learn to not be innocent if they see us acting differently—not coming to resolution and holding grudges.

It's very easy to superimpose upon children what we think energy management is supposed to look like in a disagreement; a lot of times arguing it out *is* appropriate energy management. (Not necessarily "slugging it out," though. It is rare that adults are able to do that cleanly, because we don't have the model for that in our own upbringing.) Children of different ages and different temperaments will manifest energy management differently, so do not assume that all children need to work things out the same way. To expect different age groups to have the same ways of handling things is quite unrealistic. It's easy for us to think that it's not okay for the kids to get down and wrestle it out, or yell it out, or whatever. Yet, I'm beginning to consider more and more that it is okay; really quite healthy. Learning how to come to resolve at six, seven and eight years of age gives them something very, very different than when they are thirty or thirty-five and trying to come to resolution without having tools and context.

11

BODY AND SOUL:
Food, Health, Sex and God

FOOD AND EATING

The key to a child's healthy relationship to food, as in all areas, is our non-judgmental and sane perspective—understanding what is clean, nutritious food and what is unhealthy and toxic food, while at the same time allowing a child some leeway to experiment occasionally.

Where are you ever going to get *totally* pure food, anyway? Nowhere! Do you think the water tables in all these places that grow organic vegetables are clean? Do you think the air is totally clean? When you bite into an apple you're not just getting the wax and the coloring on the skin, but all the air in the orchard that the apple grew in, and all the stuff in the water. So, you don't need to be too righteous or dogmatic, but just eat basically healthy, live food, and don't worry about it having to be perfect. Because, if you worry about it, and complain about it, you are going to prejudice your children toward zealous exclusivity. Give them a break, and yourself too. Just use common sense, get as clean food as you can, and relax.

* * *

When I was a child, I had the same thing six nights a week: steak (the best available cut), burnt vegetables and salad. Six nights a week! I never ate the salad, I hated it; as for the burnt vegetables, I would stuff down the minimum unless it was something I really liked, like spinach or asparagus, in which case I would eat a lot. (But if it was cauliflower, forget it!) I had the same breakfast food everyday for twenty years too; exactly the same thing: a half grapefruit, toast, eggs, bacon, glass of milk and cereal. Always in the same order. The only variation was that I had Cheerios for ten years, Wheaties for five years and then back to Cheerios; and occasionally in place of the half grapefruit I had a glass of fresh orange juice. My family went out to eat about once a week, sometimes more, and we tried every variety of food available. Even though our home-fare was basically limited—simple and predictable—my parents encouraged me to try every taste I could find, and my mother was always bringing home exotic fruits and treats. I was not in any way biased against any type of food. And the food served was clean and fresh, so that impression was strong.

What do I eat now? Salad, fruit and vegetables— everything I didn't eat when I was a child, but which *was* available and healthy. As a child I ate whatever my parents let me have —all the bread I wanted, as much butter as I wanted on the bread, but no more. Since I was not conditioned to the "wrongness" of any kind of food, not psychologically biased, when I grew up I was free to make choices based on open-minded consideration. I now choose a basic vegetarian diet (with some exceptions) of clean, fresh, wholesome food. But I will have junk food, now and then, depending on the company I'm with and the situation.

Once, I was with a five-year-old who wanted a quarter-pound stick of butter, so I said okay. She picked the stick of butter up and ate it, completely. You know what happened? Nothing. Some of the women reading this are saying, "You're lying. She got sick. I *know* she got sick. Maybe you didn't notice it, but she ran in her room and threw up. Something must have happened." No. Nothing happened. And you know what? She never asked to do it again. In fact, she developed a very conservative (and the best, natural need-level for the body) relationship to butter.

When she was devouring the butter my eyes were wide. "How was it?" I asked.

"Oh, it was good." That was it.

Obviously we should use common sense, but a child will not eat too much ice cream more than once or twice. Healthily-raised children aren't self-abusive as many of us are. They get sick once, they learn.

Along the same lines, sometimes kids will eat the same thing, consistently, for a long time. My daughter went through a period where she ate maybe five or six bananas a day, and very little else, for months— frozen bananas. And there was no problem. Let children eat what they want, and every once in a while you can say, for example, "Wouldn't you like a little salad or a bit of rice?" Children's bodies, unprogrammed by righteous or closed-minded adults, will define desires and tastes. If they need greens or carrots, and these foods are available, that's what they will eat and enjoy.

* * *

You don't want to prejudice your children. If there is some food you don't like, let your children make up their *own* minds about it. I would cook oatmeal for one of my daughters when she was young; she would eat it, fine. One time her mother tasted it and said, "There's no salt in this oatmeal," with such an emotional attachment to salt that every time thereafter my daughter would ask, "Is there salt in it?" She had been shockingly impressed by the internal intensity of a prejudice for salt. If I would cook the oatmeal without salt, she would eat it and she would enjoy it, but if her mother came into the room the child would go for the salt shaker, every time. One reaction—that's all it took. The oatmeal had tasted fine to her, so the addition of salt became pure habit, a psychosomatic taste expectation ... it had nothing to do with her natural taste buds.

Another way we prejudice our children: Take the average mother with a child. Let's say the child is a year old and tastes garlic, cayenne, spinach, beets, anything, and doesn't like it. In that mother's mind the child doesn't like that thing, and won't ever like it, unless it's one of the mother's favorite foods. Then, every time it's served, the mother will try to feed it to the child. But if the mother doesn't like the food, or has decided the child doesn't—based on the one time the child rejected it—the mother will assume that the child doesn't and won't like it *forever*. For the next twenty years, every time somebody says to the child or young adult, "Have some beets," the mother will say, "She doesn't like them." Automatically.

To anyone functioning from the context of ego, the past is a living, viable, meaningful entity, and it is *real* and no change is possible. Because the past is real to ego, anyone functioning from the context of ego has a linear relationship to everything. Ego protects itself and sustains its own independent and autonomous authority by establishing a continuity through memory of the past and projecting itself into the future. Ego protects itself by always assuming that it is going to survive in the future, and by utilizing its experience in the past to define future behavior. It never deals with the present moment, because the present moment is the only moment that is free.

With genuinely free behavior, however, the only thing that is taken into consideration is the present moment, and all free behavior is a spontaneous manifestation or response to stimuli in that moment. Completely free behavior functions in many ways, but the principle is always the same.

So, we should allow our children lots of space to like something one day, not the next, and like it again the next. Children's tastes will change, sometimes quite dramatically as they grow. In this domain of food, as well as in every other area of life, so we should not cram our children into immovable lines of preference and taste.

TRUSTING IN FOOD

Trusting that the food their parents are giving them is good for them is most important for a child, and if we are constantly picking apart the food, "Oh, you know, that doesn't have your daily requirement of protein, you need your proteins, and you need your vitamins, don't forget your vitamin C, and oh, vitamin B's, gotta have your vitamin B12, and don't forget your calcium, and nah-nah-nah-nah-nah ...," we are liable to have one sick little puppy, neurotic and obsessive.

We don't need to overeducate our children about the food they eat. We aren't bound to give them a choice between organic brown rice and a greasy fast-food cheeseburger or fried chicken nuggets; just offer them a variety of natural, fresh healthy food and let them eat what they like of what we offer. Let them eat whatever is on the table, as much as they want, and if they are stuffing themselves and that's clear, all we need to say is, "I think you've had enough."

My essential view is that children need limits that make sense both to them and to the adults in their lives, and never limits that are arbitrary. Making sense when it comes to food, for example, means not taking our own beliefs so seriously that we become nutrition cops. So, we don't have to say, "Don't have so many fried potatoes. Do you know how much fat and grease you're eating? Your liver nah-nah-nah-nah-nah-.... " Or, "Do you have any idea what sugar does to you? Why if you had donuts now you would be bouncing off the walls. You'd be up until three in the morning and I'd never get you to sleep tonight, blah, blah, blah!" That is not a reasonable limit. That is nutritional hysteria, of which there is plenty. What we can say, when they ask for donuts, for example, is: "We already had a big bunch of sugar today, and it's best if we take a break, but we will have them soon." And when the child asks, "Why is it best we take a break?" then it behooves (and beclaws) us to know our dietary ABC's (and P's and Q's). Not: "... sugar, sugar, sugar, sugar, caffeine, caffeine, caffeine, meat, meat, meat, meat, bad, bad, bad ..." That is no way to educate a child about vitamins and nutrition. That's a way to turn a child off, good and proper. Simply feed them properly *and* include lots of "treats" to supplement their right, holistic dietary intake. As they grow, if we are into nutritional optimization, they will ask about information when they are ready and willing to learn.

Don't ever tell children that what they eat is expensive and is costing you money. Just make sure your children are supported in their bounteous love of nutritious food. And how will they be supported? When we aren't hovering over their shoulders worrying that their diet is terrible and that we've got to pump some vitamins and some greens into them.

Face it, they will be healthy anyway. Kids, with their vital energy, will gravitate to what they actually *need*, and besides that, kids can eat practically anything. It's the adults who are all screwed up.

And obviously we would not feed a child chocolate all day long, so I assume any intelligent adult will have a modicum of common sense (I know, I know! An assumption like that and two dollars will get me on the New York subway).

VARIETY IS THE SPICE

It is helpful with children to vary their diet a little bit. If the child is rigidly brought up on a certain diet, they will grow up with a pattern that becomes extremely limited and exclusive, and they will have a very hard time, later on, expanding that pattern to include other possibilities that come into their lives. The issue of giving or not giving their children sugar and other "treats" is a big one for many parents. And, although I would introduce them to sugar as late as possible, personally, I'm very much in favor of allowing children who are brought up as strict vegetarians to sometimes eat meat, to sometimes have sugar—not often, but once in a while, just so their bodies don't grow up without the recognition of those other food substances. It doesn't have to be once a week or once a month, but every few months a little good meat, a little fish, a little chicken, some cheap chocolate pudding ... lets the body know, organically, that there are many patterns of many kinds of substances. The body doesn't get too locked into something that is so pure that it also defines that child's whole chemical relationship to life.

In our community we eat a primarily vegetarian diet, with very little processed food, chemical additives, food substitute products ..., but we also have many exceptions, both at special holiday times and at times of personal celebration as well. If we are traveling and eating away from home, we will get the kids ice cream and lots of whatever the local food favorites are, including meat and special desserts. Consistently I have been more strict at home and more loose on the road. So, when we do travel with the kids, whenever we are in Europe or wherever, it's "open season" on foods that we normally wouldn't have, or foods that are cultural specialties that help broaden a child's spectrum of experience. They can have anything they want, within reason. After all, it is an adventure, a vacation. They know that when they come home, no bratwurst (Germany), no lapin (France), no goat (Mexico) and no sugar (everywhere). Traveling should not be work for children. It should be fun, it should be exploration, full of wonder, delight and discovery.

Adults who are vegetarians, and whose parents and families are not, can certainly tolerate a small piece of meat once in awhile when going home to visit. Such behavior is also very fine teaching in the domain of hospitality—to eat what we are served when we are a guest, even in our old home. If Mother serves a pot roast or a ham, just like we used to love, we should eat it and please her. Mother's happiness is more important (in this case!) than the righteousness of a confirmed vegetarian.

If our children's dietary habits are sound when they are home, they may indulge when they are eighteen or twenty-one or when they go to college, but whatever they do they will come back to their most stable habits. That's the overview that I have seen experientially. We often don't know how effective our childraising has been until our children are thirty years old and raising their own children.

FOOD & LOVE

How we cripple children, of course, is to train them that food equals "love." I have known a number of people for whom their diet is "love," and if they have to go without certain dietary supplements, or if they are denied food as punishment, even if the circumstances make it impossible to eat the type or volume of food they feel they need, their body goes into panic and recoil because they feel they are unworthy to be a human being, to even live and walk on the face of the Earth, and that they are unloved and never will be loved unless they get their iron or their ice-cream treat or their third helping.

Many adults use food instead of affection and respect to train children to do what the adult wants; a way of making the child adaptive. "Go wash or you get no dinner," etc... is the usual substitute for a hug and a kiss and an honoring request to wash hands, after playing in the sewer, before eating a sandwich. Food becomes the payment, or the payoff, for "good" behavior—the child gets an ice-cream cone in the place of loving attention, and learns quickly that food, special food, equals love. It is usually sweet food, and children know how sweet *love* is. They crave it. So, we often train them, sometimes unwittingly, to be sweets addicts. Of course, for some severe cases, it is food itself that is the addiction.

Some adults are so repressed, so bound up in their ability to offer free affection, that food treats become a way of trying to tell the child that they are loved. But children don't understand such subtle psychological dynamics. They need touch, lots of physical contact, wrestling, hugs, kisses—both gentler and affectionate touch and strong confident touch. So, don't stuff their mouths when what they need is a reassuring smile, a word of praise or acknowledgment, or a hug.

* * *

Snacking for children is just a matter of keeping their bodies well-attended to. There is immense energy involved in growing to adulthood, so lots of fuel of various kinds is required. Snacks are fine as long as they generally don't interfere with active participation at mealtime. However, we should help children develop a relationship to snacks that is not neurotic (i.e., just something to keep them busy). Children will move out of snacking naturally when they are ready, that is, if we don't offer them a snack every time they are bored.

I wouldn't encourage feeding them nothing but potato chips, cookies and cheese-products washed down with "fruit drinks" ("made with real fruit juice"). Snacks for children can run the range of raw vegetables and dips, to sandwiches, fruit, cereals and other healthy choices.

EATING PROTOCOL

An expectation for mealtime should be that children decide, once they have grown to decision-making age, about their own food likes and dislikes, and what they are going to eat, particularly when the food is served buffet style. Also, however, they should be trusted to use discretion sensitively, not just take *all* the olives, or drown everything on their plate in ketchup. But even so, if we took a five-year-old to a fine buffet-style restaurant and all they ate for dinner was a whole plate of olives, no harm would come of it. We don't need to force them to eat a big casserole just because we are out in a restaurant, if all they want is pickles and saltines.

Children don't always have to be fed first. Sometimes that is held by the adults as an automatic thing, out of a parental sense of "protecting the young." Our children are not helpless and needn't be treated as if there will be no food left for them if they aren't served first, or immediately. I would not expect a two-year-old to wait unnecessarily, so I would ask the waiter or waitress in a restaurant to bring their meals as quickly as possible, but with a seven-year-old I would expect them to understand that restaurants don't exist to cater to their needs exclusively and singularly. I would not wish to burden any child with endless waiting, but a small bit of patience is not out of line. It sets up a neurotic mood of scarcity to always panic around getting our child's food right away. Just integrate children into the timing of meal service very simply. That should not require any great effort.

If everybody in the family brings their own dish to the kitchen to be washed, children should as well. If a small child is helping with clean up, or is just bringing their dish to the kitchen and drops a bit of salad on the floor, or that uneaten cauliflower, they should be responsible for at least picking it up, and possibly cleaning up the floor, depending on their age. But certainly don't expect a three-year-old to have the facility or responsibility you would expect of a twelve-year-old.

Children love to help to clean up, and it is worth helping them develop responsible habits even if, at very young ages, they will demonstrate more enthusiasm than practical skills. Let them help, and then clean up the messes they make in their unbridled delight at being an integral part of things. (Clean up their omissions after they are out of the space, i.e., not in front of them.)

In principle, if we are always doing for children what they can do for themselves, they learn to develop that relationship of helplessness to other people as a life strategy. Then, when they become adults, they have tremendous difficulties because they expect their mate or friends, or even their boss, to do for them what they easily and rightly should do themselves. It becomes a way of manipulating, a way of dominating, and can be very unpleasant.

We can allow children to "work with" their food a little—often it's a sort of love affair. If they are three and they know what is going on, and they sit there intentionally whipping spoonfuls of food on the floor, then I would stop them. If they are six months old, then they are going to play with their food with delight—and delight should not be construed to be an intentional and malicious attempt to personally disturb us. It isn't at all.

Every individual has a very unique eating style, so to try to get our children to eat, in form and gesture, exactly like we do may not be allowing them leeway to find their own "medium." Food is a more primal domain than sex, so to be unhealthy in relation to eating, to ingestion, to the nurturance that food is, is a basic disease that can easily affect all areas of adult life negatively. So, be very clear about the distinctions between eating idiosyncratically, and using food as a weapon of mischief. A seven-year-old may absent-mindedly knock food off their plate and onto the table in the midst of an excited conversation or a consuming day-dream, but a simple, gentle reminder to pay attention will suffice. We don't need to lecture them on table manners!

HEALTH

There's a downside to the kind of conscious childraising that we attempt to practice. And the downside is "smother-mothering," where we're so indulgent of our children's health and innocence that we actually train them to *be sick*, and to lack innocence, so that they continue to have our pandering to them.

Someone said the other day, "Shouldn't we try to keep the children from getting this idea of having to take something ever time they get sick?" and I said, "Are you kidding, they've already got that." For *years* the women here would walk around with their eyes peeled for every minor incident. They had little holsters—you know how in the Wild West they used to carry their six-shooters, well they (the women here) used to have little holsters with Rescue Remedy[1] and they would walk around, waiting, and the second a child would fall down on the tennis court they would rush over, literally, at the speed of light. You should have seen some of these mothers move—if we could get them to move like that when they were washing dishes, or going on a trip, we'd have it knocked, or walking through the Mall, but no! We used to have fast-draw contests with Rescue Remedy; they'd be all over the child: Rescue Remedy on the head, Rescue Remedy in the mouth, Rescue Remedy up the butt, you name it, there was Rescue Remedy for everything. And the children learned by the time they were two—it was "in" already—that every little nudge, every little "uumph," every little something had to have Rescue Remedy, and little white pills and a big bandage. Now, when they get little cuts, maybe a 32nd of an inch, and you pull out a little bandage, they say: "That's not big enough." They need BIG bandages, four of them, so it looks like a big star, with colors and pictures on them. It's "in," that's how they're going to be the rest of their lives. That's how they're going to raise their children.

We don't let our children fall down and scrape their knees. We get hysterical. I was thrilled the first time my daughter fell down and scraped her knee. I was so happy. I was like: "Oh my God, she's bleeding. Thank God she's a normal kid." Not quite that dramatically. But let's not imagine our children to be these perfect little things, these angels, these porcelain dolls. We should tend towards this perspective of—kids grow up: they fall down, they get bumps, they get bangs, they get cuts, so what? Children recover with amazing facility. Treat the symptom directly, neither more nor less than it calls for.

I never had an infection—I haven't had an infection except in India, years ago, and I don't put all that stuff on. You get a cut, you get a cut. Wash it out, go about your business. And we are like: "Oh my God, they're gonna be infected, put this in the mouth, in the eyes, up the butt ...."

So, one day the healing team will entirely appreciate the context of this, and will not indulge anyone in their need to be given affection because they're sick; given love because they're sick. Some of us probably even *get* a little sick sometimes because that's the only time we get compensated with exceptional care and attention. You all probably know the dynamic: for many children the only time one of their parents stays home from work and really gives them attention is when the child is sick. So, often we develop *getting sick* to get attention. I'm sure anybody in the health profession knows this—a lot of people go to health practitioners because that's where they get the most attention in their lives. If a doctor's got a really welcoming bedside manner, people will come. I mean, every doctor has a number of patients who are total psychosomatics, total hypochondriacs. That's where they go to get attention; they go to the healer, in whatever form, to get attention.

I'm on the other side of the coin. Once when someone was in the hospital, she had appendicitis, and they cut it (her appendix) out. And after a couple of days, Nurse Ratched was on the floor (I don't remember her name exactly, but she looked like her), and they wouldn't let "the patient" out of the hospital. I went down (I shouldn't do this kind of thing), and I said "Put your clothes on." She was saying: "Get me out of here." We started walking out and the nurse came in and said, "What are you doing?" And I said, "What do you mean what are we doing? Is this a prison or a hospital?" (I shouldn't have said that). I was really annoyed, yes very heated up, because they wouldn't let her out of the hospital. I said: "What? Is it a law, are the police going to come or what? Does she have to stay in the hospital?" And the nurse said "No, but she's not recovered yet," (at $3000 a day or so). I said, "Well, she's healthy, she's fine, we're going home." And the nurse said, "You're going to have to sign a release. We will not take responsiblity for this." And I said, "Well, stop *trying* to take responsibility for it, and let me get her out of here."

She ran and got the doctor, and the doctor

shrugged his shoulders and said to her: "Let them sign the release. Relax. It's their problem."

So we signed the release. They wanted three or four more days in the hospital, and we refused. And she was perfectly healthy. Nothing terrible happened. Nothing *would have* happened. Except, if she'd stayed in, she would have had more jello and more instant potatoes and more chocolate milk for lunch.

Don't teach the children to be little whiners over nothing. If one of their fingers is falling off and hanging on by one tendon, okay, then it's time to get a little excited. But, if they fall down and bang their head, give 'em a break. Kiss them, sympathize and let them get on with their play.

Everybody says: "How do we *know*? How do we know there's not a *problem*?" I don't know how you know. I guess if you're a mother, you should *know* whether your child is *hurt*—whether their pride is hurt or whether their body is hurt. And if they scratch their knee, only their pride is hurt, not their body. So you put a little stuff on, and "Okay, it's fine."

"No, it hurts."

"Yea, I know it hurts. It'll hurt for fifteen mintues, then it won't hurt anymore."

Every once in a while we need to have a little bit of demand on our children. Like, "You're all right. I can see you're all right, I know it hurts—paper cuts hurt, scraped knees hurt ... but you're really okay ... you'll heal quickly. It's not that big a deal."

"It is it is, it really hurts."

"Yes, I know it hurts. It hurts me when I do that too. It's okay though, it's cool. It's fine. You can manage it."

So, to really have that attitude is healthy. But don't overdo it and expect heroic suppression of pain and reactions of shock or surprise over hurts or illnesses as if our child was Rambo or something. Remember above all that children are children, not adults, and need lots of understanding, nurturing, care, affection and acceptance.

Our Beliefs Can Be Abusive

Much of what we considered about food can apply to the consideration of health as well. Our beliefs can be abusive. While many mothers in the alternative, "natural foods, natural living" camp are radically devoted to the natural process of health and healing (as I am too), I've come to the conclusion, based on experience, that to withhold healing from a child, because what they have is "only a virus and they'll get through it," and because we don't want the child to become artificially dependent on drugs—even homeopathic remedies ... because "pills are pills," you know—is a very subtle form of manipulation, which could easily become a more rigid form of child abuse. It is a form of child abuse to let a child suffer because we are purists. It may not be as bad as some orthodox zealot letting their child die because they refuse to take the child to the hospital for a blood transfusion, but it is still taking the child's health into our own hands when we might be better off consulting a naturopath or some other form of physician.

When children are too young to take care of their own healing it is our responsibility to do so. It is not our job to try to convince them that there is "no such thing as suffering," or that "all illnesses are psychosomatic" or to unnecessarily let them suffer, when there are ways of relieving the immediate stress and anxiety of an illness. There are no excuses for our own lack of clarity in this regard. It is our job to care for our children, and if our principles of living are genuine and true, our children will learn them. A one-year-old can't learn about natural healing by suffering through an illness without being given a remedy.

If we live a healthy life, our children will learn that from us as they observe us and practice our lifestyle over time. No matter how many children's aspirin we give them, if *we* don't take aspirin, then when the child gets old enough to communicate and observe us, they will stop taking aspirin.

As I have stressed over and over, our children want no more than to be exactly like us. That's their primary aim in life. A child's parents are their idols. And they will be like us! You may doubt this at times, but believe me you have more of an impact on their lives, beliefs and behavior than Luke Skywalker, Hans Solo or Princess Leia even if it doesn't seem that way for a while. If our life has integrity to it, they will learn that. We don't have to worry about them being corrupted by an aspirin when they are suffering when they are two years old.

ABOUT SEX

I read an article in *Playboy* about "love maps." The author said that each of us has a hidden agenda in our relationship—a "love map" that contains an idealized lover, a love scene, and a program of erotic activities that will guide us through our adult sexual life. He said that these patterns are laid down in early childhood, perhaps as early as the age of three.

This is an important consideration, particularly

330

for those of us who have children. We already have our "love map," and we are stuck with it, healthy or not; but we can still give our children healthy, natural, unaffected "love maps" by not impressing or focusing our perversities onto them.

Some influence does come from movies, which often keep children's attention totally rapt. (Which is why we don't want to take young children to movies with a lot of violent sexual encounters, because they could well end up being unable to pleasurably make love without violence, if the impressions are deeply affective enough.) But generally the "love map" that a child develops depends upon the relationship to sex and to the body itself that is held by their parents or the adults in their environment.

It's like, if you are a man and you are in the shower, and a child—boy or girl—comes in by accident, and you hide yourself as if nakedness was something to be ashamed of, that gives them a very clear, negative message which gets included in their own relationship to their body and their whole sexuality and eventual sexual dynamics. And, of course, some men march around "showing it off," another variety of the unhealthy demonstration of lack of sexual confidence and clarity. There is a middle ground where we can be naked in front of our children without undue exhibitionism or fear of vulnerability. It is very healthy for children to observe their parents' non-judgmental and easeful relationships to their bodies, both naked and clothed.

Whether sex and sexuality (two very distinct things) are overall healthy, or overall unhealthy and twisted, depends on our body-image, and with the feelings associated with bodily pleasure (and our love of pleasing others) or the suppression of or disgust with bodily functions and feelings. All of these impressions are taught us very early in life, from infancy, long before an adult sexual relationship is ever at issue.

I remember one incident where I unexpectedly walked into the bathroom in my home—I never saw a towel move that fast. I thought it levitated, but actually my aunt grabbed it off the towel rack to cover her lower anatomy. That thing moved at supersonic speed! As a result, when I'm with a woman, if there's not a towel in between us I have problems. So you might find me skulking around the laundry lines—it takes me an hour and a half to hang four or five pieces of laundry out there. I just have to hang out, play with the clothespins, look at the towels, wondering what's behind them. Logically I know there's nothing behind them—I know it's a towel hanging on a clothes line; I know there's nothing behind it except the scenery. But once you have a "love map" you have a "love map." I want to know what's behind these towels! Even though as an adult I know there is nothing behind them but air, as a child I knew there was something behind there and I wanted to know what. It is fascinating. Like a mystery. It's forbidden territory. I want to examine it and satisfy curiosity I didn't even know I had until I was denied the sight of ... of what? I still don't know. But there is something real interesting behind that towel.

The author of the "Love Maps" article also said that it is repressive sexual attitudes, not permissive values, that will increasingly breed aberrant behavior. I agree. It would be much better for our child to walk into our bedroom and find us making love and have us just turn around when they say "What are you doing?" and reply, "Making love. Could you go out and close the door and we'll talk to you when we're done," than for us to scream, pull the covers up, and shout, "Get the hell out of here. Haven't I told you a hundred times to knock, God dammit," and like that—which some of us were probably at the effect of as children, having innocently walked into our parents' bedroom while they were "doing it."

If we have raised our child with a good sense of humor, when they are eight or nine and they accidentally walk in on us, they'll say, "Hey Dad, you got a pimple on your ass." Be cool. And don't correct their language, even if it is "*You've* got ...."

Another example: When little children want to look at their dad's penis, it is a great conflict for many men. If a man is embarrassed by their curiosity (his children may still want to see it flop around and float in the bathtub ... whatever those things do), there has to be a way of dealing with that kind of thing firmly, but without trauma to the child. There is no way of explaining *how* to do that—it is a situation by situation call. The more we are with children, the more we can handle such issues without getting too flustered.

Don't hide your body and don't unnecessarily expose your body. Unaffected naturalness is the key.

MASTURBATION

Children play with their genitals, which, if we are repressed and easily embarrassed, can generate some confusion in us as to how to handle it all. Because they *really play* with them. They don't just touch them, they lie there feeling good—stroking and poking and pulling and what not. After all, genitals are in a handy place— easily reached, quite accessible to fingers. The little girls get as much pleasure playing with their little equipment as the little boys get playing with their little equipment.

If we really get uptight and brush their hand away, they learn that it's wrong somehow, and that is the beginning of a negative body-image. The less we moralize, the more they will just go through stages and grow up fine.

So what to do? Nothing. Let them play.

Some of us are pretty ashamed that we even have genitals. We watch our children caressing themselves and we are so embarrassed we don't know whether to shit or turn green. We can't believe the innocent freedom children express! We don't want them to sit around when they are thirteen masturbating in front of guests, of course, but on the other hand pulling their hand away from their private parts when they are little children isn't so good either. If we let them follow their inclinations they will develop a natural social etiquette. It is when we don't allow them to develop as instinct demands that aberrant sexuality develops.

My hands must have been tied behind my back when I was little. I don't remember at all, it is a blank, but somehow I've managed to overcome it. (Hey, lighten up will you? It's just a joke. We're only talking about wanking, not vivisection. Chill, folks.)

SEX AND THE FAMILY BED

When you and your mate and a young child are in the same bed together, I recommend that you and your mate make love when the child is sound asleep. But you *can* make love in the same bed if you want to. If you are really uncomfortable, put a mat on the floor and put the child on it for the time being, then bring the child back into the bed later. Or leave the child asleep on the bed and *you* use the floor (or the desk). Perhaps a little variety wouldn't hurt!

I would not make love while the child is watching, but in terms of a child being asleep in the same room when the parents are making love, I don't think there is a problem. It's natural after all. Regularly talk to the child about it, so the child's unconscious is relaxed and comfortable. I wouldn't necessarily explain to the child the laws of biology or procreation, but just: "Mommy and Daddy are going to be making love, and if you hear any noise ... or if the bed's bouncing all over the room ... that's the way it's supposed to be." It is also a healthy impression for the child to know that when they grow up they can be expressive in lovemaking, rather than isolated and insular. It could save them years of therapy. On the other hand, once the child gets their own room, if they have been fairly well buffered from the sex-act issue, be aware that if a child hears their mother screaming like the dickens (whatever *the dickens* is!), the child will almost always assume the mother is in terrible trouble and will be very scared for her ... concerned. So, be sensitive to whether your child is awake or asleep when you make love. And if you don't scream out of respecting the child's space, well and good; but if you can't scream, too bad, you don't know what you're missing (men too).

UNCENSORED EXPRESSIVENESS

Children raised in a conscious, open, loving and supportive environment can go up to people and ask them questions that interest them, without fear or embarrassment. Sometimes the clarity and forthrightness of such children is startling to adults who are themselves shut-down and repressed.

Have you seen little kids brought up without prejudice and rigidity playing at giving birth? They

335

open their legs and take the doll out from between them, from under their dress. I bet some of you would be pretty worried about taking the kids home to Grandma, huh? What would Grandma do when a three-year-old spreads her legs and pulls a doll out? She probably would have apoplexy. It would be the end of Grandma's peace of mind, either that or she'd roar with delight.

Nonetheless, it's a wonderful thing to see children for whom all the natural elements of life—birth, death, mood swings, peeing and pooping, and having genitals and so on—are just taken in stride in the course of things. It's a very freeing observation to know that our children aren't as bound up, i.e., as psychologically constipated, as most of us are about birth, sex and death.

Typically, children are naturally curious and naturally enthusiastic about sharing their discoveries, and it is very healthy to accept these qualities of theirs. Besides, given half the chance, children are fabulous and delightful conversationalists—fascinating and engaging.

GOD, RELIGION, AND SPIRITUALITY

A book of Claudio Naranjo's, called *The End of Patriarchy, The Triune Society*,[2] is about his concepts of the ideal education and the ideal culture, based on the ideal relationship between mother, father and child. In general, he says that a lot of the things that we are educated in are really expendable—that we would learn them in the course of our lives anyway, and probably better and more practically. The two things that formal education *is* crucial for, for holistic training, are mathematics and music. Dr. Naranjo notes many different experiments where music and mathematics have been taught from an early age and have been foundational in the skills needed which could then be applied to so many other areas.

In his opinion, religion should not be formally taught until puberty. Certainly if one lives in a religious environment, if one's home is by its nature religious, the children will pick it up, but formal instruction should not be given until puberty. The consciousness of puberty is a consciousness of breaking out of dependence, breaking out of the security and the sanctuary of the home, and really coming into one's own as an adult. That is the ideal time in which to teach religion, because in essence that is what people entering into their independent adulthood are looking for at that time—universal answers. If religion is not taught until then, children will not have been exposed to the very likely danger of having religion become just some kind of rote thing that they learned when they were little; something that they really could have had no organic feel for, except in some really subtle intuitive sense. (But that subtle sense would be universal, not "religious" in an organized way.) Young people would not have been already turned off or damaged to the possibility of a real immersion in the true principles of religion by some dogmatic or doctrinaire conditioning that is way beyond their possible level of understanding or appreciation.

Dr. Naranjo is very critical of organized religious circumstances, because children are conditioned into a mechanical or rote practice rather than initiated into true religious realities. This, he says, really can't happen before puberty, because we just don't have the full formulation of consciousness that can get what the reality is. Before puberty we are still in the formative stages of other less subtle domains.

That is why in most native cultures, initiatory experiences are given at puberty. Maybe early on in a child's life the family will discuss dreams, or whatever, and involve the child in the whole ordinary flow of family life including spirituality, but they don't actually *try* to give children the experience of transcendental reality, they just allow children to perceive what they perceive at any given developmental level, answering questions they may have, but not filling them with preformulated data.

In teaching who Jesus or Buddha is, to three- and four- and five-year-olds, we are trying to instruct children in a transcendental reality that needs to be purely experiential and requires all the faculties of adult development. It *must* become artificial, because at three, four and five, children are only in the developmental stage of basic physical skills. At seven, eight, nine, ten, they are then growing into emotional realities. The thinking center hasn't naturally come to its developmental stage, which is one of the ingredients required for a full and thorough comprehension and appreciation of what the spiritual reality is.

Stories are different—with stories, children are not required to animate the moral, the transcendental reality, except vicariously of course. Storytelling is very healthy, particularly when the story is something that a child can follow along with and imagine, not something they are required to learn before they can appreciate, in their own experience, the moral of it all. So, we can allow children a gradual integration into higher

338

truths, but we should not expect them to understand such things practically when their experience is purely intuitive or instinctual.

* * *

Talking to our children about God, if we believe in such a thing, should be natural. They are going to ask questions and it should not be problematical to answer them, just a matter of using the right language. The way an adult may abstractly or philosophically understand God is far beyond what a child can understand in those terms. But understanding God, or whatever we choose to call it, is not beyond them. We need to speak the language they know, that's all. Somehow we have to translate our knowing into terms of "felt knowing" of reality or life-as-it-is. To try to explain the complex ways in which we might understand is much too intricate for children.

* * *

For children to live a life of spiritual practice, or holistic beliefs and lifestyle, they need to see adults who are living this way. The ineffective way to communicate is through all the ways of forced indoctrination. (There is a big difference between education and indoctrination—even learning to read and write, learning the three R's, can either be educational or by indoctrination, depending on whether or not the teachers are actually teaching or simply beating information into their students.) Indoctrination often produces the opposite of what we are hoping will "take." Heavy-handed handling of subjects that should be full of joy, freedom and exhilaration usually causes the indoctrinee to reject the doctrines.

We don't really need to thoroughly introduce our children into whatever spiritual practices we might be doing. Personally, I think that showing them a few minutes of meditation, or whatever we practice, is enough, until they wonder what it is that we get out of it and decide to experiment on their own. If they see us meditating that is the most important thing. Until a child reaches puberty, they are naturally "where we are" when we practice meditation, anyway. That is, children don't need to meditate in the same way we do because *they are meditation*, whether they are sitting still or playing raucously. The dynamic that this practice creates in our bodies is already in them. So, as long as they keep some sense of innocence, they are meditating. They automatically do what we employ meditation to do.

Children don't need to be taught to sense the ever-present blessing of Divine Presence in their lives and in all life. But the key element to their knowing this is *how* they are made aware of it. Children learn of this Presence through adults who are aware of it and who live on the basis of it, and that's it. And if adults are living this, then there can be verbal adjuncts to that—language can be used to explain it— but children will know already what we are talking about. Any struggle in explaining will be merely our own confusions and discomforts with it.

MAKING UP THEIR OWN MINDS

The first time I ever thought about God was when I was seventeen years old. Before then I thought about animals; I collected all kinds of stuff: bugs and snakes and turtles and lizards and fish and birds and

340

cats, but I never thought about God.

My father was this guy who had all the answers to everything. In fact, when I was in grade school I had a big encyclopedia but I never used it, because whenever I wanted to know anything I would just ask him. When I needed to know how something was spelled, I would always ask my father, and after awhile he would say, "Why don't you go use the dictionary?" He figured that if he kept giving me the spelling I would never even know how to use a dictionary.

Anyway, when I was seventeen I thought about God one day, so I said to myself, "Well, I wonder what my father thinks about God, since he's sort of like God?" So I went to him and asked, "Do you believe in God?" And he said, "Well, I have my beliefs, but I think, with something like that, it's important that you come to your own conclusions and make your own decisions." He wouldn't tell me anything. Just, "If you want to know if there's a God, or about God, you investigate yourself." I didn't, for about the next six or seven years. I said, "Oh, well, I'm not ready yet."

When I got into my own form of spirituality, and I was passionately interested in all these ideas, I looked at my father and thought, "He's an artist; I bet this is a whole area of life undiscovered for him." So I went to him, "Do you know anything about esotericism and mysticism?"

He started reeling off names. "Oh," he said, "when I was in my twenties in Europe I exhaustively studied theosophy—Blavatsky and Besant. I studied all the contemporary religions, Hinduism and Buddhism ...."

I was like amazed, because he had never mentioned a word about such studies. Literally, never mentioned a word, except about the injustices of man to man. He left me to discover my own views.

When I look back, I realize that my parents were passionately involved in social movements. At one point, early in ... I guess it was the Korean War, I'm not sure ... there were candlelight marches around where we lived in New Jersey. They never asked me to go. The baby-sitter would come, and I would ask my parents, "Where are you going?" and they would say, "We're going on a march against the war," and that was it. That was all I ever heard. Around the dinner table, in our family, when we would have guests over, the only things we discussed were family, life, art and the like. When politics were going to be discussed the men would go off in one room, the women would go off in the other room—very traditional. The men would discuss politics, and the women discussed politics, or gossip, or whatever. The children were allowed to come and go, to listen or join in as they wished.

I was never indoctrinated, never had opinions put on me. I was left to develop my own. They never said, "War is bad." Just, if I said, "Where are you going tonight?" they would tell me, "We're going to the march against the war." I never asked, and they never volunteered unless I asked *specifically* about what was going on.

I wasn't fed an ideology, even with religion. In the town that I grew up in there was a lot of prejudice towards Jews—we couldn't join the country club because it wasn't open to Jews, and we couldn't join the swim club because it wasn't open to Jews. (Although I didn't know any of this.) We lived on the poor side of town, so in my school there were Blacks and Orientals, and a little of everything: Catholics, Episcopalians, Presbyterians and me. I was friends with everybody and everybody was friends with me. When I realized there was such a thing as prejudice at about eleven years old, I had never even known of its existence before, never even imagined such a thing.

Once a year we would do a Jewish ceremony with the religious, practicing side of the family, at Passover. So, when I was about fourteen I said to my parents, "What's this all about? Jewish? Christian? What's going on? How come we don't go to a temple?"

They said, "If you want to study the Jewish religion, there is a man who gives lessons in Jewish culture to children who haven't gone to a synagogue school. You can go and learn about it, and then if you want to go to the temple, you can go." So I went for about six months. I lasted six months because there was a girl in the class who was the most beautiful thing I had ever seen in my entire life, even more beautiful than my cats, which was saying something. When she left, I left.

My parents let me make up my own mind, which was really healthy. I opted for girls at that time. They weren't worried (much!). In due time I came to develop a worldview quite resonant with my parents' deep humanitarian beliefs.

* * *

Where religion and other many other issues are concerned we can trust and allow our children to come to their own sensitivities about things. Of course we can guide them, steer them gently, but that's very different than forcing them to narrow or exclusive beliefs or experiences.

We live in a world that is extremely politicized in many ways—a world in which there is a lot of injustice, a tremendous amount of social inequality and inhumane acts—like all the torture that goes on, all the crime and bigotry. It is important to allow children to learn about those things through observation not by being trained to be a zealot, a sadist or a bigot, sexist, ageist, racist, classist or other.

Children are basically innocent, and in their innocence they are basically good. They genuinely care about other people and animals and the environment until they are taught to be selfish, greedy, hostile and suspicious of others. Still, it is important to allow them to come to their own opinions rather than turning them into radicals with lots of fiery invective. It is very strange in the U.S., for instance, if there is a protest against abortion, to see five- and six-year-old children with big signs like: "Murder! Fetuses are people too," standing out in front of abortion clinics. These are children! They don't know what the fuss is about. They are just parroting their parents, wanting to feel like they are contributing. Some contribution!

We can provide our children with information and experience about religious and social issues, and then we must allow their own sensitivities and natures to unfold. Children who are allowed to come to their own opinions will come to the opinion that there are injustices in the world. They will feel the suffering of the starving and the tortured and will do their part to eliminate such horrors. *They will!* But they will feel these things from within their own being, not from the superficiality of an attitude that they were force-fed by the adults in their environment.

— 12 —

SPIRITUAL PRACTICE
FOR PARENTS

Parenting is a practice which, if truly engaged, is more consuming than that of a Zen monk sitting zazen during a sesshin. It lasts not three days or a month, but almost twenty years, day and night, without interruption. It is also a practice that, once begun, cannot be dismissed or forgotten. Like the labor of birth, or like the Work itself, once this process is entered into there is no way out but through. Only deepening engagement and Enquiry will help us face both the heartache and the pure joy that parenting inevitably brings at times, and helps us open to the profound change of heart that is possible through conscious parenting. This is a practice that, once accepted, carries its own built-in momentum that requires our ever-deepening attention, vulnerability, service, sacrifice and surrender.

In our community we are trying to give children something ideal, and at the same time we find ourselves frustrated because we're not ideal, and life isn't ideal. Of course, if our lives were defined by a deep relationship to the Divine, particularly as that manifests as the ongoing nature of Life itself, then we wouldn't have to worry about whether our children had their needs met or not. There would be no question about it. When we are living in this domain—I'd call it the domain of a spiritual practitioner—our relationship to children is naturally and spontaneously appropriate. When we're not living there, then maybe our relationship is appropriate and maybe it isn't, and that depends upon the health of our psyche, and the depth and breadth of our education, wisdom and creativity.

If our psyche is not healthy, neither will be our relationship to children. And if our psyche *is* healthy and we're not living as a spiritual practitioner, our relationship to children may still be great—full of integrity and warmth. But, if we *are* a spiritual practitioner, we *can't* relate to children any other way than with the attention that effectively demonstrates our love for them as they are.

Children will tell us whether we are really participating in this Work or not. They are an instant feedback mechanism as to the resonance or dissonance of our relationship to them, to truth, to Reality, to Right Life and to objective justice.

* * *

Having a child can wreak havoc with relationships, including our relationship to our usual life practices. The grind is—you're raising a child, and you have to learn to practice in the midst of this overwhelming demand.

346

Parenting is a great opportunity then, to learn how to "practice" without spiraling down into confusion and insecurity. This does not mean putting in six hours a day doing formal meditation and prayer, for instance, because we can't do that when we are raising a child. Instead, we learn how to practice internally *within this primary relationship* with our child—a relationship that requires external time, energy, attention and every kind of adjustment.

When a couple has a child, more often than not the man is working full time, so the woman usually ends up taking on significant parental responsibilities. Those responsibilities are time-consuming and exhausting, there is no doubt about that, and the woman will often stop studying, meditating and exercising, or whatever her spiritual practices are, and will feel, "I've got no practice. I must be losing my connection to the Divine." Such beliefs are nonsense, however. If we just live our life the way it is, from the right context, and do what is required of us *now*, and don't moan and cry about the way it used to be, then that serves God. We don't have to look for special or exclusive actions to make us more attractive to the Divine. That is action—just living our life *as it is*. If our life itself is transformational, then, as ordinary as it may seem, that's *it*: get up in the morning, eat, go to work and come home to be with the family, or stay home and work and play with the children all day, or whatever, then go to bed. And occasionally we may have time for formal prayer or ritual. For a parent, that day-to-day "as it is-ness" can be as worthy and valuable a *sadhana* (spiritual practice) as leading the masses may be for someone else; as valuable as some fancy and exciting job with a lot of responsibility— a job in which someone gets their name and photograph in the paper.

A lot of people feel, when they have a life circumstance in which they aren't able to participate in all the formal practices that they were used to, and as they would like to, that they are "out of it"—out of the flow of grace, out of the flow of practice. But that need not be true, especially for parents of young children. Just being a good parent, if lived from the right context, is practice, and it serves God directly and profoundly. Of course it is exceptionally healthy and valuable for a child to see his or her parent in moods of prayer or worship, and to see them demonstrating qualities of discipline, discrimination, reliability and integrity, but these qualities, when demonstrated in immediate relationship to childraising, give children the model of them, and can always be routed specifically into their own spiritual practices when children get older.

With the practices in our school (daily meditation, daily exercise and daily study, etc.), we suggest that these recommended conditions are secondary to the right and attentive care of children. There is also a whole level of subtle conditions (like elements of relationship, generosity, compassion, patience, kindness), and one certainly doesn't need to abandon those for a child, but simply apply them in parenting.

It is very significant for one's spiritual life if one is disciplined, does yoga or whatever exercise, meditates and all that, but the greatest discipline is to raise a child with love and responsibility. So, the spiritual responsibility of the mother is to provide an environment in which the child will maintain a relationship to God. For a mother not to pay attention to that responsibility, but to be proud about meditating every day and exercising every day while the child is neglected or shuffled off to a "baby-sitter," is plain ridiculous.

The mother (and father) is essentially creating a being who will either add to the suffering of God or who will help alleviate the suffering of God. The mother is almost like God in that sense, creating something that will either *serve* the process of life on Earth, and even throughout the Universe, or distort and disorient it.

LOSING SOMETHING?

When you have a child, unless you're extremely mature, completely developed in your first four chakras[1], basically you give something of yourself (you *give up* something) to the development of that child. Even if you *are* mature you give something, but then you have a clear, conscious understanding of it and don't "lose" what you've given, so to speak. Rather you gain, by virtue of your child's maturity as a human being.

Before you have a child you may be functioning fine as a single practitioner, and feeling like you've "got non-duality" really down.[2] Then, all of a sudden you have a child and non-duality goes out the window ... unless you've *really* got it down. Non-duality goes out the window, so you "lose" something, which is the attachment that you give to your child. And you have to reclaim that wisdom, if you ever had it of course, by allowing your children to be entirely who they are as *human beings*—not as "your" children.

On the other hand, it's ridiculous to attempt to mimic non-attachment, to go around saying "the" child. There are some people for whom that is their survival mechanism, to say that. They can't even speak the words "*my* child"— it is too threatening to be so intimate, so connected, and so responsible. Saying "the child," as in: "Honey, the child just spilled its milk," is a way of denying and even rejecting relationship, and no child is dense enough not to pick this up, and it is devastating for them. Children *assume* relationship—it is a given, a tacit constant in the reality of life. To realize that a parent *rejects* them cannot help but be a shock, shattering the truth of their view and encouraging them to live a lie.

At the same time, an unconscious perception of that human being in the possessive sense is attachment. So, our children *are* ours, but they *are not objects*. For example, for a woman whose flesh and blood has fed off her for nine months, it will be very hard for her to not have some, even unconscious, relationship to "that" as hers in the possessive rather than acknowledging sense. And, to have no sense of that being as "her possession," her "territory," her "thing" (except in the ultimate sense—that each of us is everything!)—is the only way a woman can reclaim what it is that she has given of herself when she had a child. Our children are ours in the same way that we are theirs—not in the exclusive way that they are our objects and we are theirs, but only because we are mother (or father) and child, and the reality of that is totally natural, organic and as-it-is.

KNOWING WHERE WE STAND

Of all the communities I've seen, ours is one of the few that offers as much leeway as we do to the children in terms of allowing them to fully engage formal spaces, speak their minds as much as they do, get lots of "treats" off of our normal diet, and things like that. I don't want to change that. Childraising is one area in which my students actually have more difficult sadhana than people in most other communities.

In most communities the children don't go into the formal meditation and prayer spaces (unless their behavior is what German parents—perhaps not contemporary German parents but certainly the last generation—would call "good"). We make a lot of compromises in that, and rightfully so I think. It's very difficult to be a community of child advocates, the way we are, and also to maintain the kind of elegance towards spaces that we try to maintain.

It is not an easy job to give our children the freedom to express themselves and yet for us not to become tyrants. It's a very difficult, sometimes confusing task to be able to manage the way we are suggesting. Of course, in the long run, it's to our benefit, as well as to our children's, to figure out all of the things that need to be figured out in order to allow children to grow confidently, wisely and elegantly. (And not only to figure out what needs to be figured out, but to be able to manage once we have figured it out.)

In one spiritual community I know of the rules were very clear, and anybody who didn't follow them didn't get to be in the space. Everything was lined out. There was no subjectivity to it, and no tolerance: you come into the meditation hall, you sit, you do not move, you do not cough, you don't make a noise, you don't move a muscle. It was very very exact and there was no room left for interpretation. Once, a small child, perhaps two-and-a-half years old, farted, and the mother was asked by the space monitor to leave the room with the child. This is, to my way of thinking, teaching children to be totally anal-retentive, or implying to them that they are bad because they "passed wind."

In a school like that, the demands may be difficult, even unrealistic or cruel, but actually it's much easier to meet those demands than to be in a school like this, where there are so many things that one has to discover for oneself, so many circumstance-by-circumstance decisions, and where one has to then manage six things at the same time after one has made these discoveries. One has to manage their children, their own attention in the space, and one has to remember all the protocol of the space. We are being called to something that is very unusual, and much more difficult than the average adult even conceives of.

Often, we may feel "critically parented,"[3] by other nosy or righteous adults, especially out in public, "worldly" spaces, where so few people are attempting to raise children consciously. These people will all disagree with our parenting choices, and often feel that it is their sovereign right to correct us or interfere. So, we need to be particularly patient, diplomatic and skillful in negotiating the territory of public spaces.

Also, if we are feeling critically-parented, we should not react to that like an insolent teenager, with "an eye for an eye," or with sullen resentment or active reactivity. We should understand how difficult our choices are to maintain and practice, and we should just dig very deeply into our strength of commitment and our sanity. Because it *is* difficult. We have an immensely difficult task to accomplish. Not just parents, because in one sense all adults are responsible for all children. So, it is not just parents who have to take care of their children exclusively without help from anyone else. All of us must commit to the conscious and loving raising of children, education of children, and maintenance of environments where children can grow fully, protected in their freedom to be who they are, to be loved, cared for, acknowledged and supported. The usual adult is so terrified of such innocence, so crippled in their own aliveness and expression, that the threat of such fullness in others, even children, is anathema to them.

IN CONCLUSION

Relationship grows through an interplay of renunciation and embrace. In marriage, we renounce all other possible mates to embrace the one we have chosen to spend our life with. Through choice and commitment, as aspects of love, we feed this relationship so that it can grow as a sacred medium of service and surrender in our work. In spiritual life, we renounce many worldly distractions so as to commit our energy to attention and service to the Divine. In the choice to open our hearts to children, both as parents and friends, we let go of many other possible endeavors. This choice, made wholly, allows us to embrace the practice of being with children as a central aspect of our work. And within this embrace, we then discover what other forms of service may blend with our work and play with children.

As sadhana demands that we let go of the small and large attachments that (though they seem to make life more bearable) actually distract us from true life, we make space in the field of our attention for that which is real. When we let go of having a night of unbroken sleep, or regular times of lovemaking with our mate, or the movies and entertainment we were once used to so frequently, to respond as needed to our children, we actually free ourselves to reconnect to our own unencumbered innocence, as we connect to theirs. As we sacrifice the attachments, seductions, distractions and fascinations that distract and isolate us from our children, mates and intimates, we can discover the pure joy of objective and truly human relationship—the overwhelming reality of love in its infinite and ultimate possibilities.

NOTES

Chapter 2

1. The "cramp" refers to a whole range of physical, mental and emotional—or psycho-physical— manifestations that are analogous to muscular cramping. These cramps affect the body in obvious or subtle ways. They also affect the emotions and the mind by binding or handicapping free and "enlightened" activity.

2. Alice Miller is the author of numerous books, including: *The Drama of The Gifted Child: The Search for the True Self* (New York: Basic Books, 1981); *For Your Own Good: Hidden Cruelty in Child-Rearing and the Roots of Violence* (New York: Farrar Straus Giroux, 1983), and *Thou Shalt Not Be Aware: Society's Betrayal of the Child* (New York: Meridian Books, Penguin, 1990). Her work is essential and foundational reading for anyone who wishes to practice conscious parenting.

3. Stettbacher, J. Konrad. *Making Sense of Suffering.* (New York: E.P.Dutton), 1991 pp. 32, 34.

4. *Hohm Sahaj Mandir Study Manual*, pp. xx

Chapter 3

1. "Real emotion" or "higher" emotion here is used in contrast to lower emotion as explained in the teaching work of Gurdjieff. The lower emotions are essentially romanticized and ego-centered versions of certain genuine states, like sadness, joy, fear, while real emotion arises from the essential being, as a true response to a circumstance.

Chapter 4

1. essence or Essence: The basic or essential quality of a person, place or thing which is not the manifestation of psyche, personality or separate self.

2. Crystallizing: In this case referring to a type of hardening or rigidifying of the individual psyche based on the need to defend itself against the threatening demands or onslaughts of the people and the conditions (including the media's assaults on the child's senses) in it's environment.

3. George Gurdjieff described three different types of "food" which the human organism needs for survival: physical food, impression food, and breath or subtle food.

4. "Bummer," 1975, Sandy Song. Used by permission.

5. Satya Sai Baba, and Swami Premananda are both contemporary Indian sages who are renowned for their ability to materialize objects (pieces of candy or sacred stones, and other small objects) out of "thin air", or in the case of Premananda, out of his own body. Uri Geller is an Israeli who demonstrated a wide range of fascinating parapsychological phenomena such as psychokinesis, telekinesis and teletransportation, many under strict laboratory conditions. Swami Rama was a great yogi who was studied at Menninger Foundation and was tested and observed slowing his heartrate to unmeasurable degrees, creating different temperatures in either hand at the same time, and so on.

6. Content and context: Context is the overall matrix or field within whichall specific events, objects, and all specific forms arise. To hold the context for a child's life, as the author uses that term here, would be to hold broad and universal principles or values, like kindness, generosity and compassion as the framework for their lives. Content, on a macrocosmic level, refers to all the myriad, specific forms and appearances of creation. As it is used here, on a more microcosmic level, it refers to the details, minutiae and particulars which make up the components of any given situation, idea or thing.

Chapter 5

1. Louis Lozowick was one of the foremost lithographers of the twentieth century. His work is in the permanent collections of the Smithsonian Institute, the Whitney Museum and the Metropolitan

Museum of Art in New York, as well as other museums worldwide. See: *Survivor From a Dead Age: The Memoirs of Louis Lozowick*, Virginia Hagelstein Marquardt, editor. (Washington, D.C.: Smithsonian Institution Press), 1997.

2. Ramakrishna was an 19th century Indian (Hindu) saint known for his devotion to the Goddess Kali.

3. Shiva/Shakti: In Hinduism, the archetypal male and female aspects of the Divine referring to Context or consciousness (Shiva), and form and manifestation (Shakti).

Chapter 6

1. The work of both John Holt and Jean Liedloff have been strongly influential in the educational approach advocated by Lee Lozowick. More on these principles will be presented in Chapter 9: *Education For Life.*

Chapter 8

1. The *est course*, Erhard Seminar Training, was developed by Werner Erhard in the early 1970s. Parts of it contained a powerfully confrontative methodology for telling oneself the truth that one had been denying.

Chapter 9

1. Liedloff, Jean. *The Continuum Concept.* (New York and London: Penguin Books), 1975, 1987, p. 35.

2. Shah, Idries. *Learning How to Learn*. (New York: Penguin, Arkana), 1978.

Chapter 10

1. In the Taoist system, the two dynamic energy forces at play in the universe are labeled "yin"and "yang." The yin force is sometimes described as the feminine, the dark, the wet, the lunar, the centripetal or drawing-inward force, while the yang force is described as the masculine, the light, the dry, the ground, the centrifugal or outgoing force, etc.. In the example cited here, if a child was experiencing yin energy for a period, he or she would be restrained, inward, focused, while the yang energy would be outgoing, moving, expansive.

Chapter 11

1. Rescue Remedy: a Bach Flower tincture used to rebalance the system after shock or trauma of any kind.

2. Naranjo, Claudio. *The End of Patriarchy and The Dawning of a Tri-une Society*. (Oakland, CA: Amber Lotus), 1994.

Chapter 12

1. Chakras: energy plexes as defined in Eastern systems of physiology and metaphysics.
2. Nonduality: non-dual, i.e., not two. The objective

principle of the nature of reality in which all things are one. In spiritual realization, the understanding is that all is One or all is God.

3. "Critical parent": a termed coined by psychologist Eric Berne, the founder of Transactional Analysis, which refers to the negative aspect of the Parent ego-state within each person which judges everything, usually finding cause for disapproval.

RECOMMENDED READING

Baldwin, Rahima. *You Are Your Child's First Teacher.* Berkeley, CA: Celestial Arts, 1989.

Berends, Polly Berrien. *Whole Child/Whole Parent.* NY, NY: Harper & Row, 1983.

Elkind, David. *Miseducation: Preschoolers at Risk.* NY, NY: Alfred A. Knopf, 1987.

_____ *The Hurried Child.* NY, NY: Alfred A. Knopf, 1984.

Gaskin, Ina May. *Spiritual Midwifery.* Summertown, TN: The Book Publishing Co., 1978.

Holt, John. *Escape From Childhood: The Needs and Rights of Children.* NY: Ballantine Books, 1974.

_____ *How Children Learn.* NY, NY: Dell Publishing Co., 1967.

_____ *How Children Fail*. NY, NY: Pitman, 1964.

_____ *Teach Your Own*. NY, NY: Delacorte Press, 1981.

La Leche League International. *The Womanly Art of Breastfeeding*. NY, NY: New American Library, 1981.

Leboyer, Frederick. *Birth Without Violence*. NY, NY: Alfred A. Knopf, 1975.

Liedloff, Jean. *The Continuum Concept*. Reading, MA: Addison-Wesley, 1977.

Martin, Chia. *We Like To Nurse*. Prescott, AZ: Hohm Press, 1995.

Miller, Alice. *Banished Knowledge: Facing Childhood Injuries*. NY, NY: Doubleday, 1990.

_____ *The Drama of the Gifted Child: Prisoners of Childhood*. NY, NY: Basic Books, 1981

_____ *For Your Own Good: Hidden Cruelty in Child-Rearing and the Roots of Violence*. NY, NY: Farrar, Straus, Giroux, 1984.

_____ *Thou Shalt Not Be Aware: Society's Betrayal of the Child*. NY, NY: Meridian Books (Penguin), 1990.

Neill, A.S. *Summerhill: A Radical Approach to Childrearing*. NY, NY: Hart Publishing Co., 1960.

Pearce, Joseph. *The Magical Child Matures.* NY, NY: E.P. Dutton, 1985.

Shah, Idries. *Learning How To Learn.* NY, NY: Penguin, Arkana, 1978.

Stettbacher, J. Konrad. *Making Sense of Suffering: The Healing Confrontation with Your Own Past.* NY, NY: Dutton, 1991.

INDEX

Abandonment 185
Abuse, child 5, 204-
  217, 221-225, 233,
  256, 291, 329
Acknowledgement 56,
  71, 72, 143
Affection 64-66, 68,
  75, 246, 298
Attention 57, 59, 66,
  72, 75, 76-83, 254,
  260, 272, 275, 299,
  327
Babysitters 84
Bedtime, *see* Rituals
Behavior, unconscious
  56, 57
Birth 21, 25-26, 33-
  36, *see also* Labor
  father's role 37
Birth control 26
Blame 213
Bonding 43, 51, 160-
  161, 259
Books, children's 93-
  94
Boundaries 58, 75,
  156, 163-166, 168-

171, 199, 232, 278,
  285, 287
  bedtime 192-193
  mealtime 189-192,
    195
  non-arbitrary, *see*
    Discipline, non-
    arbitrary
  protocol 187-199,
    278
  setting 101, 172-
    187, 201, 249, 318
Breast-feeding, *see*
  Nursing
C-section 29, 30
Circumcision 39
Communication 17,
  38, 77, 85, 108-110,
  138, 239-240, 251,
  295, 297, 303, 306-
  307
Compassion 9, 87, 90,
  112, 114, 144, 145,
  146
Complaining 142-144
Compliments 241-243
Computers 97

Conception, conscious
15-20
Cruelty, *see* Negative
influences
Crystallization 125,
126
Defense mechanisms
137-140
Discipline, non-
arbitrary 8, 10, 165,
170, 172, 176-180,
185, 200, 278, *see
also* Boundaries
Education 5, 12, 273,
276-278, 282, 283,
290, 337, *see also*
Home schooling
Emotions, expressions
of 293-295
Energy management
301-303, 312
Energy, feminine 72-
74
masculine 72-74
Enlightened witness
102-103, 105
Environments, child
centered 108-109,
265
Expectations 14, 18,
124, 268, 271-272,
302
Fairy tales 93-94

Family bed 42, 141,
334-335
Farm, The 28-29
Fatherhood 159-162
Fertility 27
Food, *see* Relationship
to food
Freedom 120, 127,
262
Gaskin, Steven, *see*
Farm, The
Grief 113
Health 329-330
Heroes, *see* Role
models
Holt, John 164, 275
Home schooling 287-
290
Honesty 80, 243-245,
247-249, 253
self 63, 140, 142,
159, 253-256, 295
Identification with the
body 32-33
Illness, *see* Sickness
Impressions 91-107,
109
Incarnation 19, 35,
113, 127
Independence 167
Innocence 2, 5, 6, 8,
9, 87-91, 94, 97, 99,
99, 112, 194, 233,

Innocence *continued*
253, 270, 344, 352
lack of 107, 137
Integrity 3, 20, 126,
144, 172, 271
Labor, *see also* Birth
Language, *see also*
Communication
parental 78-79, 108,
182, 186-187
Liedloff, Jean 164,
259, 268, 269
"in-arms" stage 261
Limits 124-126, 142,
164, 169-170, *see
also* Boundaries
Love 10-12, 58, 64,
67, 137, 300
"un-", *see* "Unlove"
unconditional 56,
59, 81
Miller, Alice 7, 51,
102, 105, 203, 223
Motherhood 22-23,
37, 153-154, 347,
350
Movies and children
94-95, 193-194, 331
Masturbation 333-334
Nakedness 101, 331,
333
Naranjo, Claudio 336-
337

Negative influences
96, 104-107, 110,
111, 114-115, 137,
144, 270-271, 343-
344
Nudity, *see* Nakedness
Nursing 40-46, 48
Passions, children's
284-285
Patience 191
Pearce, Joseph Chilton
96, 263, 275
Peer group 307
Photographs 127-128,
129-130
Polarity principles, *see*
Energy management
Post-Partum seclusion
37-38
Pregnancy 21-24
Prejudice 111
Priorities 83
Problems, resolving
311-312
Projection 122-123,
124
Puberty 337-338, 340
Punishment 44, 67-68,
75, 184, 321
Relationship 3, 4, 11,
245, 256, 279, 350,
353
to the divine 16-17,

to the divine
continued 346
to food 23, 281,
313-320, 322-325
to sex 331-335
Religion 337-339
Respect 229, 233, 279
Responsibility of
parents 1-2, 10-11,
20, 85, 126, 196-
197, 199, 222, 262,
264, 329
Rituals 35
bedtime 193
Role models 73, 133-
136, 140, 168, 172,
266, 303
Sacrifice 27, 85, 353
Scarcity, disposition of
52, 54-57, 63
Self-confidence 272-
273
Self-esteem, child 48,
59, 69, 76, 249
parent 12
Self hatred 207, 216
Service 124
Sex, *see* Relationship
to sex
Shah, Idries 273
Shame 60, 99, 207-
208, 232, 306
Shoes 100-101

Siblings 69-70
Sickness 4, 102, 105,
235, 237, 325-328
Smothering 9, 155,
157, 325, *see also*
Spoiling
Spoiling 74-76
Stettbacher, J. Konrad
39
Storytelling 93, 127,
338
Suffering 9, 113-114,
211
Support system 31,
158
Survival strategy 33,
46-47, 207
Television 96-97, 110
Tantrum 243-244,
297-301
Teasing 309
Threats 182-183, 184
Touch 74, 322
Toys 97-98, 181
Travel 101-102
Transformation,
personal 224
Trust 5, 65, 184, 215-
216, 297, 317
Trustworthiness 252-
253
Underworld influences,
see Negative

influences
"Unlove" 53-54, 56,
    57, 58, 60, 62-63,
    64, 76, 169, 218-219
Video games, *see*
    Computers
Weaning 47
Wisdom 88, 146
Women's culture 158

ADDITIONAL TITLES OF INTEREST FROM HOHM PRESS

THE ALCHEMY OF TRANSFORMATION
by Lee Lozowick
Foreword by: Claudio Naranjo, M.D.

"I really appreciate Lee's message. The world needs to hear his God-talk. It's insightful and healing."—(John White, author, and editor, *What is Enlightenment?: Exploring the Goal of the Spiritual Path.*
A concise and straightforward overview of the principles of spiritual life as developed and taught by Lee Lozowick for the past twenty years in the West. Subjects of use to seekers and serious students of any spiritual tradition include: • From self-centeredness to God-centeredness • The role of a Teacher and a practice in spiritual life • The job of the community in "self"-liberation • Longing and devotion. Lee Lozowick's spiritual tradition is that of the western Baul, related in teaching and spirit to the Bauls of Bengal, India. *The Alchemy of Transformation* presents his radical, elegant and irreverent approach to human alchemical transformation.

Paper, 192 pages, $14.95   ISBN: 0-934252-62-9

• • •

THE ALCHEMY OF LOVE AND SEX
by Lee Lozowick
Foreword by Georg Feuerstein, Ph.D., author of *Sacred Sexuality*

Discover 70 "secrets" about love, sex and relationships. Lozowick recognizes the immense conflict and confusion surrounding love and sex, and tantric spiritual practice. Preaching neither asceticism nor hedonism, he presents a middle path—one grounded in the appreciation of simple human relatedness. Topics include: • what men want from women in sex, and what women want from men • the development of a passionate love affair with life • how to balance the essential masculine and essential feminine • the dangers and possibilities of sexual Tantra • the reality of a genuine, sacred marriage. . .and much more. The author is an American "Crazy Wisdom teacher" in the tradition of those whose enigmatic life and madcap teaching styles have affronted the polite society of their day. Lozowick is the author of 14 books in English and several in French and German translations only. " ... attacks Western sexuality with a vengeance." —*Library Journal.*

Paper, 312 pages, $16.95   ISBN: 0-934252-58-0

TO ORDER, PLEASE SEE ACCOMPANYING ORDER FORM.

ADDITIONAL TITLES OF INTEREST FROM HOHM PRESS

THE ART OF TOUCH: A Massage Manual For Young People
by Chia Martin

Provides young people (ages 9 and up) with a simple, step-by-step method for learning massage techniques to use on themselves and others for health, pain relief and increased self-esteem. Encourages a young person to respect his/her own body and the bodies of others.

Photographs clearly demonstrate proper hand placement and capture the mood of gentleness and playfulness which the author encourages throughout the text. Adults will also enjoy reading about and practicing these techniques.

Paper, 72 pages, 92 photographs, $15.95   ISBN: 0-934252-57-2

• • •

WE LIKE TO NURSE
by Chia Martin
Illustrations by Shukyo Lin Rainey

This unique book honors the mother-child relationship, reminding young children and mothers alike of their deep feelings for the bond created by nursing. Captivating and colorful illustrations present mother animals nursing their young. The text is simple and warmly encouraging.

La Leche League International has documented that the advantages of breastfeeding far outweigh the disadvantages in the overall health of the child. Advantages to the child include: greater immunity, prevention of allergy, the superior digestibility of mother's milk, and better tooth and jaw development. This book is Hohm Press' contribution to the health of children everywhere.

Paper, 32 pages, 16 full-color illustrations, $9.95   ISBN: 0-934252-45-9

TO ORDER, PLEASE SEE ACCOMPANYING ORDER FORM.

ADDITIONAL TITLES OF INTEREST FROM HOHM PRESS

THE JUMP INTO LIFE: *Moving Beyond Fear*
by Arnaud Desjardins
Foreword by Richard Moss, M.D.

"Say Yes to life," the author continually invites in this welcome guidebook to the spiritual path. For anyone who has ever felt oppressed by the life-negative seriousness of religion, this book is a timely antidote. In language that translates the complex to the obvious, Desjardins applies his simple teaching of happiness and gratitude to a broad range of weighty topics, including sexuality and intimate relationships, structuring an "inner life," the relief of suffering, and overcoming fear.

Paper, 216 pages, $12.95   ISBN: 0-934252-42-4

• • •

TEN ESSENTIAL FOODS
by Lalitha Thomas

Lalitha has done for food what she did with such wit and wisdom for herbs in her best-selling *10 Essential Herbs*. This new book presents 10 ordinary, but *essential* and great-tasting foods that can: • Strengthen a weakened immune system • Rebalance brain chemistry • Fight cancer and other degenerative diseases • Help you lose weight, simply and naturally.

Carrots, broccoli, almonds, grapefruit and six other miracle foods will enhance your health when used regularly and wisely. Lalitha gives in-depth nutritional information plus flamboyant and good-humored stories about these foods, based on her years of health and nutrition counseling. Each chapter contains easy and delicious recipes, tips for feeding kids and helpful hints for managing your food dollar. A bonus section supports the use of 10 Essential Snacks.

This book's focus is squarely on target: fruits, vegetables and whole grains— everything comes in the right natural proportions."—Charles Attwood, M.D., F.A.A.P.; author, *Dr. Attwood's Low-Fat Prescription for Kids* (Viking).

Paper, 324 pages, $16.95   ISBN: 0-934252-74-2

TO ORDER, PLEASE SEE ACCOMPANYING ORDER FORM.

ADDITIONAL TITLES OF INTEREST FROM HOHM PRESS

TOWARD THE FULLNESS OF LIFE: The Fullness of Love
by Arnaud Desjardins

Renowned French spiritual teacher, Arnaud Desjardins, offers elegant and wise counsel, arguing that a successful love relationship requires the heart of a child joined with the maturity of an adult. This book points the way to that blessed union. Topics include: happiness, marriage, absolute love and male and female energy.

Paper, 182 pages, $12.95   ISBN: 0-934252-55-6

• • •

WHEN SONS AND DAUGHTERS
CHOOSE ALTERNATIVE LIFESTYLES
by Mariana Caplan, M.A.

A guidebook for families in building workable relationships based on trust and mutual respect, despite the fears and concerns brought on by differences in lifestyle. Practical advice on what to do when sons and daughters (brothers, sisters, grandchildren...) join communes, go to gurus, follow rock bands around the country, marry outside their race or within their own gender, or embrace a religious belief that is alien to yours.

"Recommended for all public libraries."—*Library Journal.*

"Entering an arena too often marked by bitter and wounding conflict between worried parents and their adult children who are living in non-traditional communities or relationships, Mariana Caplan has produced a wise and thoughtful guide to possible reconciliation and healing...An excellent book."
—Alan F. Leveton, M.D.; Association of Family Therapists, past president

Paper, 264 pages, $14.95   ISBN: 0-934252-69-6

TO ORDER, PLEASE SEE ACCOMPANYING ORDER FORM.

ADDITIONAL TITLES OF INTEREST FROM HOHM PRESS

TRANSFORMATION THROUGH INSIGHT:
Enneatypes in Clinical Practice
by Claudio Naranjo, M.D.
Foreword by Will Schutz, Ph.D.

The Enneagram, an ancient system of understanding human nature, divides human personalities into 9 basic types (*ennea* means nine). Whether one is a newcomer to the field of Enneagram studies, or an experienced therapist using this material with clients, Dr. Naranjo's latest book will provide a wealth of invaluable data about the Enneatypes presented in a unique format which turns a scholarly text into a fascinating page-gripper. Each of the nine Enneagram types is illustrated by passages from famous pieces of literature, case studies by famous therapists, and a therapeutic dialogue between Dr. Naranjo and one of his own clients who demonstrates the type being considered. Claudio Naranjo is a world-renowned authority on the Enneagram.

Paper, 544 pages, $24.95   ISBN: 0-934252-73-4

• • •

CONSCIOUS PARENTING
by Lee Lozowick

Any individual who cares for children needs to attend to the essential message of this book: that the first two years are the most crucial time in a child's education and development, and that children learn to be healthy and "whole" by living with healthy, whole adults. Offers practical guidance and help for anyone who wishes to bring greater consciousness to every aspect of childraising, including:
• conception, pregnancy and birth • emotional development • language usage
• role modeling: the mother's role, the father's role • the exposure to various influences • establishing workable boundaries • the choices we make on behalf of our children's education ... and much more.

Paper, 384 pages, $17.95   ISBN: 0-934252-67-X

TO ORDER, PLEASE SEE ACCOMPANYING ORDER FORM.

RETAIL ORDER FORM FOR HOHM PRESS BOOKS

Name_____ Phone (   ) _____

Street Address or P.O. Box _____

City _____ State _____ Zip Code _____

	QTY	TITLE	ITEM PRICE	TOTAL PRICE
1		THE ALCHEMY OF LOVE AND SEX	$16.95	
2		THE ALCHEMY OF TRANSFORMATION	$14.95	
3		THE ART OF TOUCH	$15.95	
4		WE LIKE TO NURSE	$9.95	
5		THE JUMP INTO LIFE	$12.95	
6		TOWARD THE FULLNESS OF LIFE	$12.95	
7		TEN ESSENTIAL FOODS	$16.95	
8		WHEN SONS AND DAUGHTERS...	$14.95	
9		TRANSFORMATION THROUGH INSIGHT	$24.95	
10		CONSCIOUS PARENTING	$17.95	

SURFACE SHIPPING CHARGES

1st book $4.00

Each additional item $1.00

SUBTOTAL:	
SHIPPING: (see below)	
TOTAL:	

SHIP MY ORDER

☐ Surface U.S. Mail—Priority   ☐ UPS (Mail + $2.00)

☐ 2nd-Day Air (Mail + $5.00)   ☐ Next-Day Air (Mail + $15.00)

METHOD OF PAYMENT:

☐ Check or M.O.   Payable to Hohm Press, P.O. Box 2501, Prescott, AZ 86302

☐ Call 1-800-381-2700 to place your credit card order

☐ Or call 1-520-717-1779 to fax your credit card order

☐ Information for Visa/MasterCard order only:

Card #_____–_____–_____–_____

Expiration Date_____

ORDER NOW!
Call 1-800-381-2700 or fax your order to 1-520-717-1779.
(Remember to include your credit card information.)